LIFE OF LORD BYRON, VOL. 4 : WITH HIS LETTERS AND JOURNALS
BY
Thomas Moore

LIFE OF LORD BYRON, VOL. 4 : WITH HIS LETTERS AND JOURNALS

Published by Wallachia Publishers

New York City, NY

First published circa 1852

Copyright © Wallachia Publishers, 2015

All rights reserved

Except in the United States of America, this book is sold subject to the condition that it shall not, by way of trade or otherwise, be lent, re-sold, hired out, or otherwise circulated without the publisher's prior consent in any form of binding or cover other than that in which it is published and without a similar condition including this condition being imposed on the subsequent purchaser.

ABOUT WALLACHIA PUBLISHERS

Wallachia Publishers mission is to publish the world's finest European history texts. More information on our recent publications and catalog can be found on our website.

CONTENTS OF VOL. IV.

LETTERS AND JOURNALS OF LORD BYRON, WITH NOTICES OF HIS LIFE, from April, 1817, to October, 1820.

NOTICES: OF THE: LIFE OF LORD BYRON.

LETTER 272. TO MR. MURRAY.
"Venice, April 9. 1817.
"Your letters of the 18th and 20th are arrived. In my own I have given you the rise, progress, decline, and fall, of my recent malady. It is gone to the devil: I won't pay him so bad a compliment as to say it came from him;—he is too much of a gentleman. It was nothing but a slow fever, which quickened its pace towards the end of its journey. I had been bored with it some weeks—with nocturnal burnings and morning perspirations; but I am quite well again, which I attribute to having had neither medicine nor doctor thereof.

"In a few days I set off for Rome: such is my purpose. I shall change it very often before Monday next, but do you continue to direct and address to Venice, as heretofore. If I go, letters will be forwarded: I say 'if,' because I never know what I shall do till it is done; and as I mean most firmly to set out for Rome, it is not unlikely I may find myself at St. Petersburg.

"You tell me to 'take care of myself;'—faith, and I will. I won't be posthumous yet, if I can help it. Notwithstanding, only think what a 'Life and Adventures,' while I am in full scandal, would be worth, together with the 'membra' of my writing-desk, the sixteen beginnings of poems never to be finished! Do you think I would not have shot myself last year, had I not luckily recollected that Mrs. C * * and Lady N * *, and all the old women in England would have been delighted;—besides the agreeable 'Lunacy,' of the 'Crowner's Quest,' and the regrets of two or three or half a dozen? Be assured that I would live for two reasons, or more;—there are one or two people whom I have to put out of the world, and as many into it, before I can 'depart in peace;' if I do so before, I have not fulfilled my mission. Besides, when I turn thirty, I will turn devout; I feel a great vocation that way in Catholic churches, and when I hear the organ.

"So * * is writing again! Is there no Bedlam in Scotland? nor thumb-screw? nor gag? nor hand-cuff? I went upon my knees to him almost, some years ago, to prevent him from publishing a political pamphlet, which would have given him a livelier idea of 'Habeas Corpus' than the world will derive from his present production upon that suspended subject, which will doubtless be followed by the suspension of other of his Majesty's subjects.

"I condole with Drury Lane and rejoice with * *,—that is, in a modest way,—on the tragical end of the new tragedy.

"You and Leigh Hunt have quarrelled then, it seems? I introduce him and his poem to you, in the hope that (malgré politics) the union would be beneficial to both, and the end is eternal enmity; and yet I did this with the best intentions: I introduce * * *, and * * * runs away with your money: my friend Hobhouse quarrels, too, with the Quarterly: and (except the last) I am the innocent Istmhus (damn the word! I can't spell it, though I have crossed that of Corinth a dozen times) of these enmities.

"I will tell you something about Chillon.—A Mr. De Luc, ninety years old, a Swiss, had it read to him, and is pleased with it,—so my sister writes. He said that he was with Rousseau at Chillon, and that the description is perfectly correct. But this is not all: I recollected something of the name, and find the following passage in 'The Confessions,' vol. iii. page 247. liv. viii.:—

"'De tous ces amusemens celui qui me plût davantage fut une promenade autour du Lac, que je fis en bateau avec De Luc père, sa bru, ses deux fils, et ma Therése. Nous mimes sept jours à cette tournée par le plus beau temps du monde. J'en gardai le vif souvenir des sites qui m'avoient frappé à l'autre extrémité du Lac, et dont je fis la description, quelques années après, dans la Nouvelle Heloise'

"This nonagenarian, De Luc, must be one of the 'deux fils.' He is in England—infirm, but still in faculty. It is odd that he should have lived so long, and not wanting in oddness that he should have made this voyage with Jean Jacques, and afterwards, at such an interval, read a poem by an Englishman (who had made precisely the same circumnavigation) upon the same scenery.

"As for 'Manfred,' it is of no use sending proofs; nothing of that kind comes. I sent the whole at different times. The two first Acts are the best; the third so so; but I was blown with the first and second heats. You must call it 'a Poem,' for it is no Drama, and I do not choose to have it called by so * * a name—a 'Poem in dialogue,' or—Pantomime, if you will; any thing but a green-room synonyme; and this is your motto—

"'There are more things in heaven and earth, Horatio,
Than are dreamt of in your philosophy.'

"Yours ever, &c.
"My love and thanks to Mr. Gifford."
LETTER 273. TO MR. MOORE.
"Venice, April 11. 1817.

"I shall continue to write to you while the fit is on me, by way of penance upon you for your former complaints of long silence. I dare say you would blush, if you could, for not answering. Next week I set out for Rome. Having seen Constantinople, I should like to look at t'other fellow. Besides, I want to see the Pope, and shall take care to tell him that I vote for the Catholics and no Veto.

"I sha'n't go to Naples. It is but the second best sea-view, and I have seen the first and third, viz. Constantinople and Lisbon, (by the way, the last is but a river-view; however, they reckon it after Stamboul and Naples, and before Genoa,) and Vesuvius is silent, and I have passed by Ætna. So I shall e'en return to Venice in July; and if you write, I pray you to address to Venice, which is my head, or rather my heart, quarters.

"My late physician, Dr. Polidori, is here on his way to England, with the present Lord G * * and the widow of the late earl. Dr. Polidori has, just now, no more patients, because his patients are no more. He had lately three, who are now all dead—one embalmed. Horner and a child of Thomas Hope's are interred at Pisa and Rome. Lord G * * died of an inflammation of the bowels: so they took them out, and sent them (on account of their discrepancies), separately from the carcass, to England. Conceive a man going one way, and his intestines another, and his immortal soul a third!—was there ever such a distribution? One certainly has a soul; but how it came to allow itself to be enclosed in a body is more than I can imagine. I only know if once mine gets out, I'll have a bit of a tussle before I let it get in again to that or any other.

"And so poor dear Mr. Maturin's second tragedy has been neglected by the discerning public! * * will be d——d glad of this, and d——d without being glad, if ever his own plays come upon 'any stage.'

"I wrote to Rogers the other day, with a message for you. I hope that he flourishes. He is the Tithonus of poetry—immortal already. You and I must wait for it.

"I hear nothing—know nothing. You may easily suppose that the English don't seek me, and I avoid them. To be sure, there are but few or none here, save passengers. Florence and Naples are their Margate and Ramsgate, and much the same sort of company too, by all accounts, which hurts us among the Italians.

"I want to hear of Lalla Rookh—are you out? Death and fiends! why don't you tell me where you are, what you are, and how you are? I shall go to Bologna by Ferrara, instead of Mantua: because I would rather see the cell where they caged Tasso, and where he became mad and * *, than his own MSS. at Modena, or the Mantuan birthplace of that harmonious plagiary and miserable flatterer, whose cursed hexameters were drilled into me at Harrow. I saw Verona and Vicenza on my way here—Padua too.

"I go alone,—but alone, because I mean to return here. I only want to see Rome. I have not the least curiosity about Florence, though I must see it for the sake of the Venus, &c. &c.; and I wish also to see the Fall of Terni. I think to return to Venice by Ravenna and Rimini, of both of which I mean to take notes for Leigh Hunt, who will be glad to hear of the scenery of his Poem. There was a devil of a review of him in the Quarterly, a year ago, which he answered. All answers are imprudent: but, to be sure, poetical flesh and blood must have the last word—that's certain. I thought, and think, very highly of his Poem; but I warned him of the row his favourite antique phraseology would bring him into.

"You have taken a house at Hornsey: I had much rather you had taken one in the Apennines. If you think of coming out for a summer, or so, tell me, that I may be upon the hover for you.

"Ever," &c.

LETTER 274. TO MR. MURRAY.

"Venice, April 14. 1817.

"By the favour of Dr. Polidori, who is here on his way to England with the present Lord G * *, (the late earl having gone to England by another road, accompanied by his bowels in a separate coffer,) I remit to you, to deliver to Mrs. Leigh, two miniatures; previously you will have the goodness to desire Mr. Love (as a peace-offering between him and me) to set them in plain gold, with my arms complete, and 'Painted by Prepiani—Venice, 1817,' on the back. I wish also that you would desire Holmes to make a copy of each—that is, both—for myself, and that you will retain the said copies till my return. One was done while I was very unwell; the other in my health, which may account for their dissimilitude. I trust that they will reach their destination in safety.

"I recommend the Doctor to your good offices with your government friends; and if you can be of any use to him in a literary point of view, pray be so.

"To-day, or rather yesterday, for it is past midnight, I have been up to the battlements of the highest tower in Venice, and seen it and its view, in all the glory of a clear Italian sky. I also went over the Manfrini Palace, famous for its pictures. Amongst them, there is a portrait of Ariosto by Titian, surpassing all my anticipation of the power of painting or human expression: it is the poetry of portrait, and the portrait of poetry. There was also one of some learned lady, centuries old, whose name I forget, but whose features must always be remembered. I never saw greater beauty, or sweetness, or wisdom:—it is the kind of face to go mad for, because it cannot walk out of its frame. There is also a famous dead Christ and live Apostles, for which Buonaparte offered in vain five thousand louis; and of which, though it is a capo d'opera of Titian, as I am no connoisseur, I say little, and thought less, except of one figure in it. There are ten thousand others, and some very fine Giorgiones amongst them, &c. &c. There is an original Laura and Petrarch, very hideous both. Petrarch has not only the dress, but the features and air of an old woman, and Laura looks by no means like a young one, or a pretty one. What struck me most in the general collection was the extreme resemblance of the style of the female faces in the mass of pictures, so many centuries or generations old, to those you see and meet every day among the existing Italians. The queen of Cyprus and Giorgione's wife, particularly the latter, are Venetians as it were of yesterday; the same eyes and expression, and, to my mind, there is none finer.

"You must recollect, however, that I know nothing of painting; and that I detest it, unless it reminds me of something I have seen, or think it possible to see, for which reason I spit upon and abhor all the Saints and subjects of one half the impostures I see in the churches and palaces; and when in Flanders, I never was so disgusted in my life, as with Rubens and his eternal wives and infernal glare of colours, as they appeared to me; and in Spain I did not think much of Murillo and Velasquez. Depend upon it, of all the arts, it is the most artificial and unnatural, and that by which the nonsense of mankind is most imposed upon. I never yet saw the picture or the statue which came a league within my conception or expectation; but I have seen many mountains, and seas, and rivers, and views, and two or three women, who went as far beyond it,—besides some horses; and a lion (at Veli Pacha's) in the Morea; and a tiger at supper in Exeter Change.

"When you write, continue to address to me at Venice. Where do you suppose the books you sent to me are? At Turin! This comes of 'the Foreign Office' which is foreign enough, God knows, for any good it can be of to me, or any one else, and be d——d to it, to its last clerk and first charlatan, Castlereagh.

"This makes my hundredth letter at least.

"Yours," &c.

TO MR. MURRAY.

"Venice, April 14. 1817.

"The present proofs (of the whole) begin only at the 17th page; but as I had corrected and sent back the first Act, it does not signify.

"The third Act is certainly d——d bad, and, like the Archbishop of Grenada's homily (which savoured of the palsy), has the dregs of my fever, during which it was written. It must on no account be published in its present state. I will try and reform it, or rewrite it altogether; but the impulse is gone, and I have no chance of making any thing out of it. I would not have it published as it is on any account. The speech of Manfred to the Sun is the only part of this act I thought good myself; the rest is certainly as bad as bad can be, and I wonder what the devil possessed me.

"I am very glad indeed that you sent me Mr. Gifford's opinion without deduction. Do you suppose me such a booby as not to be very much obliged to him? or that in fact I was not, and am not, convinced and convicted in my conscience of this same overt act of nonsense?

"I shall try at it again: in the mean time, lay it upon the shelf (the whole Drama, I mean): but pray correct your copies of the first and second Acts from the original MS.

"I am not coming to England; but going to Rome in a few days. I return to Venice in June; so, pray, address all letters, &c. to me here, as usual, that is, to Venice. Dr. Polidori this day left this city with Lord G * * for England. He is charged with some books to your care (from me), and two miniatures also to the same address, both for my sister.

"Recollect not to publish, upon pain of I know not what, until I have tried again at the third Act. I am not sure that I shall try, and still less that I shall succeed, if I do; but I am very sure, that (as it is) it is unfit for publication or perusal; and unless I can make it out to my own satisfaction, I won't have any part published.

"I write in haste, and after having lately written very often. Yours," &c.
LETTER 276. TO MR. MURRAY.
"Foligno, April 26. 1817.

"I wrote to you the other day from Florence, inclosing a MS. entitled 'The Lament of Tasso.' It was written in consequence of my having been lately at Ferrara. In the last section of this MS. but one (that is, the penultimate), I think that I have omitted a line in the copy sent to you from Florence, viz. after the line—

"And woo compassion to a blighted name,

insert,

"Sealing the sentence which my foes proclaim.

The context will show you the sense, which is not clear in this quotation. Remember, I write this in the supposition that you have received my Florentine packet.

"At Florence I remained but a day, having a hurry for Rome, to which I am thus far advanced. However, I went to the two galleries, from which one returns drunk with beauty. The Venus is more for admiration than love; but there are sculpture and painting, which for the first time at all gave me an idea of what people mean by their cant, and what Mr. Braham calls 'entusimusy' (i.e. enthusiasm) about those two most artificial of the arts. What struck me most were, the mistress of Raphael, a portrait; the mistress of Titian, a portrait; a Venus of Titian in the Medici gallery— the Venus; Canova's Venus also in the other gallery: Titian's mistress is also in the other gallery (that is, in the Pitti Palace gallery): the Parcæ of Michael Angelo, a picture: and the Antinous, the Alexander, and one or two not very decent groups in marble; the Genius of Death, a sleeping figure, &c. &c.

"I also went to the Medici chapel—fine frippery in great slabs of various expensive stones, to commemorate fifty rotten and forgotten carcasses. It is unfinished, and will remain so.

"The church of 'Santa Croce' contains much illustrious nothing. The tombs of Machiavelli, Michael Angelo, Galileo Galilei, and Alfieri, make it the Westminster Abbey of Italy. I did not admire any of these tombs—beyond their contents. That of Alfieri is heavy, and all of them seem to me overloaded. What is necessary but a bust and name? and perhaps a date? the last for the unchronological, of whom I am one. But all your allegory and eulogy is infernal, and worse than the long wigs of English numskulls upon Roman bodies in the statuary of the reigns of Charles II., William, and Anne.

"When you write, write to Venice, as usual; I mean to return there in a fortnight. I shall not be in England for a long time. This afternoon I met Lord and Lady Jersey, and saw them for some time: all well; children grown and healthy; she very pretty, but sunburnt; he very sick of travelling; bound for Paris. There are not many English on the move, and those who are, mostly homewards. I shall not return till business makes me, being much better where I am in health, &c. &c.

"For the sake of my personal comfort, I pray you send me immediately to Venice—mind, Venice—viz. Waites' tooth-powder, red, a quantity; calcined magnesia, of the best quality, a quantity; and all this by safe, sure, and speedy means; and, by the Lord! do it.

"I have done nothing at Manfred's third Act. You must wait; I'll have at it in a week or two, or so. Yours ever," &c.

LETTER 277. TO MR. MURRAY.

"Rome, May 5. 1817.

"By this post, (or next at farthest) I send you in two other covers, the new third Act of 'Manfred.' I have re-written the greater part, and returned what is not altered in the proof you sent me. The Abbot is become a good man, and the Spirits are brought in at the death. You will find I think, some good poetry in this new act, here and there; and if so, print it, without sending me farther proofs, under Mr. Gifford's correction, if he will have the goodness to overlook it. Address all answers to Venice, as usual; I mean to return there in ten days.

"'The Lament of Tasso,' which I sent from Florence, has, I trust, arrived: I look upon it as a 'these be good rhymes,' as Pope's papa said to him when he was a boy. For the two—it and the Drama—you will disburse to me (via Kinnaird) six hundred guineas. You will perhaps be surprised that I set the same price upon this as upon the Drama; but, besides that I look upon it as good, I won't take less than three hundred guineas for any thing. The two together will make you a larger publication than the 'Siege' and 'Parisina;' so you may think yourself let off very easy: that is to say, if these poems are good for any thing, which I hope and believe.

"I have been some days in Rome the Wonderful. I am seeing sights, and have done nothing else, except the new third Act for you. I have this morning seen a live pope and a dead cardinal: Pius VII. has been burying Cardinal Bracchi, whose body I saw in state at the Chiesa Nuova. Rome has delighted me beyond every thing, since Athens and Constantinople. But I shall not remain long this visit. Address to Venice.

"Ever, &c.

"P.S. I have got my saddle-horses here, and have ridden, and am riding, all about the country."

From the foregoing letters to Mr. Murray, we may collect some curious particulars respecting one of the most original and sublime of the noble poet's productions, the Drama of Manfred. His failure (and to an extent of which the reader shall be enabled presently to judge), in the completion of a design which he had, through two Acts, so magnificently carried on,—the impatience with which, though conscious of this failure, he as usual hurried to the press, without deigning to woo, or wait for, a happier moment of inspiration,—his frank docility in, at once, surrendering up his third Act to reprobation, without urging one parental word in its behalf,—the doubt he evidently felt, whether, from his habit of striking off these creations at a heat, he should be able to rekindle his imagination on the subject,—and then, lastly, the complete success with which, when his mind did make the spring, he at once cleared the whole space by which he before fell short of perfection,—all these circumstances, connected with the production of this grand poem, lay open to us features, both of his disposition and genius, in the highest degree interesting, and such as there is a pleasure, second only to that of perusing the poem itself, in contemplating.

As a literary curiosity, and, still more, as a lesson to genius, never to rest satisfied with imperfection or mediocrity, but to labour on till even failures are converted into triumphs, I shall here transcribe the third Act, in its original shape, as first sent to the publisher:—

ACT III.—SCENE I.

A Hall in the Castle of Manfred.

MANFRED and HERMAN.

Man. What is the hour?

Her. It wants but one till sunset,
And promises a lovely twilight.

Man. Say,
Are all things so disposed of in the tower
As I directed?

Her. All, my lord, are ready:
Here is the key and casket.

Man. It is well:
Thou may'st retire. [Exit HERMAN.

Man. (alone.) There is a calm upon me—
Inexplicable stillness! which till now
Did not belong to what I knew of life.
If that I did not know philosophy
To be of all our vanities the motliest,
The merest word that ever fool'd the ear
From out the schoolman's jargon, I should deem
The golden secret, the sought 'Kalon,' found,

And seated in my soul. It will not last,
But it is well to have known it, though but once:
It hath enlarged my thoughts with a new sense,
And I within my tablets would note down
That there is such a feeling. Who is there?
Re-enter HERMAN.
Her. My lord, the Abbot of St. Maurice craves
To greet your presence.
Enter the ABBOT OF ST. MAURICE.
Abbot.Peace be with Count Manfred!
Man. Thanks, holy father! welcome to these walls;
Thy presence honours them, and blesseth those
Who dwell within them.
Abbot.Would it were so, Count!
But I would fain confer with thee alone.
Man. Herman, retire. What would my reverend guest?
Exit HERMAN.
Abbot. Thus, without prelude:—Age and zeal, my office,
And good intent, must plead my privilege;
Our near, though not acquainted neighbourhood,
May also be my herald. Rumours strange,
And of unholy nature, are abroad,
And busy with thy name—a noble name
For centuries; may he who bears it now
Transmit it unimpair'd.
Man.Proceed,—I listen.
Abbot. 'Tis said thou boldest converse with the things
Which are forbidden to the search of man;
That with the dwellers of the dark abodes,
The many evil and unheavenly spirits
Which walk the valley of the shade of death,
Thou communest. I know that with mankind,
Thy fellows in creation, thou dost rarely
Exchange thy thoughts, and that thy solitude
Is as an anchorite's, were it but holy.
Man. And what are they who do avouch these things?
Abbot. My pious brethren—the scared peasantry—
Even thy own vassals—who do look on thee
With most unquiet eyes. Thy life's in peril.
Man. Take it.

Abbot. I come to save, and not destroy—
I would not pry into thy secret soul;
But if these things be sooth, there still is time
For penitence and pity: reconcile thee
With the true church, and through the church to heaven.
Man. I hear thee. This is my reply; Whate'er
I may have been, or am, doth rest between
Heaven and myself.—I shall not choose a mortal
To be my mediator. Have I sinn'd
Against your ordinances? prove and punish!
Abbot. Then, hear and tremble! For the headstrong wretch
Who in the mail of innate hardihood
Would shield himself, and battle for his sins,
There is the stake on earth, and beyond earth eternal—
Man. Charity, most reverend father,
Becomes thy lips so much more than this menace,
That I would call thee back to it; but say,
What wouldst thou with me?
Abbot. It may be there are
Things that would shake thee—but I keep them back,
And give thee till to-morrow to repent.
Then if thou dost not all devote thyself
To penance, and with gift of all thy lands
To the monastery—
Man. I understand thee,—well!
Abbot. Expect no mercy; I have warned thee.
Man. (opening the casket.) Stop—
There is a gift for thee within this casket.
MANFRED opens the casket, strikes a light, and burns some incense.
Ho! Ashtaroth!
The DEMON ASHTAROTH appears, singing as follows:—

The raven sits On the raven-stone, And his black wing flits O'er the milk-white bone; To and fro, as the night-winds blow, The carcass of the assassin swings; And there alone, on the raven-stone, The raven flaps his dusky wings.

The fetters creak—and his ebon beak Croaks to the close of the hollow sound; And this is the tune by the light of the moon To which the witches dance their round— Merrily, merrily, cheerily, cheerily, Merrily, speeds the ball: The dead in their shrouds, and the demons in clouds, Flock to the witches' carnival.

Abbot. I fear thee not—hence—hence—
Avaunt thee, evil one!—help, ho! without there!

Man. Convey this man to the Shreckhorn—to its peak—
To its extremest peak—watch with him there
From now till sunrise; let him gaze, and know
He ne'er again will be so near to heaven.
But harm him not; and, when the morrow breaks,
Set him down safe in his cell—away with him!
Ash. Had I not better bring his brethren too,
Convent and all, to bear him company?
Man. No, this will serve for the present. Take him up.
Ash. Come, friar! now an exorcism or two,
And we shall fly the lighter.
ASHTAROTH disappears with the ABBOT, singing as follows:—
   A prodigal son and a maid undone, And a widow re-wedded within the year; And a worldly monk and a pregnant nun, Are things which every day appear.
MANFRED alone.
Man. Why would this fool break in on me, and force
My art to pranks fantastical?—no matter,
It was not of my seeking. My heart sickens,
And weighs a fix'd foreboding on my soul;
But it is calm—calm as a sullen sea
After the hurricane; the winds are still,
But the cold waves swell high and heavily,
And there is danger in them. Such a rest
Is no repose. My life hath been a combat.
And every thought a wound, till I am scarr'd
In the immortal part of me—What now?
Re-enter HERMAN.
Her. My lord, you bade me wait on you at sunset:
He sinks behind the mountain.
Man. Doth he so?
I will look on him.
[MANFRED advances to the window of the hall.
Glorious orb! the idol
Of early nature, and the vigorous race
Of undiseased mankind, the giant sons
Of the embrace of angels, with a sex
More beautiful than they, which did draw down
The erring spirits who can ne'er return.—
Most glorious orb! that wert a worship, ere
The mystery of thy making was reveal'd!

Thou earliest minister of the Almighty,
Which gladden'd, on their mountain tops, the hearts
Of the Chaldean shepherds, till they pour'd
Themselves in orisons! Thou material God!
And representative of the Unknown—
Who chose thee for his shadow! Thou chief star!
Centre of many stars! which mak'st our earth
Endurable, and temperest the hues
And hearts of all who walk within thy rays!
Sire of the seasons! Monarch of the climes,
And those who dwell in them! for, near or far,
Our inborn spirits have a tint of thee,
Even as our outward aspects;—thou dost rise,
And shine, and set in glory. Fare thee well!
I ne'er shall see thee more. As my first glance
Of love and wonder was for thee, then take
My latest look: thou wilt not beam on one
To whom the gifts of life and warmth have been
Of a more fatal nature. He is gone:
I follow.[Exit MANFRED.
SCENE II.
The Mountains—The Castle of Manfred at some distance—A Terrace before
a Tower—Time, Twilight.
HERMAN, MANUEL, and other dependants of MANFRED.
Her. 'Tis strange enough; night after night, for years,
He hath pursued long vigils in this tower,
Without a witness. I have been within it,—
So have we all been oft-times; but from it,
Or its contents, it were impossible
To draw conclusions absolute of aught
His studies tend to. To be sure, there is
One chamber where none enter; I would give
The fee of what I have to come these three years,
To pore upon its mysteries.
Manuel.'Twere dangerous;
Content thyself with what thou know'st already.
Her. Ah! Manuel! thou art elderly and wise,
And couldst say much; thou hast dwelt within the castle—
How many years is't?
Manuel.Ere Count Manfred's birth,

I served his father, whom he nought resembles.
Her. There be more sons in like predicament.
But wherein do they differ?
Manuel.I speak not
Of features or of form, but mind and habits:
Count Sigismund was proud,—but gay and free,—
A warrior and a reveller; he dwelt not
With books and solitude, nor made the night
A gloomy vigil, but a festal time,
Merrier than day; he did not walk the rocks
And forests like a wolf, nor turn aside
From men and their delights.
Her.Beshrew the hour,
But those were jocund times! I would that such
Would visit the old walls again; they look
As if they had forgotten them.
Manuel.These walls
Must change their chieftain first. Oh! I have seen
Some strange things in these few years.
Her.Come, be friendly;
Relate me some, to while away our watch:
I've heard thee darkly speak of an event
Which happened hereabouts, by this same tower.
Manuel. That was a night indeed! I do remember
'Twas twilight, as it may be now, and such
Another evening;—yon red cloud, which rests
On Eigher's pinnacle, so rested then,—
So like that it might be the same; the wind
Was faint and gusty, and the mountain snows
Began to glitter with the climbing moon;
Count Manfred was, as now, within his tower,—
How occupied, we knew not, but with him
The sole companion of his wanderings
And watchings—her, whom of all earthly things
That lived, the only thing he seemed to love,—
As he, indeed, by blood was bound to do,
The lady Astarte, his—
Her.Look—look—the tower—
The tower's on fire. Oh, heavens and earth! what sound,
What dreadful sound is that?[A crash like thunder.

Manuel. Help, help, there!—to the rescue of the Count,—
The Count's in danger,—what ho! there! approach!
The Servants, Vassals, and Peasantry approach, stupified with terror.
If there be any of you who have heart
And love of human kind, and will to aid
Those in distress—pause not—but follow me—
The portal's open, follow.   [MANUEL goes in.
Her.Come—who follows?
What, none of ye?—ye recreants! shiver then
Without. I will not see old Manuel risk
His few remaining years unaided.[HERMAN goes in.
Vassal.Hark!—
No—all is silent—not a breath—the flame
Which shot forth such a blaze is also gone;
What may this mean? Let's enter!
Peasant.Faith, not I,—
Not that, if one, or two, or more, will join,
I then will stay behind; but, for my part,
I do not see precisely to what end.
Vassal. Cease your vain prating—come.
Manuel. (speaking within.)'Tis all in vain—
He's dead.
Her. (within.) Not so—even now methought he moved;
But it is dark—so bear him gently out—
Softly—how cold he is! take care of his temples
In winding down the staircase.
Re-enter MANUEL and HERMAN, bearing MANFRED in their arms.
Manuel. Hie to the castle, some of ye, and bring
What aid you can. Saddle the barb, and speed
For the leech to the city—quick! some water there!
Her. His cheek is black—but there is a faint beat
Still lingering about the heart. Some water.
[They sprinkle MANFRED with water; after a pause, he gives some signs of life.
Manuel. He seems to strive to speak—come—cheerly, Count!
He moves his lips—canst hear him? I am old,
And cannot catch faint sounds.
[HERMAN inclining his head and listening.
Her.I hear a word
Or two—but indistinctly—what is next?
What's to be done? let's bear him to the castle.

[MANFRED motions with his hand not to remove him.
Manuel. He disapproves—and 'twere of no avail—
He changes rapidly.
Her.'Twill soon be over.
Manuel. Oh! what a death is this! that I should live
To shake my gray hairs over the last chief
Of the house of Sigismund.—And such a death!
Alone—we know not how—unshrived—untended—
With strange accompaniments and fearful signs—
I shudder at the sight—but must not leave him.
Manfred. (speaking faintly and slowly.) Old man! 'tis not so difficult to die.[MANFRED having said this expires.
Her. His eyes are fixed and lifeless.—He is gone.—
Manuel. Close them.—My old hand quivers.—He departs—
Whither? I dread to think—but he is gone!
LETTER 278. TO MR. MURRAY.
"Rome, May 9. 1817.
"Address all answers to Venice; for there I shall return in fifteen days, God willing.

"I sent you from Florence 'The Lament of Tasso,' and from Rome the third Act of Manfred, both of which, I trust, will duly arrive. The terms of these two I mentioned in my last, and will repeat in this, it is three hundred for each, or six hundred guineas for the two—that is, if you like, and they are good for any thing.

"At last one of the parcels is arrived. In the notes to Childe Harold there is a blunder of yours or mine: you talk of arrival at St. Gingo, and, immediately after, add—'on the height is the Château of Clarens.' This is sad work: Clarens is on the other side of the Lake, and it is quite impossible that I should have so bungled. Look at the MS.; and at any rate rectify it.

"The 'Tales of my Landlord' I have read with great pleasure, and perfectly understand now why my sister and aunt are so very positive in the very erroneous persuasion that they must have been written by me. If you knew me as well as they do, you would have fallen, perhaps, into the same mistake. Some day or other, I will explain to you why—when I have time; at present, it does not much matter; but you must have thought this blunder of theirs very odd, and so did I, till I had read the book. Croker's letter to you is a very great compliment; I shall return it to you in my next.

"I perceive you are publishing a Life of Raffael d'Urbino: it may perhaps interest you to hear that a set of German artists here allow their hair to grow, and trim it into his fashion, thereby drinking the cummin of the disciples of the old philosopher; if they would cut their hair, convert it into brushes, and paint like him, it would be more 'German to the matter.'

"I'll tell you a story: the other day, a man here—an English—mistaking the statues of Charlemagne and Constantine, which are equestrian, for those of Peter and Paul, asked another which was Paul of these same horsemen?—to which the reply was,—'I thought, sir, that St. Paul had never got on horseback since his accident?'

"I'll tell you another: Henry Fox, writing to some one from Naples the other day, after an illness, adds—'and I am so changed, that my oldest creditors would hardly know me.'

"I am delighted with Rome—as I would be with a bandbox, that is, it is a fine thing to see, finer than Greece; but I have not been here long enough to affect it as a residence, and I must go back to Lombardy, because I am wretched at being away from Marianna. I have been riding my saddle-horses every day, and been to Albano, its Lakes, and to the top of the Alban Mount, and to Frescati, Aricia, &c. &c. with an &c. &c. &c. about the city, and in the city: for all which—vide Guide-book. As a whole, ancient and modern, it beats Greece, Constantinople, every thing—at least that I have ever seen. But I can't describe, because my first impressions are always strong and confused, and my memory selects and reduces them to order, like distance in the landscape, and blends them better, although they may be less distinct. There must be a sense or two more than we have, us mortals; for * * * * * where there is much to be grasped we are always at a loss, and yet feel that we ought to have a higher and more extended comprehension.

"I have had a letter from Moore, who is in some alarm about his poem. I don't see why.

"I have had another from my poor dear Augusta, who is in a sad fuss about my late illness; do, pray, tell her (the truth) that I am better than ever, and in importunate health, growing (if not grown) large and ruddy, and congratulated by impertinent persons on my robustious appearance, when I ought to be pale and interesting.

"You tell me that George Byron has got a son, and Augusta says, a daughter; which is it?—it is no great matter: the father is a good man, an excellent officer, and has married a very nice little woman, who will bring him more babes than income; howbeit she had a handsome dowry, and is a very charming girl;—but he may as well get a ship.

"I have no thoughts of coming amongst you yet awhile, so that I can fight off business. If I could but make a tolerable sale of Newstead, there would be no occasion for my return; and I can assure you very sincerely, that I am much happier (or, at least, have been so) out of your island than in it.

"Yours ever.

"P.S. There are few English here, but several of my acquaintance; amongst others, the Marquis of Lansdowne, with whom I dine to-morrow. I met the Jerseys on the road at Foligno—all well.

"Oh—I forgot—the Italians have printed Chillon, &c. a piracy,—a pretty little edition, prettier than yours—and published, as I found to my great astonishment on arriving here; and what is odd, is, that the English is quite correctly printed. Why they did it, or who did it, I know not; but so it is;—I suppose, for the English people. I will send you a copy."

LETTER 279. TO MR. MOORE.

"Rome, May 12. 1817.

"I have received your letter here, where I have taken a cruise lately; but I shall return back to Venice in a few days, so that if you write again, address there, as usual. I am not for returning to England so soon as you imagine; and by no means at all as a residence. If you cross the Alps in your projected expedition, you will find me somewhere in Lombardy, and very glad to see you.

Only give me a word or two beforehand, for I would readily diverge some leagues to meet you.

"Of Rome I say nothing; it is quite indescribable, and the Guide-book is as good as any other. I dined yesterday with Lord Lansdowne, who is on his return. But there are few English here at present; the winter is their time. I have been on horseback most of the day, all days since my arrival, and have taken it as I did Constantinople. But Rome is the elder sister, and the finer. I went some days ago to the top of the Alban Mount, which is superb. As for the Coliseum, Pantheon, St. Peter's, the Vatican, Palatine, &c. &c.—as I said, vide Guide-book. They are quite inconceivable, and must be seen. The Apollo Belvidere is the image of Lady Adelaide Forbes—I think I never saw such a likeness.

"I have seen the Pope alive, and a cardinal dead,—both of whom looked very well indeed. The latter was in state in the Chiesa Nuova, previous to his interment.

"Your poetical alarms are groundless; go on and prosper. Here is Hobhouse just come in, and my horses at the door, so that I must mount and take the field in the Campus Martius, which, by the way, is all built over by modern Rome.

"Yours very and ever, &c.

"P.S. Hobhouse presents his remembrances, and is eager, with all the world, for your new poem."

LETTER 280. TO MR. MURRAY.

"Venice, May 30. 1817.

"I returned from Rome two days ago, and have received your letter; but no sign nor tidings of the parcel sent through Sir C. Stuart, which you mention. After an interval of months, a packet of 'Tales,' &c. found me at Rome; but this is all, and may be all that ever will find me. The post seems to be the only sure conveyance; and that only for letters. From Florence I sent you a poem on Tasso, and from Rome the new third Act of 'Manfred,' and by Dr. Polidori two portraits for my sister. I left Rome and made a rapid journey home. You will continue to direct here as usual. Mr. Hobhouse is gone to Naples: I should have run down there too for a week, but for the quantity of English whom I heard of there. I prefer hating them at a distance; unless an earthquake, or a good real irruption of Vesuvius, were ensured to reconcile me to their vicinity.

"The day before I left Rome I saw three robbers guillotined. The ceremony—including the masqued priests; the half-naked executioners; the bandaged criminals; the black Christ and his banner; the scaffold; the soldiery; the slow procession, and the quick rattle and heavy fall of the axe; the splash of the blood, and the ghastliness of the exposed heads—is altogether more impressive than the vulgar and ungentlemanly dirty 'new drop,' and dog-like agony of infliction upon the sufferers of the English sentence. Two of these men behaved calmly enough, but the first of the three died with great terror and reluctance. What was very horrible, he would not lie down; then his neck was too large for the aperture, and the priest was obliged to drown his exclamations by still louder exhortations. The head was off before the eye could trace the blow; but from an attempt to draw back the head, notwithstanding it was held forward by the hair, the first head was cut off close to the ears: the other two were taken off more cleanly. It is better than the oriental way, and (I should think) than the axe of our ancestors. The pain seems little, and yet the effect to the spectator, and the preparation to the criminal, is very striking and chilling. The first turned me quite hot and thirsty, and made me shake so that I could hardly hold the opera-glass (I was close, but was determined to see, as one should see every thing, once, with attention); the second and third (which shows how dreadfully soon things grow indifferent), I am ashamed to say, had no effect on me as a horror, though I would have saved them if I could. Yours," &c.

LETTER 281. TO MR. MURRAY.

"Venice, June 4. 1817.

"I have received the proofs of the 'Lament of Tasso,' which makes me hope that you have also received the reformed third Act of Manfred, from Rome, which I sent soon after my arrival there. My date will apprise you of my return home within these few days. For me, I have received none of your packets, except, after long delay, the 'Tales of my Landlord,' which I before acknowledged. I do not at all understand the why nots, but so it is; no Manuel, no letters, no tooth-powder, no extract from Moore's Italy concerning Marino Faliero, no NOTHING—as a man hallooed out at one of Burdett's elections, after a long ululatus of 'No Bastille! No governor-ities! No—'God knows who or what;—but his ne plus ultra was, 'No nothing!'—and my receipts of your packages amount to about his meaning. I want the extract from Moore's Italy very much, and the tooth-powder, and the magnesia; I don't care so much about the poetry, or the letters, or Mr. Maturin's by-Jasus tragedy. Most of the things sent by the post have come—I mean proofs and letters; therefore send me Marino Faliero by the post, in a letter.

"I was delighted with Rome, and was on horseback all round it many hours daily, besides in it the rest of my time, bothering over its marvels. I excursed and skirred the country round to Alba, Tivoli, Frescati, Licenza, &c. &c.; besides, I visited twice the Fall of Terni, which beats every thing. On my way back, close to the temple by its banks, I got some famous trout out of the river Clitumnus—the prettiest little stream in all poesy, near the first post from Foligno and Spoletto.—I did not stay at Florence, being anxious to get home to Venice, and having already seen the galleries and other sights. I left my commendatory letters the evening before I went, so I saw nobody.

"To-day, Pindemonte, the celebrated poet of Verona, called on me; he is a little thin man, with acute and pleasing features; his address good and gentle; his appearance altogether very philosophical; his age about sixty, or more. He is one of their best going. I gave him Forsyth, as he speaks, or reads rather, a little English, and will find there a favourable account of himself. He enquired after his old Cruscan friends, Parsons, Greathead, Mrs. Piozzi, and Merry, all of whom he had known in his youth. I gave him as bad an account of them as I could, answering, as the false 'Solomon Lob' does to 'Totterton' in the farce, 'all gone dead,' and damned by a satire more than twenty years ago; that the name of their extinguisher was Gifford; that they were but a sad set of scribes after all, and no great things in any other way. He seemed, as was natural, very much pleased with this account of his old acquaintances, and went away greatly gratified with that and Mr. Forsyth's sententious paragraph of applause in his own (Pindemonte's) favour. After having been a little libertine in his youth, he is grown devout, and takes prayers, and talks to himself, to keep off the devil; but for all that, he is a very nice little old gentleman.

"I forgot to tell you that at Bologna (which is celebrated for producing popes, painters, and sausages) I saw an anatomical gallery, where there is a deal of waxwork, in which * *.

"I am sorry to hear of your row with Hunt; but suppose him to be exasperated by the Quarterly and your refusal to deal; and when one is angry and edites a paper, I should think the temptation too strong for literary nature, which is not always human. I can't conceive in what, and for what, he abuses you: what have you done? you are not an author, nor a politician, nor a public character; I know no scrape you have tumbled into. I am the more sorry for this because I introduced you to Hunt, and because I believe him to be a good man; but till I know the particulars, I can give no opinion.

"Let me know about Lalla Rookh, which must be out by this time.

"I restore the proofs, but the punctuation should be corrected. I feel too lazy to have at it myself; so beg and pray Mr. Gifford for me.—Address to Venice. In a few days I go to my villeggiatura, in a cassino near the Brenta, a few miles only on the main land. I have determined on another year, and many years of residence if I can compass them. Marianna is with me, hardly recovered of the fever, which has been attacking all Italy last winter. I am afraid she is a little hectic; but I hope the best.

"Ever, &c.

"P.S. Torwaltzen has done a bust of me at Rome for Mr. Hobhouse, which is reckoned very good. He is their best after Canova, and by some preferred to him.

"I have had a letter from Mr. Hodgson. He is very happy, has got a living, but not a child: if he had stuck to a curacy, babes would have come of course, because he could not have maintained them.

"Remember me to all friends, &c. &c.

"An Austrian officer, the other day, being in love with a Venetian, was ordered, with his regiment, into Hungary. Distracted between love and duty, he purchased a deadly drug, which dividing with his mistress, both swallowed. The ensuing pains were terrific, but the pills were purgative, and not poisonous, by the contrivance of the unsentimental apothecary; so that so much suicide was all thrown away. You may conceive the previous confusion and the final laughter; but the intention was good on all sides."

LETTER 282. TO MR. MURRAY.

"Venice, June 8. 1817.

"The present letter will be delivered to you by two Armenian friars, on their way, by England, to Madras. They will also convey some copies of the grammar, which I think you agreed to take. If you can be of any use to them, either amongst your naval or East Indian acquaintances, I hope you will so far oblige me, as they and their order have been remarkably attentive and friendly towards me since my arrival at Venice. Their names are Father Sukias Somalian and Father Sarkis Theodorosian. They speak Italian, and probably French, or a little English. Repeating earnestly my recommendatory request, believe me, very truly, yours,

"BYRON.

"Perhaps you can help them to their passage, or give or get them letters for India."
LETTER 283. TO MR. MURRAY.
"La Mira, near Venice, June 14. 1817.
"I write to you from the banks of the Brenta, a few miles from Venice, where I have colonised for six months to come. Address, as usual, to Venice.

"Three months after date (17th March),—like the unnegotiable bill despondingly received by the reluctant tailor,—your despatch has arrived, containing the extract from Moore's Italy and Mr. Maturin's bankrupt tragedy. It is the absurd work of a clever man. I think it might have done upon the stage, if he had made Manuel (by some trickery, in a masque or vizor) fight his own battle, instead of employing Molineux as his champion; and, after the defeat of Torismond, have made him spare the son of his enemy, by some revulsion of feeling, not incompatible with a character of extravagant and distempered emotions. But as it is, what with the Justiza, and the ridiculous conduct of the whole dram. pers. (for they are all as mad as Manuel, who surely must have had more interest with a corrupt bench than a distant relation and heir presumptive, somewhat suspect of homicide,) I do not wonder at its failure. As a play, it is impracticable; as a poem, no great things. Who was the 'Greek that grappled with glory naked?' the Olympic wrestlers? or Alexander the Great, when he ran stark round the tomb of t'other fellow? or the Spartan who was fined by the Ephori for fighting without his armour? or who? And as to 'flaying off life like a garment,' helas! that's in Tom Thumb—see king Arthur's soliloquy:

"'Life's a mere rag, not worth a prince's wearing;
I'll cast it off.'

And the stage-directions—'Staggers among the bodies;'—the slain are too numerous, as well as the blackamoor knights-penitent being one too many: and De Zelos is such a shabby Monmouth Street villain, without any redeeming quality—Stap my vitals! Maturin seems to be declining into Nat. Lee. But let him try again; he has talent, but not much taste. I 'gin to fear, or to hope, that Sotheby, after all, is to be the Eschylus of the age, unless Mr. Shiel be really worthy his success. The more I see of the stage, the less I would wish to have any thing to do with it; as a proof of which, I hope you have received the third Act of Manfred, which will at least prove that I wish to steer very clear of the possibility of being put into scenery. I sent it from Rome.

"I returned the proof of Tasso. By the way, have you never received a translation of St. Paul which I sent you, not for publication, before I went to Rome?

"I am at present on the Brenta. Opposite is a Spanish marquis, ninety years old; next his casino is a Frenchman's,—besides the natives; so that, as somebody said the other day, we are exactly one of Goldoni's comedies (La Vedova Scaltra), where a Spaniard, English, and Frenchman are introduced: but we are all very good neighbours, Venetians, &c. &c. &c.

"I am just getting on horseback for my evening ride, and a visit to a physician, who has an agreeable family, of a wife and four unmarried daughters, all under eighteen, who are friends of Signora S * *, and enemies to nobody. There are, and are to be, besides, conversaziones and I know not what, a Countess Labbia's and I know not whom. The weather is mild; the thermometer 110 in the sun this day, and 80 odd in the shade. Yours, &c.

"N."

LETTER 284. TO MR. MURRAY.

"La Mira, near Venice, June 17. 1817.

"It gives me great pleasure to hear of Moore's success, and the more so that I never doubted that it would be complete. Whatever good you can tell me of him and his poem will be most acceptable: I feel very anxious indeed to receive it. I hope that he is as happy in his fame and reward as I wish him to be; for I know no one who deserves both more—if any so much.

"Now to business; * * * * * * I say unto you, verily, it is not so; or, as the foreigner said to the waiter, after asking him to bring a glass of water, to which the man answered, 'I will, sir,'—'You will!—G——d d——n,—I say, you mush!' And I will submit this to the decision of any person or persons to be appointed by both, on a fair examination of the circumstances of this as compared with the preceding publications. So there's for you. There is always some row or other previously to all our publications: it should seem that, on approximating, we can never quite get over the natural antipathy of author and bookseller, and that more particularly the ferine nature of the latter must break forth.

"You are out about the third Canto: I have not done, nor designed, a line of continuation to that poem. I was too short a time at Rome for it, and have no thought of recommencing.

"I cannot well explain to you by letter what I conceive to be the origin of Mrs. Leigh's notion about 'Tales of my Landlord;' but it is some points of the characters of Sir E. Manley and Burley, as well as one or two of the jocular portions, on which it is founded, probably.

"If you have received Dr. Polidori as well as a parcel of books, and you can be of use to him, be so. I never was much more disgusted with any human production than with the eternal nonsense, and tracasseries, and emptiness, and ill humour, and vanity of that young person; but he has some talent, and is a man of honour, and has dispositions of amendment, in which he has been aided by a little subsequent experience, and may turn out well. Therefore, use your government interest for him, for he is improved and improvable.

"Yours," &c.

LETTER 285. TO MR. MURRAY.

"La Mira, near Venice, June 18. 1817.

"Enclosed is a letter to Dr. Holland from Pindemonte. Not knowing the Doctor's address, I am desired to enquire, and, perhaps, being a literary man, you will know or discover his haunt near some populous churchyard. I have written to you a scolding letter—I believe, upon a misapprehended passage in your letter—but never mind: it will do for next time, and you will surely deserve it. Talking of doctors reminds me once more to recommend to you one who will not recommend himself,—the Doctor Polidori. If you can help him to a publisher, do; or, if you have any sick relation, I would advise his advice: all the patients he had in Italy are dead—Mr. * *'s son, Mr. Horner, and Lord G * *, whom he embowelled with great success at Pisa.

"Remember me to Moore, whom I congratulate. How is Rogers? and what is become of Campbell and all t'other fellows of the Druid order? I got Maturin's Bedlam at last, but no other

parcel; I am in fits for the tooth-powder, and the magnesia. I want some of Burkitt's soda-powders. Will you tell Mr. Kinnaird that I have written him two letters on pressing business, (about Newstead, &c.) to which I humbly solicit his attendance. I am just returned from a gallop along the banks of the Brenta—time, sunset. Yours,
"B."
LETTER 286. TO MR. MURRAY.
"La Mira, near Venice, July 1. 1817.
"Since my former letter, I have been working up my impressions into a fourth Canto of Childe Harold, of which I have roughened off about rather better than thirty stanzas, and mean to go on; and probably to make this 'Fytte' the concluding one of the poem, so that you may propose against the autumn to draw out the conscription for 1818. You must provide moneys, as this new resumption bodes you certain disbursements. Somewhere about the end of September or October, I propose to be under way (i.e. in the press); but I have no idea yet of the probable length or calibre of the Canto, or what it will be good for; but I mean to be as mercenary as possible, an example (I do not mean of any individual in particular, and least of all, any person or persons of our mutual acquaintance) which I should have followed in my youth, and I might still have been a prosperous gentleman.
"No tooth-powder, no letters, no recent tidings of you.
"Mr. Lewis is at Venice, and I am going up to stay a week with him there—as it is one of his enthusiasms also to like the city.
       "I stood in Venice on the 'Bridge of Sighs,' &c. &c.
"The 'Bridge of Sighs' (i.e. Ponte de'i Sospiri) is that which divides, or rather joins, the palace of the Doge to the prison of the state. It has two passages: the criminal went by the one to judgment, and returned by the other to death, being strangled in a chamber adjoining, where there was a mechanical process for the purpose.
"This is the first stanza of our new Canto; and now for a line of the second:—
       "In Venice, Tasso's echoes are no more,
       And silent rows the songless gondolier,
       Her palaces, &c. &c.

"You know that formerly the gondoliers sung always, and Tasso's Gierusalemme was their ballad. Venice is built on seventy-two islands.
"There! there's a brick of your new Babel! and now, sirrah! what say you to the sample?
"Yours, &c.
"P.S. I shall write again by and by."
LETTER 287. TO MR. MURRAY.
"La Mira, near Venice, July 8. 1817
"If you can convey the enclosed letter to its address, or discover the person to whom it is directed, you will confer a favour upon the Venetian creditor of a deceased Englishman. This epistle is a dun to his executor, for house-rent. The name of the insolvent defunct is, or was,

Porter Valter, according to the account of the plaintiff, which I rather suspect ought to be Walter Porter, according to our mode of collocation. If you are acquainted with any dead man of the like name a good deal in debt, pray dig him up, and tell him that 'a pound of his fair flesh' or the ducats are required, and that 'if you deny them, fie upon your law!'

"I hear nothing more from you about Moore's poem, Rogers, or other literary phenomena; but to-morrow, being post-day, will bring perhaps some tidings. I write to you with people talking Venetian all about, so that you must not expect this letter to be all English.

"The other day, I had a squabble on the highway, as follows: I was riding pretty quickly from Dolo home about eight in the evening, when I passed a party of people in a hired carriage, one of whom, poking his head out of the window, began bawling to me in an inarticulate but insolent manner. I wheeled my horse round, and overtaking, stopped the coach, and said, 'Signor, have you any commands for me?' He replied, impudently as to manner, 'No.' I then asked him what he meant by that unseemly noise, to the discomfiture of the passers-by. He replied by some piece of impertinence, to which I answered by giving him a violent slap in the face. I then dismounted, (for this passed at the window, I being on horseback still,) and opening the door desired him to walk out, or I would give him another. But the first had settled him except as to words, of which he poured forth a profusion in blasphemies, swearing that he would go to the police and avouch a battery sans provocation. I said he lied, and was a * *, and if he did not hold his tongue, should be dragged out and beaten anew. He then held his tongue. I of course told him my name and residence, and defied him to the death, if he were a gentleman, or not a gentleman, and had the inclination to be genteel in the way of combat. He went to the police, but there having been bystanders in the road,—particularly a soldier, who had seen the business,—as well as my servant, notwithstanding the oaths of the coachman and five insides besides the plaintiff, and a good deal of paying on all sides, his complaint was dismissed, he having been the aggressor;—and I was subsequently informed that, had I not given him a blow, he might have been had into durance.

"So set down this,—'that in Aleppo once' I 'beat a Venetian;' but I assure you that he deserved it, for I am a quiet man, like Candide, though with somewhat of his fortune in being forced to forego my natural meekness every now and then.

"Yours, &c. B."

LETTER 288. TO MR. MURRAY.

"Venice, July 9, 1817.

"I have got the sketch and extracts from Lalla Rookh. The plan, as well as the extracts, I have seen, please me very much indeed, and I feel impatient for the whole.

"With regard to the critique on 'Manfred,' you have been in such a devil of a hurry, that you have only sent me the half: it breaks off at page 294. Send me the rest; and also page 270., where there is 'an account of the supposed origin of this dreadful story,'—in which, by the way, whatever it may be, the conjecturer is out, and knows nothing of the matter. I had a better origin than he can devise or divine, for the soul of him.

"You say nothing of Manfred's luck in the world; and I care not. He is one of the best of my misbegotten, say what they will.

"I got at last an extract, but no parcels. They will come, I suppose, some time or other. I am come up to Venice for a day or two to bathe, and am just going to take a swim in the Adriatic; so, good evening—the post waits. Yours, &c.

"B.

"P.S. Pray, was Manfred's speech to the Sun still retained in Act third? I hope so: it was one of the best in the thing, and better than the Colosseum. I have done fifty-six of Canto fourth, Childe Harold; so down with your ducats."

LETTER 289. TO MR. MOORE.

"La Mira, Venice, July 10. 1817.

"Murray, the Mokanna of booksellers, has contrived to send me extracts from Lalla Rookh by the post. They are taken from some magazine, and contain a short outline and quotations from the two first Poems. I am very much delighted with what is before me, and very thirsty for the rest. You have caught the colours as if you had been in the rainbow, and the tone of the East is perfectly preserved. I am glad you have changed the title from 'Persian Tale.'

"I suspect you have written a devilish fine composition, and I rejoice in it from my heart; because 'the Douglas and the Percy both together are confident against a world in arms.' I hope you won't be affronted at my looking on us as 'birds of a feather;' though on whatever subject you had written, I should have been very happy in your success.

"There is a simile of an orange-tree's 'flowers and fruits,' which I should have liked better if I did not believe it to be a reflection on * * *.

"Do you remember Thurlow's poem to Sam—'When Rogers;' and that d——d supper of Rancliffe's that ought to have been a dinner? 'Ah, Master Shallow, we have heard the chimes at midnight.' But

> "My boat is on the shore,
> And my bark is on the sea;
> But, before I go, Tom Moore,
> Here's a double health to thee!

"This should have been written fifteen moons ago—the first stanza was. I am just come out from an hour's swim in the Adriatic; and I write to you with a black-eyed Venetian girl before me, reading Boccacio.

"Last week I had a row on the road (I came up to Venice from my casino, a few miles on the Paduan road, this blessed day, to bathe) with a fellow in a carriage, who was impudent to my horse. I gave him a swingeing box on the ear, which sent him to the police, who dismissed his complaint. Witnesses had seen the transaction. He first shouted, in an unseemly way, to frighten my palfry. I wheeled round, rode up to the window, and asked him what he meant. He grinned, and said some foolery, which produced him an immediate slap in the face, to his utter discomfiture. Much blasphemy ensued, and some menace, which I stopped by dismounting and opening the carriage door, and intimating an intention of mending the road with his immediate remains, if he did not hold his tongue. He held it.

"Monk Lewis is here—'how pleasant!' He is a very good fellow, and very much yours. So is Sam—so is every body—and amongst the number,

"Yours ever,

"B.

"P.S. What think you of Manfred?"

LETTER 290. TO MR. MURRAY.

"La Mira, near Venice, July 15. 1817.

"I have finished (that is, written—the file comes afterwards) ninety and eight stanzas of the fourth Canto, which I mean to be the concluding one. It will probably be about the same length as the third, being already of the dimensions of the first or second Cantos. I look upon parts of it as very good, that is, if the three former are good, but this we shall see; and at any rate, good or not, it is rather a different style from the last—less metaphysical—which, at any rate, will be a variety. I sent you the shaft of the column as a specimen the other day, i.e. the first stanza. So you may be thinking of its arrival towards autumn, whose winds will not be the only ones to be raised, if so be as how that it is ready by that time.

"I lent Lewis, who is at Venice, (in or on the Canalaccio, the Grand Canal,) your extracts from Lalla Rookh and Manuel, and, out of contradiction, it may be, he likes the last, and is not much taken with the first, of these performances. Of Manuel, I think, with the exception of a few capers, it is as heavy a nightmare as was ever bestrode by indigestion.

"Of the extracts I can but judge as extracts, and I prefer the 'Peri' to the 'Silver Veil.' He seems not so much at home in his versification of the 'Silver Veil,' and a little embarrassed with his horrors; but the conception of the character of the impostor is fine, and the plan of great scope for his genius,—and I doubt not that, as a whole, it will be very Arabesque and beautiful.

"Your late epistle is not the most abundant in information, and has not yet been succeeded by any other; so that I know nothing of your own concerns, or of any concerns, and as I never hear from any body but yourself who does not tell me something as disagreeable as possible, I should not be sorry to hear from you: and as it is not very probable,—if I can, by any device or possible arrangement with regard to my personal affairs, so arrange it,—that I shall return soon, or reside ever in England, all that you tell me will be all I shall know or enquire after, as to our beloved realm of Grub Street, and the black brethren and blue sisterhood of that extensive suburb of Babylon. Have you had no new babe of literature sprung up to replace the dead, the distant, the tired, and the retired? no prose, no verse, no nothing?"

LETTER 291. TO MR. MURRAY.

"Venice, July 20. 1817.

"I write to give you notice that I have completed the fourth and ultimate Canto of Childe Harold. It consists of 126 stanzas, and is consequently the longest of the four. It is yet to be copied and polished; and the notes are to come, of which it will require more than the third Canto, as it necessarily treats more of works of art than of nature. It shall be sent towards autumn;—and now for our barter. What do you bid? eh? you shall have samples, an' it so please you: but I wish to know what I am to expect (as the saying is) in these hard times, when poetry does not let for half its value. If you are disposed to do what Mrs. Winifred Jenkins calls 'the handsome thing,' I may perhaps throw you some odd matters to the lot,—translations, or slight originals; there is no saying what may be on the anvil between this and the booking season. Recollect that it is the last Canto, and completes the work; whether as good as the others, I cannot judge, in course—least of all as yet,—but it shall be as little worse as I can help. I may, perhaps, give some little gossip in the notes as to the present state of Italian literati and literature, being acquainted with some of their capi—men as well as books;—but this depends upon my humour at the time. So, now, pronounce: I say nothing.

"When you have got the whole four Cantos, I think you might venture on an edition of the whole poem in quarto, with spare copies of the two last for the purchasers of the old edition of the first two. There is a hint for you, worthy of the Row; and now, perpend—pronounce.

"I have not received a word from you of the fate of 'Manfred' or 'Tasso,' which seems to me odd, whether they have failed or succeeded.

"As this is a scrawl of business, and I have lately written at length and often on other subjects, I will only add that I am," &c.

LETTER 292. TO MR. MURRAY.

"La Mira, near Venice, August 7, 1817

"Your letter of the 18th, and, what will please you, as it did me, the parcel sent by the good-natured aid and abetment of Mr. Croker, are arrived.—Messrs. Lewis and Hobhouse are here: the former in the same house, the latter a few hundred yards distant.

"You say nothing of Manfred, from which its failure may be inferred; but I think it odd you should not say so at once. I know nothing, and hear absolutely nothing, of any body or any thing in England; and there are no English papers, so that all you say will be news—of any person, or thing, or things. I am at present very anxious about Newstead, and sorry that Kinnaird is leaving England at this minute, though I do not tell him so, and would rather he should have his pleasure, although it may not in this instance tend to my profit.

"If I understand rightly, you have paid into Morland's 1500 pounds: as the agreement in the paper is two thousand guineas, there will remain therefore six hundred pounds, and not five hundred, the odd hundred being the extra to make up the specie. Six hundred and thirty pounds will bring it to the like for Manfred and Tasso, making a total of twelve hundred and thirty, I believe, for I am not a good calculator. I do not wish to press you, but I tell you fairly that it will be a convenience to me to have it paid as soon as it can be made convenient to yourself.

"The new and last Canto is 130 stanzas in length; and may be made more or less. I have fixed no price, even in idea, and have no notion of what it may be good for. There are no metaphysics in it; at least, I think not. Mr. Hobhouse has promised me a copy of Tasso's Will, for notes; and I have some curious things to say about Ferrara, and Parisina's story, and perhaps a farthing candle's worth of light upon the present state of Italian literature. I shall hardly be ready by October; but that don't matter. I have all to copy and correct, and the notes to write.

"I do not know whether Scott will like it; but I have called him the 'Ariosto of the North' in my text. If he should not, say so in time.

"An Italian translation of 'Glenarvon' came lately to be printed at Venice. The censor (Sr. Petrotini) refused to sanction the publication till he had seen me on the subject. I told him that I did not recognise the slightest relation between that book and myself; but that, whatever opinions might be upon that subject, I would never prevent or oppose the publication of any book, in any language, on my own private account; and desired him (against his inclination) to permit the poor translator to publish his labours. It is going forwards in consequence. You may say this, with my compliments, to the author.

"Yours."

LETTER 293. TO MR. MURRAY.

"Venice, August 12. 1817.

"I have been very sorry to hear of the death of Madame de Staël, not only because she had been very kind to me at Copet, but because now I can never requite her. In a general point of view, she will leave a great gap in society and literature.

"With regard to death, I doubt that we have any right to pity the dead for their own sakes.

"The copies of Manfred and Tasso are arrived, thanks to Mr. Croker's cover. You have destroyed the whole effect and moral of the poem by omitting the last line of Manfred's speaking; and why this was done, I know not. Why you persist in saying nothing of the thing itself, I am equally at a loss to conjecture. If it is for fear of telling me something disagreeable, you are wrong; because sooner or later I must know it, and I am not so new, nor so raw, nor so inexperienced, as not to be able to bear, not the mere paltry, petty disappointments of authorship, but things more serious,—at least I hope so, and that what you may think irritability is merely mechanical, and only acts like galvanism on a dead body, or the muscular motion which survives sensation.

"If it is that you are out of humour, because I wrote to you a sharp letter, recollect that it was partly from a misconception of your letter, and partly because you did a thing you had no right to do without consulting me.

"I have, however, heard good of Manfred from two other quarters, and from men who would not be scrupulous in saying what they thought, or what was said; and so 'good morrow to you, good Master Lieutenant.'

"I wrote to you twice about the fourth Canto, which you will answer at your pleasure. Mr. Hobhouse and I have come up for a day to the city; Mr. Lewis is gone to England; and I am

"Yours."

LETTER 294. TO MR. MURRAY.

"La Mira, near Venice, August 21. 1817.

"I take you at your word about Mr. Hanson, and will feel obliged if you will go to him, and request Mr. Davies also to visit him by my desire, and repeat that I trust that neither Mr. Kinnaird's absence nor mine will prevent his taking all proper steps to accelerate and promote the sale of Newstead and Rochdale, upon which the whole of my future personal comfort depends. It is impossible for me to express how much any delays upon these points would inconvenience me; and I do not know a greater obligation that can be conferred upon me than the pressing these things upon Hanson, and making him act according to my wishes. I wish you would speak out, at least to me, and tell me what you allude to by your cold way of mentioning him. All mysteries at such a distance are not merely tormenting but mischievous, and may be prejudicial to my interests; so, pray expound, that I may consult with Mr. Kinnaird when he arrives; and remember that I prefer the most disagreeable certainties to hints and innuendoes. The devil take every body: I never can get any person to be explicit about any thing or any body, and my whole life is passed in conjectures of what people mean: you all talk in the style of C * * L * *'s novels.

"It is not Mr. St. John, but Mr. St. Aubyn, son of Sir John St. Aubyn. Polidori knows him, and introduced him to me. He is of Oxford, and has got my parcel. The Doctor will ferret him out, or ought. The parcel contains many letters, some of Madame de Staël's, and other people's, besides MSS., &c. By ——, if I find the gentleman, and he don't find the parcel, I will say something he won't like to hear.

"You want a 'civil and delicate declension' for the medical tragedy? Take it—

"Dear Doctor, I have read your play,
Which is a good one in its way,—
Purges the eyes and moves the bowels,
And drenches handkerchiefs like towels
With tears, that, in a flux of grief,
Afford hysterical relief
To shatter'd nerves and quicken'd pulses,
Which your catastrophe convulses.

"I like your moral and machinery;
Your plot, too, has such scope for scenery!
Your dialogue is apt and smart;
The play's concoction full of art;
Your hero raves, your heroine cries,
All stab, and every body dies.
In short, your tragedy would be
The very thing to hear and see:
And for a piece of publication,
If I decline on this occasion,
It is not that I am not sensible
To merits in themselves ostensible,
But—and I grieve to speak it—plays
Are drugs, mere drugs, sir—now-a-days.
I had a heavy loss by 'Manuel,'—
Too lucky if it prove not annual,—
And S * *, with his 'Orestes,'
(Which, by the by, the author's best is,)

  Has lain so very long on hand
  That I despair of all demand.
  I've advertised, but see my books,
  Or only watch my shopman's looks;—
  Still Ivan, Ina, and such lumber,
My back-shop glut, my shelves encumber.
"There's Byron too, who once did better,
  Has sent me, folded in a letter,
  A sort of—it's no more a drama
  Than Darnley, Ivan, or Kehama;
  So alter'd since last year his pen is,
  I think he's lost his wits at Venice.
  In short, sir, what with one and t'other,
  I dare not venture on another.
  I write in haste; excuse each blunder;
The coaches through the street so thunder!
  My room's so full—we've Gifford here
  Reading MS., with Hookham Frere,
  Pronouncing on the nouns and particles
  Of some of our forthcoming Articles.
  "The Quarterly—Ah, sir, if you
  Had but the genius to review!—
  A smart critique upon St. Helena,
  Or if you only would but tell in a
  Short compass what—but, to resume:
  As I was saying, sir, the room—
  The room's so full of wits and bards,
Crabbes, Campbells, Crokers, Freres, and Wards,
  And others, neither bards nor wits:—
  My humble tenement admits
  All persons in the dress of gent.,
  From Mr. Hammond to Dog Dent.
  "A party dines with me to-day,
  All clever men, who make their way;
  They're at this moment in discussion
  On poor De Staël's late dissolution.
  Her book, they say, was in advance—
  Pray Heaven, she tell the truth of France!
  "Thus run our time and tongues away.—
  But, to return, sir, to your play:

> Sorry, sir, but I cannot deal,
> Unless 'twere acted by O'Neill.
> My hands so full, my head so busy,
> I'm almost dead, and always dizzy;
> And so, with endless truth and hurry,
> Dear Doctor, I am yours,

"P.S. I've done the fourth and last Canto, which amounts to 133 stanzas. I desire you to name a price; if you don't, I will; so I advise you in time.

"Yours, &c.

"There will be a good many notes."

Among those minor misrepresentations of which it was Lord Byron's fate to be the victim, advantage was, at this time, taken of his professed distaste to the English, to accuse him of acts of inhospitality, and even rudeness, towards some of his fellow-countrymen. How far different was his treatment of all who ever visited him, many grateful testimonies might be collected to prove; but I shall here content myself with selecting a few extracts from an account given me by Mr. Henry Joy of a visit which, in company with another English gentleman, he paid to the noble poet this summer, at his villa on the banks of the Brenta. After mentioning the various civilities they had experienced from Lord Byron; and, among others, his having requested them to name their own day for dining with him,—"We availed ourselves," says Mr. Joy, "of this considerate courtesy by naming the day fixed for our return to Padua, when our route would lead us to his door; and we were welcomed with all the cordiality which was to be expected from so friendly a bidding. Such traits of kindness in such a man deserve to be recorded on account of the numerous slanders thrown upon him by some of the tribes of tourists, who resented, as a personal affront, his resolution to avoid their impertinent inroads upon his retirement. So far from any appearance of indiscriminate aversion to his countrymen, his enquiries about his friends in England (quorum pars magna fuisti) were most anxious and particular.

"He expressed some opinions," continues my informant, "on matters of taste, which cannot fail to interest his biographer. He contended that Sculpture, as an art, was vastly superior to Painting;—a preference which is strikingly illustrated by the fact that, in the fourth Canto of Childe Harold, he gives the most elaborate and splendid account of several statues, and none of any pictures; although Italy is, emphatically, the land of painting, and her best statues are derived from Greece. By the way, he told us that there were more objects of interest in Rome alone than in all Greece from one extremity to the other. After regaling us with an excellent dinner, (in which, by the by, a very English joint of roast beef showed that he did not extend his antipathies to all John-Bullisms,) he took me in his carriage some miles of our route towards Padua, after apologising to my fellow-traveller for the separation, on the score of his anxiety to hear all he could of his friends in England; and I quitted him with a confirmed impression of the strong ardour and sincerity of his attachment to those by whom he did not fancy himself slighted or ill treated."

LETTER 295. TO MR. MURRAY.

"Sept. 4. 1817.

"Your letter of the 15th has conveyed with its contents the impression of a seal, to which the 'Saracen's Head' is a seraph, and the 'Bull and Mouth' a delicate device. I knew that calumny had sufficiently blackened me of later days, but not that it had given the features as well as complexion of a negro. Poor Augusta is not less, but rather more, shocked than myself, and says 'people seem to have lost their recollection strangely' when they engraved such a 'blackamoor.' Pray don't seal (at least to me) with such a caricature of the human numskull altogether; and if you don't break the seal-cutter's head, at least crack his libel (or likeness, if it should be a likeness) of mine.

"Mr. Kinnaird is not yet arrived, but expected. He has lost by the way all the tooth-powder, as a letter from Spa informs me.

"By Mr. Rose I received safely, though tardily, magnesia and tooth-powder, and * * * *. Why do you send me such trash—worse than trash, the Sublime of Mediocrity? Thanks for Lalla, however, which is good; and thanks for the Edinburgh and Quarterly, both very amusing and well-written. Paris in 1815, &c.—good. Modern Greece—good for nothing; written by some one who has never been there, and not being able to manage the Spenser stanza, has invented a thing of his own, consisting of two elegiac stanzas, an heroic line, and an Alexandrine, twisted on a string. Besides, why 'modern?' You may say modern Greeks, but surely Greece itself is rather more ancient than ever it was. Now for business.

"You offer 1500 guineas for the new Canto: I won't take it. I ask two thousand five hundred guineas for it, which you will either give or not, as you think proper. It concludes the poem, and consists of 144 stanzas. The notes are numerous, and chiefly written by Mr. Hobhouse, whose researches have been indefatigable; and who, I will venture to say, has more real knowledge of Rome and its environs than any Englishman who has been there since Gibbon. By the way, to prevent any mistakes, I think it necessary to state the fact that he, Mr. Hobhouse, has no interest whatever in the price or profit to be derived from the copyright of either poem or notes directly or indirectly; so that you are not to suppose that it is by, for, or through him, that I require more for this Canto than the preceding.—No: but if Mr. Eustace was to have had two thousand for a poem on Education; if Mr. Moore is to have three thousand for Lalla, &c.; if Mr. Campbell is to have three thousand for his prose on poetry—I don't mean to disparage these gentlemen in their labours—but I ask the aforesaid price for mine. You will tell me that their productions are considerably longer: very true, and when they shorten them, I will lengthen mine, and ask less. You shall submit the MS. to Mr. Gifford, and any other two gentlemen to be named by you, (Mr. Frere, or Mr. Croker, or whomever you please, except such fellows as your * *s and * *s,) and if they pronounce this Canto to be inferior as a whole to the preceding, I will not appeal from their award, but burn the manuscript, and leave things as they are.

"Yours very truly.

"P.S. In answer to a former letter, I sent you a short statement of what I thought the state of our present copyright account, viz. six hundred pounds still (or lately) due on Childe Harold, and six hundred guineas, Manfred and Tasso, making a total of twelve hundred and thirty pounds. If we agree about the new poem, I shall take the liberty to reserve the choice of the manner in which it should be published, viz. a quarto, certes."

LETTER 296. TO MR. HOPPNER.

"La Mira, Sept. 12. 1817.

"I set out yesterday morning with the intention of paying my respects, and availing myself of your permission to walk over the premises. On arriving at Padua, I found that the march of the Austrian troops had engrossed so many horses, that those I could procure were hardly able to crawl; and their weakness, together with the prospect of finding none at all at the post-house of Monselice, and consequently either not arriving that day at Este, or so late as to be unable to return home the same evening, induced me to turn aside in a second visit to Arqua, instead of proceeding onwards; and even thus I hardly got back in time.

"Next week I shall be obliged to be in Venice to meet Lord Kinnaird and his brother, who are expected in a few days. And this interruption, together with that occasioned by the continued march of the Austrians for the next few days, will not allow me to fix any precise period for availing myself of your kindness, though I should wish to take the earliest opportunity. Perhaps, if absent, you will have the goodness to permit one of your servants to show me the grounds and house, or as much of either as may be convenient; at any rate, I shall take the first occasion possible to go over, and regret very much that I was yesterday prevented.

"I have the honour to be your obliged," &c.

LETTER 297. TO MR. MURRAY.

"September 15. 1817.

"I enclose a sheet for correction, if ever you get to another edition. You will observe that the blunder in printing makes it appear as if the Château was over St. Gingo, instead of being on the opposite shore of the Lake, over Clarens. So, separate the paragraphs, otherwise my topography will seem as inaccurate as your typography on this occasion.

"The other day I wrote to convey my proposition with regard to the fourth and concluding Canto. I have gone over and extended it to one hundred and fifty stanzas, which is almost as long as the two first were originally, and longer by itself than any of the smaller poems except 'The Corsair.' Mr. Hobhouse has made some very valuable and accurate notes of considerable length, and you may be sure that I will do for the text all that I can to finish with decency. I look upon Childe Harold as my best; and as I begun, I think of concluding with it. But I make no resolutions on that head, as I broke my former intention with regard to 'The Corsair.' However, I fear that I shall never do better; and yet, not being thirty years of age, for some moons to come, one ought to be progressive as far as intellect goes for many a good year. But I have had a devilish deal of tear and wear of mind and body in my time, besides having published too often and much already. God grant me some judgment to do what may be most fitting in that and every thing else, for I doubt my own exceedingly.

"I have read 'Lalla Rookh,' but not with sufficient attention yet, for I ride about, and lounge, and ponder, and—two or three other things; so that my reading is very desultory, and not so attentive as it used to be. I am very glad to hear of its popularity, for Moore is a very noble fellow in all respects, and will enjoy it without any of the bad feelings which success—good or evil—sometimes engenders in the men of rhyme. Of the poem, itself, I will tell you my opinion when I have mastered it: I say of the poem, for I don't like the prose at all; and in the mean time, the 'Fire-worshippers' is the best, and the 'Veiled Prophet' the worst, of the volume.

"With regard to poetry in general, I am convinced, the more I think of it, that he and all of us—Scott, Southey, Wordsworth, Moore, Campbell, I,—are all in the wrong, one as much as another; that we are upon a wrong revolutionary poetical system, or systems, not worth a damn in itself, and from which none but Rogers and Crabbe are free; and that the present and next generations will finally be of this opinion. I am the more confirmed in this by having lately gone over some of our classics, particularly Pope, whom I tried in this way,—I took Moore's poems and my own and some others, and went over them side by side with Pope's, and I was really astonished (I ought not to have been so) and mortified at the ineffable distance in point of sense, learning, effect, and even imagination, passion, and invention, between the little Queen Anne's man, and us of the Lower Empire. Depend upon it, it is all Horace then, and Claudian now, among us; and if I had to begin again, I would mould myself accordingly. Crabbe's the man, but he has got a coarse and impracticable subject, and * * * is retired upon half-pay, and has done enough, unless he were to do as he did formerly."

LETTER 298. TO MR. MURRAY.

"September 17. 1817.

"Mr. Hobhouse purposes being in England in November; he will bring the fourth Canto with him, notes and all; the text contains one hundred and fifty stanzas, which is long for that measure.

"With regard to the 'Ariosto of the North,' surely their themes, chivalry, war, and love, were as like as can be; and as to the compliment, if you knew what the Italians think of Ariosto, you would not hesitate about that. But as to their 'measures,' you forget that Ariosto's is an octave stanza, and Scott's any thing but a stanza. If you think Scott will dislike it, say so, and I will expunge. I do not call him the 'Scotch Ariosto,' which would be sad provincial eulogy, but the 'Ariosto of the North, meaning of all countries that are not the South. * *

"As I have recently troubled you rather frequently, I will conclude, repeating that I am

"Yours ever," &c.

LETTER 299. TO MR. MURRAY.

"October 12. 1817.

"Mr. Kinnaird and his brother, Lord Kinnaird, have been here, and are now gone again. All your missives came, except the tooth-powder, of which I request further supplies, at all convenient opportunities; as also of magnesia and soda-powders, both great luxuries here, and neither to be had good, or indeed hardly at all, of the natives. * * *

"In * *'s Life, I perceive an attack upon the then Committee of D.L. Theatre for acting Bertram, and an attack upon Maturin's Bertram for being acted. Considering all things, this is not very grateful nor graceful on the part of the worthy autobiographer; and I would answer, if I had not obliged him. Putting my own pains to forward the views of * * out of the question, I know that there was every disposition, on the part of the Sub-Committee, to bring forward any production of his, were it feasible. The play he offered, though poetical, did not appear at all practicable, and Bertram did;—and hence this long tirade, which is the last chapter of his vagabond life.

"As for Bertram, Maturin may defend his own begotten, if he likes it well enough; I leave the Irish clergyman and the new Orator Henley to battle it out between them, satisfied to have done the best I could for both. I may say this to you, who know it.

"Mr. * * may console himself with the fervour,—the almost religious fervour of his and W * *'s disciples, as he calls it. If he means that as any proof of their merits, I will find him as much 'fervour' in behalf of Richard Brothers and Joanna Southcote as ever gathered over his pages or round his fire-side.

"My answer to your proposition about the fourth Canto you will have received, and I await yours;—perhaps we may not agree. I have since written a poem (of 84 octave stanzas), humorous, in or after the excellent manner of Mr. Whistlecraft (whom I take to be Frere), on a Venetian anecdote which amused me:—but till I have your answer, I can say nothing more about it.

"Mr. Hobhouse does not return to England in November, as he intended, but will winter here and as he is to convey the poem, or poems,—for there may perhaps be more than the two mentioned, (which, by the way, I shall not perhaps include in the same publication or agreement,) I shall not be able to publish so soon as expected; but I suppose there is no harm in the delay.

"I have signed and sent your former copyrights by Mr. Kinnaird, but not the receipt, because the money is not yet paid. Mr. Kinnaird has a power of attorney to sign for me, and will, when necessary.

"Many thanks for the Edinburgh Review, which is very kind about Manfred, and defends its originality, which I did not know that any body had attacked. I never read, and do not know that I ever saw, the 'Faustus of Marlow,' and had, and have, no dramatic works by me in English, except the recent things you sent me; but I heard Mr. Lewis translate verbally some scenes of Goethe's Faust (which were, some good, and some bad) last summer;—which is all I know of the history of that magical personage; and as to the germs of Manfred, they may be found in the Journal which I sent to Mrs. Leigh (part of which you saw) when I went over first the Dent de Jaman, and then the Wengen or Wengeberg Alp and Sheideck, and made the giro of the Jungfrau, Shreckhorn, &c. &c. shortly before I left Switzerland. I have the whole scene of Manfred before me as if it was but yesterday, and could point it out, spot by spot, torrent and all.

"Of the Prometheus of Æschylus I was passionately fond as a boy (it was one of the Greek plays we read thrice a year at Harrow);—indeed that and the 'Medea' were the only ones, except the 'Seven before Thebes,' which ever much pleased me. As to the 'Faustus of Marlow,' I never read, never saw, nor heard of it—at least, thought of it, except that I think Mr. Gifford mentioned, in a note of his which you sent me, something about the catastrophe; but not as having any thing to do with mine, which may or may not resemble it, for any thing I know.

"The Prometheus, if not exactly in my plan, has always been so much in my head, that I can easily conceive its influence over all or any thing that I have written;—but I deny Marlow and his progeny, and beg that you will do the same.

"If you can send me the paper in question, which the Edinburgh Review mentions, do. The review in the magazine you say was written by Wilson? it had all the air of being a poet's, and was a very good one. The Edinburgh Review I take to be Jeffrey's own by its friendliness. I wonder they thought it worth while to do so, so soon after the former; but it was evidently with a good motive.

"I saw Hoppner the other day, whose country-house at Este I have taken for two years. If you come out next summer, let me know in time. Love to Gifford.

"Yours ever truly.

"Crabbe, Malcolm, Hamilton, and Chantrey,
Are all partakers of my pantry.

These two lines are omitted in your letter to the doctor, after—
"All clever men who make their way."

LETTER 300. TO MR. MURRAY.

"Venice, October 23. 1817.

"Your two letters are before me, and our bargain is so far concluded. How sorry I am to hear that Gifford is unwell! Pray tell me he is better: I hope it is nothing but cold. As you say his illness originates in cold, I trust it will get no further.

"Mr. Whistlecraft has no greater admirer than myself: I have written a story in 89 stanzas, in imitation of him, called Beppo, (the short name for Giuseppe, that is, the Joe of the Italian Joseph,) which I shall throw you into the balance of the fourth Canto, to help you round to your money; but you perhaps had better publish it anonymously; but this we will see to by and by.

"In the Notes to Canto fourth, Mr. Hobhouse has pointed out several errors of Gibbon. You may depend upon H.'s research and accuracy. You may print it in what shape you please.

"With regard to a future large edition, you may print all, or any thing, except 'English Bards,' to the republication of which at no time will I consent. I would not reprint them on any consideration. I don't think them good for much, even in point of poetry; and, as to other things, you are to recollect that I gave up the publication on account of the Hollands, and I do not think that any time or circumstances can neutralise the suppression. Add to which, that, after being on terms with almost all the bards and critics of the day, it would be savage at any time, but worst of all now, to revive this foolish lampoon.

"The review of Manfred came very safely, and I am much pleased with it. It is odd that they should say (that is somebody in a magazine whom the Edinburgh controverts) that it was taken from Marlow's Faust, which I never read nor saw. An American, who came the other day from Germany, told Mr. Hobhouse that Manfred was taken from Goethe's Faust. The devil may take both the Faustuses, German and English—I have taken neither.

"Will you send to Hanson, and say that he has not written since 9th September?—at least I have had no letter since, to my great surprise.

"Will you desire Messrs. Morland to send out whatever additional sums have or may be paid in credit immediately, and always to their Venice correspondents? It is two months ago that they sent me out an additional credit for one thousand pounds. I was very glad of it, but I don't know how the devil it came; for I can only make out 500 of Hanson's payment, and I had thought the other 500 came from you; but it did not, it seems, as, by yours of the 7th instant, you have only just paid the 1230l. balance.

"Mr. Kinnaird is on his way home with the assignments. I can fix no time for the arrival of Canto fourth, which depends on the journey of Mr. Hobhouse home; and I do not think that this will be immediate.

"Yours in great haste and very truly,

"B.

"P.S. Morlands have not yet written to my bankers apprising the payment of your balances: pray desire them to do so.

"Ask them about the previous thousand—of which I know 500 came from Hanson's—and make out the other 500—that is, whence it came."

LETTER 301. TO MR. MURRAY.

"Venice, November 15. 1817.

"Mr. Kinnaird has probably returned to England by this time, and will have conveyed to you any tidings you may wish to have of us and ours. I have come back to Venice for the winter. Mr. Hobhouse will probably set off in December, but what day or week I know not. He is my opposite neighbour at present.

"I wrote yesterday in some perplexity, and no very good humour, to Mr. Kinnaird, to inform me about Newstead and the Hansons, of which and whom I hear nothing since his departure from this place, except in a few unintelligible words from an unintelligible woman.

"I am as sorry to hear of Dr. Polidori's accident as one can be for a person for whom one has a dislike, and something of contempt. When he gets well, tell me, and how he gets on in the sick line. Poor fellow! how came he to fix there?

"I fear the Doctor's skill at Norwich
Will hardly salt the Doctor's porridge.

Methought he was going to the Brazils to give the Portuguese physic (of which they are fond to desperation) with the Danish consul.

"Your new Canto has expanded to one hundred and sixty-seven stanzas. It will be long, you see; and as for the notes by Hobhouse, I suspect they will be of the heroic size. You must keep Mr. * * in good humour, for he is devilish touchy yet about your Review and all which it inherits, including the editor, the Admiralty, and its bookseller. I used to think that I was a good deal of an author in amour propre and noli me tangere; but these prose fellows are worst, after all, about their little comforts.

"Do you remember my mentioning, some months ago, the Marquis Moncada—a Spaniard of distinction and fourscore years, my summer neighbour at La Mira? Well, about six weeks ago, he fell in love with a Venetian girl of family, and no fortune or character; took her into his mansion; quarrelled with all his former friends for giving him advice (except me who gave him none), and installed her present concubine and future wife and mistress of himself and furniture. At the end of a month, in which she demeaned herself as ill as possible, he found out a correspondence between her and some former keeper, and after nearly strangling, turned her out of the house, to the great scandal of the keeping part of the town, and with a prodigious éclat, which has occupied all the canals and coffee-houses in Venice. He said she wanted to poison him; and she says—God knows what; but between them they have made a great deal of noise. I know a little of both the parties: Moncada seemed a very sensible old man, a character which he has not quite kept up on this occasion; and the woman is rather showy than pretty. For the honour of religion, she was bred in a convent, and for the credit of Great Britain, taught by an Englishwoman.

"Yours," &c.

LETTER 302. TO MR. MURRAY.

"Venice, December 3. 1817.

"A Venetian lady, learned and somewhat stricken in years, having, in her intervals of love and devotion, taken upon her to translate the Letters and write the Life of Lady Mary Wortley Montague,—to which undertaking there are two obstacles, firstly, ignorance of English, and, secondly, a total dearth of information on the subject of her projected biography, has applied to me for facts or falsities upon this promising project. Lady Montague lived the last twenty or more years of her life in or near Venice, I believe; but here they know nothing, and remember nothing, for the story of to-day is succeeded by the scandal of to-morrow; and the wit, and beauty, and gallantry, which might render your countrywoman notorious in her own country, must have been here no great distinction—because the first is in no request, and the two latter are common to all women, or at least the last of them. If you can therefore tell me any thing, or get any thing told, of Lady Wortley Montague, I shall take it as a favour, and will transfer and translate it to the 'Dama' in question. And I pray you besides to send me, by some quick and safe voyager, the edition of her Letters, and the stupid Life, by Dr. Dallaway, published by her proud and foolish family.

"The death of the Princess Charlotte has been a shock even here, and must have been an earthquake at home. The Courier's list of some three hundred heirs to the crown (including the house of Wirtemberg, with that * * *, P——, of disreputable memory, whom I remember seeing at various balls during the visit of the Muscovites, &c. in 1814) must be very consolatory to all true lieges, as well as foreigners, except Signor Travis, a rich Jew merchant of this city, who complains grievously of the length of British mourning, which has countermanded all the silks which he was on the point of transmitting, for a year to come. The death of this poor girl is melancholy in every respect, dying at twenty or so, in childbed—of a boy too, a present princess and future queen, and just as she began to be happy, and to enjoy herself, and the hopes which she inspired.

"I think, as far as I can recollect, she is the first royal defunct in childbed upon record in our history. I feel sorry in every respect—for the loss of a female reign, and a woman hitherto harmless; and all the lost rejoicings, and addresses, and drunkenness, and disbursements, of John Bull on the occasion.

"The Prince will marry again, after divorcing his wife, and Mr. Southey will write an elegy now, and an ode then; the Quarterly will have an article against the press, and the Edinburgh an article, half and half, about reform and right of divorce; the British will give you Dr. Chalmers's funeral sermon much commended, with a place in the stars for deceased royalty; and the Morning Post will have already yelled forth its 'syllables of dolour.'

"Woe, woe, Nealliny!—the young Nealliny!

"It is some time since I have heard from you: are you in bad humour? I suppose so. I have been so myself, and it is your turn now, and by and by mine will come round again. Yours truly,

"B.

"P.S. Countess Albrizzi, come back from Paris, has brought me a medal of himself, a present from Denon to me, and a likeness of Mr. Rogers (belonging to her), by Denon also."

LETTER 303. TO MR. HOPPNER.

"Venice, December 15. 1817.

"I should have thanked you before, for your favour a few days ago, had I not been in the intention of paying my respects, personally, this evening, from which I am deterred by the recollection that you will probably be at the Count Goess's this evening, which has made me postpone my intrusion.

"I think your Elegy a remarkably good one, not only as a composition, but both the politics and poetry contain a far greater portion of truth and generosity than belongs to the times, or to the professors of these opposite pursuits, which usually agree only in one point, as extremes meet. I do not know whether you wished me to retain the copy, but I shall retain it till you tell me otherwise; and am very much obliged by the perusal.

"My own sentiments on Venice, &c., such as they are, I had already thrown into verse last summer, in the fourth Canto of Childe Harold, now in preparation for the press; and I think much more highly of them, for being in coincidence with yours.

"Believe me yours," &c.

LETTER 304. TO MR. MURRAY.

"Venice, January 8. 1818.

"My dear Mr. Murray,
You're in a damn'd hurry
To set up this ultimate Canto;
But (if they don't rob us)
You'll see Mr. Hobhouse
Will bring it safe in his portmanteau.

LETTER 305. TO MR. MURRAY.

"Venice, January 19. 1818.

"I send you the Story in three other separate covers. It won't do for your Journal, being full of political allusions. Print alone, without name; alter nothing; get a scholar to see that the Italian phrases are correctly published, (your printing, by the way, always makes me ill with its eternal blunders, which are incessant,) and God speed you. Hobhouse left Venice a fortnight ago, saving two days. I have heard nothing of or from him.

"Yours, &c.

"He has the whole of the MSS.; so put up prayers in your back shop, or in the printer's 'Chapel.'"

LETTER 306. TO MR. MURRAY.

"Venice, January 27. 1818.

"My father—that is, my Armenian father, Padre Pasquali—in the name of all the other fathers of our Convent, sends you the enclosed, greeting.

"Inasmuch as it has pleased the translators of the long-lost and lately-found portions of the text of Eusebius to put forth the enclosed prospectus, of which I send six copies, you are hereby implored to obtain subscribers in the two Universities, and among the learned, and the unlearned who would unlearn their ignorance—This they (the Convent) request, I request, and do you request.

"I sent you Beppo some weeks agone. You must publish it alone; it has politics and ferocity, and won't do for your isthmus of a Journal.

"Mr. Hobhouse, if the Alps have not broken his neck, is, or ought to be, swimming with my commentaries and his own coat of mail in his teeth and right hand, in a cork jacket, between Calais and Dover.

"It is the height of the Carnival, and I am in the extreme and agonies of a new intrigue with I don't exactly know whom or what, except that she is insatiate of love, and won't take money, and has light hair and blue eyes, which are not common here, and that I met her at the Masque, and that when her mask is off, I am as wise as ever. I shall make what I can of the remainder of my youth."

LETTER 307. TO MR. MOORE.

"Venice, February 2. 1818.

"Your letter of December 8th arrived but this day, by some delay, common but inexplicable. Your domestic calamity is very grievous, and I feel with you as much as I dare feel at all. Throughout life, your loss must be my loss, and your gain my gain; and, though my heart may ebb, there will always be a drop for you among the dregs.

"I know how to feel with you, because (selfishness being always the substratum of our damnable clay) I am quite wrapt up in my own children. Besides my little legitimate, I have made unto myself an illegitimate since (to say nothing of one before), and I look forward to one of these as the pillar of my old age, supposing that I ever reach—which I hope I never shall—that desolating period. I have a great love for my little Ada, though perhaps she may torture me, like * * *.

"Your offered address will be as acceptable as you can wish. I don't much care what the wretches of the world think of me—all that's past. But I care a good deal what you think of me, and, so, say what you like. You know that I am not sullen; and, as to being savage, such things depend on circumstances. However, as to being in good humour in your society, there is no great merit in that, because it would be an effort, or an insanity, to be otherwise.

"I don't know what Murray may have been saying or quoting. I called Crabbe and Sam the fathers of present Poesy; and said, that I thought—except them—all of 'us youth' were on a wrong tack. But I never said that we did not sail well. Our fame will be hurt by admiration and imitation. When I say our, I mean all (Lakers included), except the postscript of the Augustans. The next generation (from the quantity and facility of imitation) will tumble and break their necks off our Pegasus, who runs away with us; but we keep the saddle, because we broke the rascal and can ride. But though easy to mount, he is the devil to guide; and the next fellows must go back to the riding-school and the manège, and learn to ride the 'great horse.'

"Talking of horses, by the way, I have transported my own, four in number, to the Lido (beach in English), a strip of some ten miles along the Adriatic, a mile or two from the city; so that I not only get a row in my gondola, but a spanking gallop of some miles daily along a firm and solitary beach, from the fortress to Malamocco, the which contributes considerably to my health and spirits.

"I have hardly had a wink of sleep this week past. We are in the agonies of the Carnival's last days, and I must be up all night again, as well as to-morrow. I have had some curious masking adventures this Carnival; but, as they are not yet over, I shall not say on. I will work the mine of my youth to the last veins of the ore, and then—good night. I have lived, and am content.

"Hobhouse went away before the Carnival began, so that he had little or no fun. Besides, it requires some time to be thoroughgoing with the Venetians; but of all this anon, in some other letter.

"I must dress for the evening. There is an opera and ridotto, and I know not what, besides balls; and so, ever and ever yours,

"B.

"P.S. I send this without revision, so excuse errors. I delight in the fame and fortune of Lalla, and again congratulate you on your well-merited success."

Of his daily rides on the Lido, which he mentions in this letter, the following account, by a gentleman who lived a good deal with him at Venice, will be found not a little interesting:—

"Almost immediately after Mr. Hobhouse's departure, Lord Byron proposed to me to accompany him in his rides on the Lido. One of the long narrow islands which separate the Lagune, in the midst of which Venice stands, from the Adriatic, is more particularly distinguished by this name. At one extremity is a fortification, which, with the Castle of St. Andrea on an island on the opposite side, defends the nearest entrance to the city from the sea. In times of peace this fortification is almost dismantled, and Lord Byron had hired here of the Commandant an unoccupied stable, where he kept his horses. The distance from the city was not very considerable; it was much less than to the Terra Firma, and, as far as it went, the spot was not ineligible for riding.

"Every day that the weather would permit, Lord Byron called for me in his gondola, and we found the horses waiting for us outside of the fort. We rode as far as we could along the sea-shore, and then on a kind of dyke, or embankment, which has been raised where the island was very narrow, as far as another small fort about half way between the principal one which I have already mentioned, and the town or village of Malamocco, which is near the other extremity of the island,—the distance between the two forts being about three miles.

"On the land side of the embankment, not far from the smaller fort, was a boundary stone which probably marked some division of property,—all the side of the island nearest the Lagune being divided into gardens for the cultivation of vegetables for the Venetian markets. At the foot of this stone Lord Byron repeatedly told me that I should cause him to be interred, if he should die in Venice, or its neighbourhood, during my residence there; and he appeared to think, as he was not a Catholic, that, on the part of the government, there could be no obstacle to his interment in an unhallowed spot of ground by the sea-side. At all events, I was to overcome whatever difficulties might be raised on this account. I was, by no means, he repeatedly told me, to allow his body to be removed to England, nor permit any of his family to interfere with his funeral.

"Nothing could be more delightful than these rides on the Lido were to me. We were from half to three quarters of an hour crossing the water, during which his conversation was always most amusing and interesting. Sometimes he would bring with him any new book he had received, and read to me the passages which most struck him. Often he would repeat to me whole stanzas of the poems he was engaged in writing, as he had composed them on the preceding evening; and this was the more interesting to me, because I could frequently trace in them some idea which he had started in our conversation of the preceding day, or some remark, the effect of which he had been evidently trying upon me. Occasionally, too, he spoke of his own affairs, making me repeat all I had heard with regard to him, and desiring that I would not spare him, but let him know the worst that was said."

LETTER 308. TO MR. MURRAY.

"Venice, Feb. 20. 1818.

"I have to thank Mr. Croker for the arrival, and you for the contents, of the parcel which came last week, much quicker than any before, owing to Mr. Croker's kind attention and the official exterior of the bags; and all safe, except much friction amongst the magnesia, of which only two bottles came entire; but it is all very well, and I am exceedingly obliged to you.

"The books I have read, or rather am reading. Pray, who may be the Sexagenarian, whose gossip is very amusing? Many of his sketches I recognise, particularly Gifford, Mackintosh, Drummond, Dutens, H. Walpole, Mrs. Inchbald, Opie, &c., with the Scotts, Loughborough, and most of the divines and lawyers, besides a few shorter hints of authors, and a few lines about a certain 'noble author,' characterised as malignant and sceptical, according to the good old story, 'as it was in the beginning, is now, but not always shall be:' do you know such a person, Master Murray? eh?—And pray, of the booksellers, which be you? the dry, the dirty, the honest, the opulent, the finical, the splendid, or the coxcomb bookseller? Stap my vitals, but the author grows scurrilous in his grand climacteric!

"I remember to have seen Porson at Cambridge, in the hall of our college, and in private parties, but not frequently; and I never can recollect him except as drunk or brutal, and generally both: I mean in an evening, for in the hall he dined at the Dean's table, and I at the Vice-master's, so that I was not near him; and he then and there appeared sober in his demeanour, nor did I ever hear of excess or outrage on his part in public,—commons, college, or chapel; but I have seen him in a private party of undergraduates, many of them fresh men and strangers, take up a poker to one of them, and heard him use language as blackguard as his action. I have seen Sheridan drunk, too, with all the world; but his intoxication was that of Bacchus, and Porson's that of Silenus. Of all the disgusting brutes, sulky, abusive, and intolerable, Porson was the most bestial, as far as the few times that I saw him went, which were only at William Bankes's (the Nubian discoverer's) rooms. I saw him once go away in a rage, because nobody knew the name of the 'Cobbler of Messina,' insulting their ignorance with the most vulgar terms of reprobation. He was tolerated in this state amongst the young men for his talents, as the Turks think a madman inspired, and bear with him. He used to recite, or rather vomit, pages of all languages, and could hiccup Greek like a Helot; and certainly Sparta never shocked her children with a grosser exhibition than this man's intoxication.

"I perceive, in the book you sent me, a long account of him, which is very savage. I cannot judge, as I never saw him sober, except in hall or combination-room; and then I was never near enough to hear, and hardly to see him. Of his drunken deportment, I can be sure, because I saw it.

"With the Reviews I have been much entertained. It requires to be as far from England as I am to relish a periodical paper properly: it is like soda-water in an Italian summer. But what cruel work you make with Lady * * * *! You should recollect that she is a woman; though, to be sure, they are now and then very provoking; still, as authoresses, they can do no great harm; and I think it a pity so much good invective should have been laid out upon her, when there is such a fine field of us Jacobin gentlemen for you to work upon.

"I heard from Moore lately, and was sorry to be made aware of his domestic loss. Thus it is—'medio de fonte leporum'—in the acmé of his fame and his happiness comes a drawback as usual.

"Mr. Hoppner, whom I saw this morning, has been made the father of a very fine boy.—Mother and child doing very well indeed. By this time Hobhouse should be with you, and also certain packets, letters, &c. of mine, sent since his departure.—I am not at all well in health within this last eight days. My remembrances to Gifford and all friends.

"Yours, &c.

"B.

"P.S. In the course of a month or two, Hanson will have probably to send off a clerk with conveyances to sign (Newstead being sold in November last for ninety-four thousand five hundred pounds), in which case I supplicate supplies of articles as usual, for which, desire Mr. Kinnaird to settle from funds in their bank, and deduct from my account with him.

"P.S. To-morrow night I am going to see 'Otello,' an opera from our 'Othello,' and one of Rossini's best, it is said. It will be curious to see in Venice the Venetian story itself represented, besides to discover what they will make of Shakspeare in music."

LETTER 309. TO MR. HOPPNER.

"Venice, February 28. 1818.

"My dear Sir,

"Our friend, il Conte M., threw me into a cold sweat last night, by telling me of a menaced version of Manfred (in Venetian, I hope, to complete the thing) by some Italian, who had sent it to you for correction, which is the reason why I take the liberty of troubling you on the subject. If you have any means of communication with the man, would you permit me to convey to him the offer of any price he may obtain or think to obtain for his project, provided he will throw his translation into the fire, and promise not to undertake any other of that or any other of my things: I will send his money immediately on this condition.

"As I did not write to the Italians, nor for the Italians, nor of the Italians, (except in a poem not yet published, where I have said all the good I know or do not know of them, and none of the harm,) I confess I wish that they would let me alone, and not drag me into their arena as one of the gladiators, in a silly contest which I neither understand nor have ever interfered with, having kept clear of all their literary parties, both here and at Milan, and elsewhere.—I came into Italy to feel the climate and be quiet, if possible. Mossi's translation I would have prevented, if I had known it, or could have done so; and I trust that I shall yet be in time to stop this new gentleman, of whom I heard yesterday for the first time. He will only hurt himself, and do no good to his party, for in party the whole thing originates. Our modes of thinking and writing are so unutterably different, that I can conceive no greater absurdity than attempting to make any approach between the English and Italian poetry of the present day. I like the people very much, and their literature very much, but I am not the least ambitious of being the subject of their discussions literary and personal (which appear to be pretty much the same thing, as is the case in most countries); and if you can aid me in impeding this publication, you will add to much kindness already received from you by yours Ever and truly,

"BYRON.

"P.S. How is the son, and mamma? Well, I dare say."

LETTER 310. TO MR. ROGERS.

"Venice, March 3. 1828.

"I have not, as you say, 'taken to wife the Adriatic.' I heard of Moore's loss from himself in a letter which was delayed upon the road three months. I was sincerely sorry for it, but in such cases what are words?

"The villa you speak of is one at Este, which Mr. Hoppner (Consul-general here) has transferred to me. I have taken it for two years as a place of Villeggiatura. The situation is very beautiful, indeed, among the Euganean hills, and the house very fair. The vines are luxuriant to a great degree, and all the fruits of the earth abundant. It is close to the old castle of the Estes, or Guelphs, and within a few miles of Arqua, which I have visited twice, and hope to visit often.

"Last summer (except an excursion to Rome) I passed upon the Brenta. In Venice I winter, transporting my horses to the Lido, bordering the Adriatic (where the fort is), so that I get a gallop of some miles daily along the strip of beach which reaches to Malamocco, when in health; but within these few weeks I have been unwell. At present I am getting better. The Carnival was short, but a good one. I don't go out much, except during the time of masques; but there are one or two conversazioni, where I go regularly, just to keep up the system; as I had letters to their givers; and they are particular on such points; and now and then, though very rarely, to the Governor's.

"It is a very good place for women. I like the dialect and their manner very much. There is a naïveté about them which is very winning, and the romance of the place is a mighty adjunct; the bel sangue is not, however, now amongst the dame or higher orders; but all under i fazzioli, or kerchiefs (a white kind of veil which the lower orders wear upon their heads);—the vesta zendale, or old national female costume, is no more. The city, however, is decaying daily, and does not gain in population. However, I prefer it to any other in Italy; and here have I pitched my staff, and here do I purpose to reside for the remainder of my life, unless events, connected with business not to be transacted out of England, compel me to return for that purpose; otherwise I have few regrets, and no desires to visit it again for its own sake. I shall probably be obliged to do so, to sign papers for my affairs, and a proxy for the Whigs, and to see Mr. Waite, for I can't find a good dentist here, and every two or three years one ought to consult one. About seeing my children I must take my chance. One I shall have sent here; and I shall be very happy to see the legitimate one, when God pleases, which he perhaps will some day or other. As for my mathematical * * *, I am as well without her.

"Your account of your visit to Fonthill is very striking: could you beg of him for me a copy in MS. of the remaining Tales? I think I deserve them, as a strenuous and public admirer of the first one. I will return it when read, and make no ill use of the copy, if granted. Murray would send me out any thing safely. If ever I return to England, I should like very much to see the author, with his permission. In the mean time, you could not oblige me more than by obtaining me the perusal I request, in French or English,—all's one for that, though I prefer Italian to either. I have a French copy of Vathek which I bought at Lausanne. I can read French with great pleasure and facility, though I neither speak nor write it. Now Italian I can speak with some fluency, and write sufficiently for my purposes, but I don't like their modern prose at all; it is very heavy, and so different from Machiavelli.

"They say Francis is Junius;—I think it looks like it. I remember meeting him at Earl Grey's at dinner. Has not he lately married a young woman; and was not he Madame Talleyrand's cavaliere servente in India years ago?

"I read my death in the papers, which was not true. I see they are marrying the remaining singleness of the royal family. They have brought out Fazio with great and deserved success at Covent Garden: that's a good sign. I tried, during the directory, to have it done at Drury Lane, but was overruled. If you think of coming into this country, you will let me know perhaps beforehand. I suppose Moore won't move. Rose is here. I saw him the other night at Madame

Albrizzi's; he talks of returning in May. My love to the Hollands.

"Ever, &c.

"P.S. They have been crucifying Othello into an opera (Otello, by Rossini): the music good, but lugubrious; but as for the words, all the real scenes with Iago cut out, and the greatest nonsense instead; the handkerchief turned into a billet-doux, and the first singer would not black his face, for some exquisite reasons assigned in the preface. Singing, dresses, and music, very good."

LETTER 311. TO MR. MOORE.

"Venice, March 16. 1818.

"My dear Tom,

"Since my last, which I hope that you have received, I have had a letter from our friend Samuel. He talks of Italy this summer—won't you come with him? I don't know whether you would like our Italian way of life or not.

"They are an odd people. The other day I was telling a girl, 'You must not come to-morrow, because Margueritta is coming at such a time,'—(they are both about five feet ten inches high, with great black eyes and fine figures—fit to breed gladiators from—and I had some difficulty to prevent a battle upon a rencontre once before,)—'unless you promise to be friends, and'—the answer was an interruption, by a declaration of war against the other, which she said would be a 'Guerra di Candia.' Is it not odd, that the lower order of Venetians should still allude proverbially to that famous contest, so glorious and so fatal to the Republic?

"They have singular expressions, like all the Italians. For example, 'Viscere'—as we would say, 'My love,' or 'My heart,' as an expression of tenderness. Also, 'I would go for you into the midst of a hundred knives.'—'Mazza ben,' excessive attachment,—literally, 'I wish you well even to killing.' Then they say (instead of our way, 'Do you think I would do you so much harm?') 'Do you think I would assassinate you in such a manner?'—'Tempo perfido,' bad weather; 'Strade perfide,' bad roads,—with a thousand other allusions and metaphors, taken from the state of society and habits in the middle ages.

"I am not so sure about mazza, whether it don't mean massa, i.e. a great deal, a mass, instead of the interpretation I have given it. But of the other phrases I am sure.

"Three o' th' clock—I must 'to bed, to bed, to bed,' as mother S * * (that tragical friend of the mathematical * * *) says.

"Have you ever seen—I forget what or whom—no matter. They tell me Lady Melbourne is very unwell. I shall be so sorry. She was my greatest friend, of the feminine gender:—when I say 'friend,' I mean not mistress, for that's the antipode. Tell me all about you and every body—how Sam is—how you like your neighbours, the Marquis and Marchesa, &c. &c.

"Ever," &c.

LETTER 312. TO MR. MURRAY.

"Venice, March 25. 1818.

"I have your letter, with the account of 'Beppo,' for which I sent you four new stanzas a fortnight ago, in case you print, or reprint.

"Croker's is a good guess; but the style is not English, it is Italian;—Berni is the original of all. Whistlecraft was my immediate model! Rose's 'Animali' I never saw till a few days ago,—they are excellent. But (as I said above) Berni is the father of that kind of writing, which, I think, suits our language, too, very well;—we shall see by the experiment. If it does, I shall send you a volume in a year or two, for I know the Italian way of life well, and in time may know it yet better; and as for the verse and the passions, I have them still in tolerable vigour.

"If you think that it will do you and the work, or works, any good, you may put my name to it; but first consult the knowing ones. It will, at any rate, show them that I can write cheerfully, and repel the charge of monotony and mannerism.

"Yours," &c.

LETTER 313. TO MR. MURRAY.

"Venice, April 11. 1818.

"Will you send me by letter, packet, or parcel, half a dozen of the coloured prints from Holmes's miniature (the latter done shortly before I left your country, and the prints about a year ago); I shall be obliged to you, as some people here have asked me for the like. It is a picture of my upright self done for Scrope B. Davies, Esq.

"Why have you not sent me an answer, and list of subscribers to the translation of the Armenian Eusebius? of which I sent you printed copies of the prospectus (in French) two moons ago. Have you had the letter?—I shall send you another:—you must not neglect my Armenians. Tooth-powder, magnesia, tincture of myrrh, tooth-brushes, diachylon plaster, Peruvian bark, are my personal demands.

> "Strahan, Tonson, Lintot of the times,
> Patron and publisher of rhymes,
> For thee the bard up Pindus climbs,
> My Murray.

LETTER 314. TO MR. MURRAY.

"Venice, April 12. 1818.

"This letter will be delivered by Signor Gioe. Bata. Missiaglia, proprietor of the Apollo library, and the principal publisher and bookseller now in Venice. He sets out for London with a view to business and correspondence with the English booksellers: and it is in the hope that it may be for your mutual advantage that I furnish him with this letter of introduction to you. If you can be of use to him, either by recommendation to others, or by any personal attention on your own part, you will oblige him and gratify me. You may also perhaps both be able to derive advantage, or establish some mode of literary communication, pleasing to the public, and beneficial to one another.

"At any rate, be civil to him for my sake, as well as for the honour and glory of publishers and authors now and to come for evermore.

"With him I also consign a great number of MS. letters written in English, French, and Italian, by various English established in Italy during the last century:—the names of the writers, Lord

Hervey, Lady M.W. Montague, (hers are but few—some billets-doux in French to Algarotti, and one letter in English, Italian, and all sorts of jargon, to the same,) Gray, the poet (one letter), Mason (two or three), Garrick, Lord Chatham, David Hume, and many of lesser note,—all addressed to Count Algarotti. Out of these, I think, with discretion, an amusing miscellaneous volume of letters might be extracted, provided some good editor were disposed to undertake the selection, and preface, and a few notes, &c.

"The proprietor of these is a friend of mine, Dr. Aglietti,—a great name in Italy,—and if you are disposed to publish, it will be for his benefit, and it is to and for him that you will name a price, if you take upon you the work. I would edite it myself, but am too far off, and too lazy to undertake it; but I wish that it could be done. The letters of Lord Hervey, in Mr. Rose's opinion and mine, are good; and the short French love letters certainly are Lady M.W. Montague's—the French not good, but the sentiments beautiful. Gray's letter good; and Mason's tolerable. The whole correspondence must be well weeded; but this being done, a small and pretty popular volume might be made of it.—There are many ministers' letters—Gray, the ambassador at Naples, Horace Mann, and others of the same kind of animal.

"I thought of a preface, defending Lord Hervey against Pope's attack, but Pope—quoad Pope, the poet—against all the world, in the unjustifiable attempts begun by Warton and carried on at this day by the new school of critics and scribblers, who think themselves poets because they do not write like Pope. I have no patience with such cursed humbug and bad taste; your whole generation are not worth a Canto of the Rape of the Lock, or the Essay on Man, or the Dunciad, or 'any thing that is his.'—But it is three in the matin, and I must go to bed. Yours alway," &c.

LETTER 315. TO MR. MURRAY.

"Venice, April 17. 1818.

"A few days ago, I wrote to you a letter, requesting you to desire Hanson to desire his messenger to come on from Geneva to Venice, because I won't go from Venice to Geneva; and if this is not done, the messenger may be damned, with him who mis-sent him. Pray reiterate my request.

"With the proofs returned, I sent two additional stanzas for Canto fourth: did they arrive?

"Your Monthly reviewer has made a mistake: Cavaliere, alone, is well enough; but 'Cavalier' servente' has always the e mute in conversation, and omitted in writing; so that it is not for the sake of metre; and pray let Griffiths know this, with my compliments. I humbly conjecture that I know as much of Italian society and language as any of his people; but, to make assurance doubly sure, I asked, at the Countess Benzona's last night, the question of more than one person in the office, and of these 'cavalieri serventi' (in the plural, recollect) I found that they all accorded in pronouncing for 'cavalier' servente' in the singular number. I wish Mr. * * * * (or whoever Griffiths' scribbler may be) would not talk of what he don't understand. Such fellows are not fit to be intrusted with Italian, even in a quotation.

"Did you receive two additional stanzas, to be inserted towards the close of Canto fourth? Respond, that (if not) they may be sent.

"Tell Mr. * * and Mr. Hanson that they may as well expect Geneva to come to me, as that I should go to Geneva. The messenger may go on or return, as he pleases; I won't stir: and I look upon it as a piece of singular absurdity in those who know me imagining that I should;—not to say malice, in attempting unnecessary torture. If, on the occasion, my interests should suffer, it is their neglect that is to blame; and they may all be d——d together.

"It is ten o'clock and time to dress.

"Yours," &c.

LETTER 316. TO MR. MURRAY.

"April 23. 1818.

"The time is past in which I could feel for the dead,—or I should feel for the death of Lady Melbourne, the best, and kindest, and ablest female I ever knew, old or young. But 'I have supped full of horrors,' and events of this kind have only a kind of numbness worse than pain,—like a violent blow on the elbow or the head. There is one link less between England and myself.

"Now to business. I presented you with Beppo, as part of the contract for Canto fourth,—considering the price you are to pay for the same, and intending to eke you out in case of public caprice or my own poetical failure. If you choose to suppress it entirely, at Mr. * * * *'s suggestion, you may do as you please. But recollect it is not to be published in a garbled or mutilated state. I reserve to my friends and myself the right of correcting the press;—if the publication continue, it is to continue in its present form.

"As Mr. * * says that he did not write this letter, &c. I am ready to believe him; but for the firmness of my former persuasion, I refer to Mr. * * * *, who can inform you how sincerely I erred on this point. He has also the note—or, at least, had it, for I gave it to him with my verbal comments thereupon. As to 'Beppo,' I will not alter or suppress a syllable for any man's pleasure but my own.

"You may tell them this; and add, that nothing but force or necessity shall stir me one step towards places to which they would wring me.

"If your literary matters prosper let me know. If 'Beppo' pleases, you shall have more in a year or two in the same mood. And so 'Good morrow to you, good Master Lieutenant.' Yours," &c.

LETTER 317. TO MR. MOORE.

"Palazzo Mocenigo, Canal Grande,

"Venice, June 1. 1818.

"Your letter is almost the only news, as yet, of Canto fourth, and it has by no means settled its fate,—at least, does not tell me how the 'Poeshie' has been received by the public. But I suspect, no great things,—firstly, from Murray's 'horrid stillness;' secondly, from what you say about the stanzas running into each other, which I take not to be yours, but a notion you have been dinned with among the Blues. The fact is, that the terza rima of the Italians, which always runs on and in, may have led me into experiments, and carelessness into conceit—or conceit into carelessness—in either of which events failure will be probable, and my fair woman, 'superne,' end in a fish; so that Childe Harold will be like the mermaid, my family crest, with the fourth Canto for a tail thereunto. I won't quarrel with the public, however, for the 'Bulgars' are generally right; and if I miss now, I may hit another time:—and so, the 'gods give us joy.'

"You like Beppo, that's right. I have not had the Fudges yet, but live in hopes. I need not say that your successes are mine. By the way, Lydia White is here, and has just borrowed my copy of 'Lalla Rookh.'

"Hunt's letter is probably the exact piece of vulgar coxcombry you might expect from his situation. He is a good man, with some poetical elements in his chaos; but spoilt by the Christ-Church Hospital and a Sunday newspaper,—to say nothing of the Surrey gaol, which conceited him into a martyr. But he is a good man. When I saw 'Rimini' in MS., I told him that I deemed it good poetry at bottom, disfigured only by a strange style. His answer was, that his style was a system, or upon system, or some such cant; and, when a man talks of system, his case is hopeless: so I said no more to him, and very little to any one else.

"He believes his trash of vulgar phrases tortured into compound barbarisms to be old English; and we may say of it as Aimwell says of Captain Gibbet's regiment, when the Captain calls it an 'old corps,'—'the oldest in Europe, if I may judge by your uniform.' He sent out his 'Foliage' by Percy Shelley * * *, and, of all the ineffable Centaurs that were ever begotten by Self-love upon a Night-mare, I think this monstrous Sagittary the most prodigious. He (Leigh H.) is an honest charlatan, who has persuaded himself into a belief of his own impostures, and talks Punch in pure simplicity of heart, taking himself (as poor Fitzgerald said of himself in the Morning Post) for Vates in both senses, or nonsenses, of the word. Did you look at the translations of his own which he prefers to Pope and Cowper, and says so?—Did you read his skimble-skamble about * * being at the head of his own profession, in the eyes of those who followed it? I thought that poetry was an art, or an attribute, and not a profession;—but be it one, is that * * * * * * at the head of your profession in your eyes? I'll be curst if he is of mine, or ever shall be. He is the only one of us (but of us he is not) whose coronation I would oppose. Let them take Scott, Campbell, Crabbe, or you, or me, or any of the living, and throne him;—but not this new Jacob Behmen, this * * * * * * whose pride might have kept him true, even had his principles turned as perverted as his soi-disant poetry.

"But Leigh Hunt is a good man, and a good father—see his Odes to all the Masters Hunt;—a good husband—see his Sonnet to Mrs. Hunt;—a good friend—see his Epistles to different people;—and a great coxcomb and a very vulgar person in every thing about him. But that's not his fault, but of circumstances.

"I do not know any good model for a life of Sheridan but that of Savage. Recollect, however, that the life of such a man may be made far more amusing than if he had been a Wilberforce;—and this without offending the living, or insulting the dead. The Whigs abuse him; however, he never left them, and such blunderers deserve neither credit nor compassion. As for his creditors,—remember, Sheridan never had a shilling, and was thrown, with great powers and passions, into the thick of the world, and placed upon the pinnacle of success, with no other external means to support him in his elevation. Did Fox * * * pay his debts?—or did Sheridan take a subscription? Was the * *'s drunkenness more excusable than his? Were his intrigues more notorious than those of all his contemporaries? and is his memory to be blasted, and theirs respected? Don't let yourself be led away by clamour, but compare him with the coalitioner Fox, and the pensioner Burke, as a man of principle, and with ten hundred thousand in personal views, and with none in talent, for he beat them all out and out. Without means, without connection, without character, (which might be false at first, and make him mad afterwards from desperation,) he beat them all, in all he ever attempted. But alas, poor human nature! Good night—or rather, morning. It is four, and the dawn gleams over the Grand Canal, and unshadows the Rialto. I must to bed; up all night—but, as George Philpot says, 'it's life, though, damme, it's life!' Ever yours, B.

"Excuse errors—no time for revision. The post goes out at noon, and I sha'n't be up then. I will write again soon about your plan for a publication."

During the greater part of the period which this last series of letters comprises, he had continued to occupy the same lodgings in an extremely narrow street called the Spezieria, at the house of the linen-draper, to whose lady he devoted so much of his thoughts. That he was, for the time, attached to this person,—as far as a passion so transient can deserve the name of attachment,—is evident from his whole conduct. The language of his letters shows sufficiently how much the novelty of this foreign tie had caught his fancy; and to the Venetians, among whom such arrangements are mere matters of course, the assiduity with which he attended his Signora to the theatre, and the ridottos, was a subject of much amusement. It was with difficulty, indeed, that he could be prevailed upon to absent himself from her so long as to admit of that hasty visit to the Immortal City, out of which one of his own noblest titles to immortality sprung; and having, in the space of a few weeks, drunk in more inspiration from all he saw than, in a less excited state, possibly, he might have imbibed in years, he again hurried back, without extending his journey to Naples,—having written to the fair Marianna to meet him at some distance from Venice.

Besides some seasonable acts of liberality to the husband, who had, it seems, failed in trade, he also presented to the lady herself a handsome set of diamonds; and there is an anecdote related in reference to this gift, which shows the exceeding easiness and forbearance of his disposition towards those who had acquired any hold on his heart. A casket, which was for sale, being one day offered to him, he was not a little surprised on discovering them to be the same jewels which he had, not long before, presented to his fair favourite, and which had, by some unromantic means, found their way back into the market. Without enquiring, however, any further into the circumstances, he generously repurchased the casket and presented it to the lady once more, good-humouredly taxing her with the very little estimation in which, as it appeared, she held his presents.

To whatever extent this unsentimental incident may have had a share in dispelling the romance of his passion, it is certain that, before the expiration of the first twelvemonth, he began to find his lodgings in the Spezieria inconvenient, and accordingly entered into treaty with Count Gritti for his Palace on the Grand Canal,—engaging to give for it, what is considered, I believe, a large rent in Venice, 200 louis a year. On finding, however, that, in the counterpart of the lease brought for his signature, a new clause had been introduced, prohibiting him not only from underletting the house, in case he should leave Venice, but from even allowing any of his own friends to occupy it during his occasional absence, he declined closing on such terms; and resenting so material a departure from the original engagement, declared in society, that he would have no objection to give the same rent, though acknowledged to be exorbitant, for any other palace in Venice, however inferior, in all respects, to Count Gritti's. After such an announcement, he was not likely to remain long unhoused; and the Countess Mocenigo having offered him one of her three Palazzi, on the Grand Canal, he removed to this house in the summer of the present year, and continued to occupy it during the remainder of his stay in Venice.

Highly censurable, in point of morality and decorum, as was his course of life while under the roof of Madame * *, it was (with pain I am forced to confess) venial in comparison with the strange, headlong career of licence to which, when weaned from that connection, he so unrestrainedly and, it may be added, defyingly abandoned himself. Of the state of his mind on leaving England I have already endeavoured to convey some idea, and, among the feelings that went to make up that self-centred spirit of resistance which he then opposed to his fate, was an indignant scorn of his own countrymen for the wrongs he thought they had done him. For a time, the kindly sentiments which he still harboured towards Lady Byron, and a sort of vague hope, perhaps, that all would yet come right again, kept his mind in a mood somewhat more softened and docile, as well as sufficiently under the influence of English opinion to prevent his breaking out into such open rebellion against it, as he unluckily did afterwards.

By the failure of the attempted mediation with Lady Byron, his last link with home was severed; while, notwithstanding the quiet and unobtrusive life which he had led at Geneva, there was as yet, he found, no cessation of the slanderous warfare against his character;—the same busy and misrepresenting spirit which had tracked his every step at home having, with no less malicious watchfulness, dogged him into exile. To this persuasion, for which he had but too much grounds, was added all that an imagination like his could lend to truth,—all that he was left to interpret, in his own way, of the absent and the silent,—till, at length, arming himself against fancied enemies and wrongs, and, with the condition (as it seemed to him) of an outlaw, assuming also the desperation, he resolved, as his countrymen would not do justice to the better parts of his nature, to have, at least, the perverse satisfaction of braving and shocking them with the worst. It is to this feeling, I am convinced, far more than to any depraved taste for such a course of life, that the extravagances to which he now, for a short time, gave loose, are to be attributed. The exciting effect, indeed, of this mode of existence while it lasted, both upon his spirits and his genius,—so like what, as he himself tells us, was always produced in him by a state of contest and defiance,—showed how much of this latter feeling must have been mixed with his excesses. The altered character too, of his letters in this respect cannot fail, I think, to be remarked by the reader,—there being, with an evident increase of intellectual vigour, a tone of violence and bravado breaking out in them continually, which marks the high pitch of re-action to which he had now wound up his temper.

In fact, so far from the powers of his intellect being at all weakened or dissipated by these irregularities, he was, perhaps, at no time of his life, so actively in the full possession of all its energies; and his friend Shelley, who went to Venice, at this period, to see him, used to say, that all he observed of the workings of Byron's mind, during his visit, gave him a far higher idea of its powers than he had ever before entertained. It was, indeed, then that Shelley sketched out, and chiefly wrote, his poem of "Julian and Maddalo," in the latter of which personages he has so picturesquely shadowed forth his noble friend; and the allusions to "the Swan of Albion," in his "Lines written among the Euganean Hills," were also, I understand, the result of the same access of admiration and enthusiasm.

In speaking of the Venetian women, in one of the preceding letters, Lord Byron, it will be recollected, remarks, that the beauty for which they were once so celebrated is no longer now to be found among the "Dame," or higher orders, but all under the "fazzioli," or kerchiefs, of the lower. It was, unluckily, among these latter specimens of the "bel sangue" of Venice that he now, by a suddenness of descent in the scale of refinement, for which nothing but the present wayward state of his mind can account, chose to select the companions of his disengaged hours;—and an additional proof that, in this short, daring career of libertinism, he was but desperately seeking relief for a wronged and mortified spirit, and

"What to us seem'd guilt might be but woe,"—

is that, more than once, of an evening, when his house has been in the possession of such visitants, he has been known to hurry away in his gondola, and pass the greater part of the night upon the water, as if hating to return to his home. It is, indeed, certain, that to this least defensible portion of his whole life he always looked back, during the short remainder of it, with painful self-reproach; and among the causes of the detestation which he afterwards felt for Venice, this recollection of the excesses to which he had there abandoned himself was not the least prominent.

The most distinguished and, at last, the reigning favourite of all this unworthy Harem was a woman named Margarita Cogni, who has been already mentioned in one of these letters, and who, from the trade of her husband, was known by the title of the Fornarina. A portrait of this handsome virago, drawn by Harlowe when at Venice, having fallen into the hands of one of Lord Byron's friends after the death of that artist, the noble poet, on being applied to for some particulars of his heroine, wrote a long letter on the subject, from which the following are extracts:—

"Since you desire the story of Margarita Cogni, you shall be told it, though it may be lengthy.

"Her face is the fine Venetian cast of the old time; her figure, though perhaps too tall, is not less fine—and taken altogether in the national dress.

"In the summer of 1817, * * * * and myself were sauntering on horseback along the Brenta one evening, when, amongst a group of peasants, we remarked two girls as the prettiest we had seen for some time. About this period, there had been great distress in the country, and I had a little relieved some of the people. Generosity makes a great figure at very little cost in Venetian livres, and mine had probably been exaggerated as an Englishman's. Whether they remarked us looking at them or no, I know not; but one of them called out to me in Venetian, 'Why do not you, who relieve others, think of us also?' I turned round and answered her—'Cara, tu sei troppo bella e giovane per aver' bisogna del' soccorso mio.' She answered, 'If you saw my hut and my food, you would not say so.' All this passed half jestingly, and I saw no more of her for some days.

"A few evenings after, we met with these two girls again, and they addressed us more seriously, assuring us of the truth of their statement. They were cousins; Margarita married, the other single. As I doubted still of the circumstances, I took the business in a different light, and made an appointment with them for the next evening. In short, in a few evenings we arranged our affairs, and for a long space of time she was the only one who preserved over me an ascendency which was often disputed, and never impaired.

"The reasons of this were, firstly, her person;—very dark, tall, the Venetian face, very fine black eyes. She was two-and-twenty years old, * * * She was, besides, a thorough Venetian in her dialect, in her thoughts, in her countenance, in every thing, with all their naïveté and pantaloon humour. Besides, she could neither read nor write, and could not plague me with letters,—except twice that she paid sixpence to a public scribe, under the piazza, to make a letter for her, upon some occasion when I was ill and could not see her. In other respects, she was somewhat fierce and 'prepotente,' that is, over-bearing, and used to walk in whenever it suited her, with no very great regard to time, place, nor persons; and if she found any women in her way, she knocked them down.

"When I first knew her, I was in 'relazione' (liaison) with la Signora * *, who was silly enough one evening at Dolo, accompanied by some of her female friends, to threaten her; for the gossips of the villeggiatura had already found out, by the neighing of my horse one evening, that I used to 'ride late in the night' to meet the Fornarina. Margarita threw back her veil (fazziolo), and replied in very explicit Venetian, 'You are not his wife: I am not his wife: you are his Donna, and I am his Donna: your husband is a becco, and mine is another. For the rest, what right have you to reproach me? If he prefers me to you, is it my fault? If you wish to secure him, tie him to your petticoat-string.—But do not think to speak to me without a reply, because you happen to be richer than I am.' Having delivered this pretty piece of eloquence (which I translate as it was related to me by a bystander), she went on her way, leaving a numerous audience with Madame * *, to ponder at her leisure on the dialogue between them.

"When I came to Venice for the winter, she followed; and as she found herself out to be a favourite, she came to me pretty often. But she had inordinate self-love, and was not tolerant of other women. At the 'Cavalchina,' the masked ball on the last night of the carnival, where all the world goes, she snatched off the mask of Madame Contarini, a lady noble by birth, and decent in conduct, for no other reason, but because she happened to be leaning on my arm. You may suppose what a cursed noise this made; but this is only one of her pranks.

"At last she quarrelled with her husband, and one evening ran away to my house. I told her this would not do: she said she would lie in the street, but not go back to him; that he beat her, (the gentle tigress!) spent her money, and scandalously neglected her. As it was midnight I let her stay, and next day there was no moving her at all. Her husband came, roaring and crying, and entreating her to come back:—not she! He then applied to the police, and they applied to me: I told them and her husband to take her; I did not want her; she had come, and I could not fling her out of the window; but they might conduct her through that or the door if they chose it. She went before the commissary, but was obliged to return with that 'becco ettico,' as she called the poor man, who had a phthisic. In a few days she ran away again. After a precious piece of work, she fixed herself in my house, really and truly without my consent; but, owing to my indolence, and not being able to keep my countenance, for if I began in a rage, she always finished by making me laugh with some Venetian pantaloonery or another; and the gipsy knew this well enough, as well as her other powers of persuasion, and exerted them with the usual tact and success of all she-things; high and low, they are all alike for that.

"Madame Benzoni also took her under her protection, and then her head turned. She was always in extremes, either crying or laughing, and so fierce when angered, that she was the terror of men, women, and children—for she had the strength of an Amazon, with the temper of Medea. She was a fine animal, but quite untameable. I was the only person that could at all keep her in any order, and when she saw me really angry (which they tell me is a savage sight), she subsided. But she had a thousand fooleries. In her fazziolo, the dress of the lower orders, she looked beautiful; but, alas! she longed for a hat and feathers; and all I could say or do (and I said much) could not prevent this travestie. I put the first into the fire; but I got tired of burning them, before she did of buying them, so that she made herself a figure—for they did not at all become her.

"Then she would have her gowns with a tail—like a lady, forsooth; nothing would serve her but 'l'abita colla coua,' or cua, (that is the Venetian for 'la cola,' the tail or train,) and as her cursed pronunciation of the word made me laugh, there was an end of all controversy, and she dragged this diabolical tail after her every where.

"In the mean time, she beat the women and stopped my letters. I found her one day pondering over one. She used to try to find out by their shape whether they were feminine or no; and she used to lament her ignorance, and actually studied her alphabet, on purpose (as she declared) to open all letters addressed to me and read their contents.

"I must not omit to do justice to her housekeeping qualities. After she came into my house as 'donna di governo,' the expenses were reduced to less than half, and every body did their duty better—the apartments were kept in order, and every thing and every body else, except herself.

"That she had a sufficient regard for me in her wild way, I had many reasons to believe. I will mention one. In the autumn, one day, going to the Lido with my gondoliers, we were overtaken by a heavy squall, and the gondola put in peril—hats blown away, boat filling, oar lost, tumbling sea, thunder, rain in torrents, night coming, and wind unceasing. On our return, after a tight struggle, I found her on the open steps of the Mocenigo palace, on the Grand Canal, with her great black eyes flashing through her tears, and the long dark hair, which was streaming, drenched with rain, over her brows and breast. She was perfectly exposed to the storm; and the wind blowing her hair and dress about her thin tall figure, and the lightning flashing round her, and the waves rolling at her feet, made her look like Medea alighted from her chariot, or the Sibyl of the tempest that was rolling around her, the only living thing within hail at that moment except ourselves. On seeing me safe, she did not wait to greet me, as might have been expected, but calling out to me—'Ah! can' della Madonna, xe esto il tempo per andar' al' Lido?' (Ah! dog of the Virgin, is this a time to go to Lido?) ran into the house, and solaced herself with scolding the boatmen for not foreseeing the 'temporale.' I am told by the servants that she had only been prevented from coming in a boat to look after me, by the refusal of all the gondoliers of the canal to put out into the harbour in such a moment; and that then she sat down on the steps in all the thickest of the squall, and would neither be removed nor comforted. Her joy at seeing me again was moderately mixed with ferocity, and gave me the idea of a tigress over her recovered cubs.

"But her reign drew near a close. She became quite ungovernable some months after, and a concurrence of complaints, some true, and many false—'a favourite has no friends'—determined me to part with her. I told her quietly that she must return home, (she had acquired a sufficient provision for herself and mother, &c. in my service,) and she refused to quit the house. I was firm, and she went threatening knives and revenge. I told her that I had seen knives drawn before her time, and that if she chose to begin, there was a knife, and fork also, at her service on the table, and that intimidation would not do. The next day, while I was at dinner, she walked in, (having broken open a glass door that led from the hall below to the staircase, by way of prologue,) and advancing straight up to the table, snatched the knife from my hand, cutting me slightly in the thumb in the operation. Whether she meant to use this against herself or me, I know not—probably against neither—but Fletcher seized her by the arms, and disarmed her. I then called my boatmen, and desired them to get the gondola ready, and conduct her to her own house again, seeing carefully that she did herself no mischief by the way. She seemed quite quiet, and walked down stairs. I resumed my dinner.

"We heard a great noise, and went out, and met them on the staircase, carrying her up stairs. She had thrown herself into the canal. That she intended to destroy herself, I do not believe; but when we consider the fear women and men who can't swim have of deep or even of shallow water, (and the Venetians in particular, though they live on the waves,) and that it was also night, and dark, and very cold, it shows that she had a devilish spirit of some sort within her. They had got her out without much difficulty or damage, excepting the salt water she had swallowed, and the wetting she had undergone.

"I foresaw her intention to refix herself, and sent for a surgeon, enquiring how many hours it would require to restore her from her agitation; and he named the time. I then said, 'I give you that time, and more if you require it; but at the expiration of this prescribed period, if she does not leave the house, I will.'

"All my people were consternated. They had always been frightened at her, and were now paralysed: they wanted me to apply to the police, to guard myself, &c. &c. like a pack of snivelling servile boobies as they were. I did nothing of the kind, thinking that I might as well end that way as another; besides, I had been used to savage women, and knew their ways.

"I had her sent home quietly after her recovery, and never saw her since, except twice at the opera, at a distance amongst the audience. She made many attempts to return, but no more violent ones. And this is the story of Margarita Cogni, as far as it relates to me.

"I forgot to mention that she was very devout, and would cross herself if she heard the prayer time strike.

"She was quick in reply; as, for instance—One day when she had made me very angry with beating somebody or other, I called her a cow (cow, in Italian, is a sad affront). I called her 'Vacca.' She turned round, courtesied, and answered, 'Vacca tua, 'celenza' (i.e. eccelenza). 'Your cow, please your Excellency.' In short, she was, as I said before, a very fine animal, of considerable beauty and energy, with many good and several amusing qualities, but wild as a witch and fierce as a demon. She used to boast publicly of her ascendency over me, contrasting it with that of other women, and assigning for it sundry reasons. True it was, that they all tried to get her away, and no one succeeded till her own absurdity helped them.

"I omitted to tell you her answer, when I reproached her for snatching Madame Contarini's mask at the Cavalchina. I represented to her that she was a lady of high birth, 'una Dama,' &c. She answered, 'Se ella è dama mi (io) son Veneziana;'—'If she is a lady, I am a Venetian.' This would have been fine a hundred years ago, the pride of the nation rising up against the pride of aristocracy: but, alas! Venice, and her people, and her nobles, are alike returning fast to the ocean; and where there is no independence, there can be no real self-respect. I believe that I mistook or mis-stated one of her phrases in my letter; it should have been—'Can' della Madonna cosa vus' tu? esto non é tempo per andar' a Lido?'"

It was at this time, as we shall see by the letters I am about to produce, and as the features, indeed, of the progeny itself would but too plainly indicate, that he conceived, and wrote some part of, his poem of 'Don Juan;'—and never did pages more faithfully and, in many respects, lamentably, reflect every variety of feeling, and whim, and passion that, like the wrack of autumn, swept across the author's mind in writing them. Nothing less, indeed, than that singular combination of attributes, which existed and were in full activity in his mind at this moment, could have suggested, or been capable of, the execution of such a work. The cool shrewdness of age, with the vivacity and glowing temperament of youth,—the wit of a Voltaire, with the sensibility of a Rousseau,—the minute, practical knowledge of the man of society, with the abstract and self-contemplative spirit of the poet,—a susceptibility of all that is grandest and most affecting in human virtue, with a deep, withering experience of all that is most fatal to it,—the two extremes, in short, of man's mixed and inconsistent nature, now rankly smelling of earth, now breathing of heaven,—such was the strange assemblage of contrary elements, all meeting together in the same mind, and all brought to bear, in turn, upon the same task, from which alone could have sprung this extraordinary poem,—the most powerful and, in many respects, painful display of the versatility of genius that has ever been left for succeeding ages to wonder at and deplore.

I shall now proceed with his correspondence,—having thought some of the preceding observations necessary, not only to explain to the reader much of what he will find in these letters, but to account to him for much that has been necessarily omitted.

LETTER 318. TO MR. MURRAY.

"Venice, June 18. 1818.

"Business and the utter and inexplicable silence of all my correspondents renders me impatient and troublesome. I wrote to Mr. Hanson for a balance which is (or ought to be) in his hands;—no answer. I expected the messenger with the Newstead papers two months ago, and instead of him, I received a requisition to proceed to Geneva, which (from * *, who knows my wishes and opinions about approaching England) could only be irony or insult.

"I must, therefore, trouble you to pay into my bankers' immediately whatever sum or sums you can make it convenient to do on our agreement; otherwise, I shall be put to the severest and most immediate inconvenience; and this at a time when, by every rational prospect and calculation, I ought to be in the receipt of considerable sums. Pray do not neglect this; you have no idea to what inconvenience you will otherwise put me. * * had some absurd notion about the disposal of this money in annuity (or God knows what), which I merely listened to when he was here to avoid squabbles and sermons; but I have occasion for the principal, and had never any serious idea of appropriating it otherwise than to answer my personal expenses. Hobhouse's wish is, if possible, to force me back to England: he will not succeed; and if he did, I would not stay. I hate the country, and like this; and all foolish opposition, of course, merely adds to the feeling. Your silence makes me doubt the success of Canto fourth. If it has failed, I will make such deduction as you think proper and fair from the original agreement; but I could wish whatever is to be paid were remitted to me, without delay, through the usual channel, by course of post.

"When I tell you that I have not heard a word from England since very early in May, I have made the eulogium of my friends, or the persons who call themselves so, since I have written so often and in the greatest anxiety. Thank God, the longer I am absent, the less cause I see for regretting the country or its living contents. I am yours," &c.

LETTER 319. TO MR. MURRAY.

"Venice, July 10. 1818.

"I have received your letter and the credit from Morlands, &c. for whom I have also drawn upon you at sixty days' sight for the remainder, according to your proposition.

"I am still waiting in Venice, in expectancy of the arrival of Hanson's clerk. What can detain him, I do not know; but I trust that Mr. Hobhouse, and Mr. Kinnaird, when their political fit is abated, will take the trouble to enquire and expedite him, as I have nearly a hundred thousand pounds depending upon the completion of the sale and the signature of the papers.

"The draft on you is drawn up by Siri and Willhalm. I hope that the form is correct. I signed it two or three days ago, desiring them to forward it to Messrs. Morland and Ransom.

"Your projected editions for November had better be postponed, as I have some things in project, or preparation, that may be of use to you, though not very important in themselves. I have completed an Ode on Venice, and have two Stories, one serious and one ludicrous (à la Beppo), not yet finished, and in no hurry to be so.

"You talk of the letter to Hobhouse being much admired, and speak of prose. I think of writing (for your full edition) some Memoirs of my life, to prefix to them, upon the same model (though far enough, I fear, from reaching it) of Gifford, Hume, &c.; and this without any intention of making disclosures or remarks upon living people, which would be unpleasant to them: but I think it might be done, and well done. However, this is to be considered. I have materials in plenty, but the greater part of them could not be used by me, nor for these hundred years to come. However, there is enough without these, and merely as a literary man, to make a preface for such an edition as you meditate. But this is by the way: I have not made up my mind.

"I enclose you a note on the subject of 'Parisina,' which Hobhouse can dress for you. It is an extract of particulars from a history of Ferrara.

"I trust you have been attentive to Missiaglia, for the English have the character of neglecting the Italians, at present, which I hope you will redeem.

"Yours in haste, B."

LETTER 320. TO MR. MURRAY.

"Venice, July 17. 1818.

"I suppose that Aglietti will take whatever you offer, but till his return from Vienna I can make him no proposal; nor, indeed, have you authorised me to do so. The three French notes are by Lady Mary; also another half-English-French-Italian. They are very pretty and passionate; it is a pity that a piece of one of them is lost. Algarotti seems to have treated her ill; but she was much his senior, and all women are used ill—or say so, whether they are or not.

"I shall be glad of your books and powders. I am still in waiting for Hanson's clerk, but luckily not at Geneva. All my good friends wrote to me to hasten there to meet him, but not one had the good sense or the good nature, to write afterwards to tell me that it would be time and a journey thrown away, as he could not set off for some months after the period appointed. If I had taken the journey on the general suggestion, I never would have spoken again to one of you as long as I existed. I have written to request Mr. Kinnaird, when the foam of his politics is wiped away, to extract a positive answer from that * * * *, and not to keep me in a state of suspense upon the subject. I hope that Kinnaird, who has my power of attorney, keeps a look-out upon the gentleman, which is the more necessary, as I have a great dislike to the idea of coming over to look after him myself.

"I have several things begun, verse and prose, but none in much forwardness. I have written some six or seven sheets of a Life, which I mean to continue, and send you when finished. It may perhaps serve for your projected editions. If you would tell me exactly (for I know nothing, and have no correspondents except on business) the state of the reception of our late publications, and the feeling upon them, without consulting any delicacies (I am too seasoned to require them), I should know how and in what manner to proceed. I should not like to give them too much, which may probably have been the case already; but, as I tell you, I know nothing.

"I once wrote from the fulness of my mind and the love of fame, (not as an end, but as a means, to obtain that influence over men's minds which is power in itself and in its consequences,) and now from habit and from avarice; so that the effect may probably be as different as the inspiration. I have the same facility, and indeed necessity, of composition, to avoid idleness (though idleness in a hot country is a pleasure), but a much greater indifference to what is to become of it, after it has served my immediate purpose. However, I should on no account like to—but I won't go on, like the Archbishop of Granada, as I am very sure that you dread the fate of Gil Blas, and with good reason. Yours, &c.

"P.S. I have written some very savage letters to Mr. Hobhouse, Kinnaird, to you, and to Hanson, because the silence of so long a time made me tear off my remaining rags of patience. I have seen one or two late English publications which are no great things, except Rob Roy. I shall be glad of Whistlecraft."

LETTER 321. TO MR. MURRAY.

"Venice, August 26. 1818.

"You may go on with your edition, without calculating on the Memoir, which I shall not publish at present. It is nearly finished, but will be too long; and there are so many things, which, out of regard to the living, cannot be mentioned, that I have written with too much detail of that which interested me least; so that my autobiographical Essay would resemble the tragedy of Hamlet at the country theatre, recited 'with the part of Hamlet left out by particular desire.' I shall keep it among my papers; it will be a kind of guide-post in case of death, and prevent some of the lies which would otherwise be told, and destroy some which have been told already.

"The tales also are in an unfinished state, and I can fix no time for their completion: they are also not in the best manner. You must not, therefore, calculate upon any thing in time for this edition. The Memoir is already above forty-four sheets of very large, long paper, and will be about fifty or sixty; but I wish to go on leisurely; and when finished, although it might do a good deal for you at the time, I am not sure that it would serve any good purpose in the end either, as it is full of many passions and prejudices, of which it has been impossible for me to keep clear:—I have not the patience.

"Enclosed is a list of books which Dr. Aglietti would be glad to receive by way of price for his MS. letters, if you are disposed to purchase at the rate of fifty pounds sterling. These he will be glad to have as part, and the rest I will give him in money, and you may carry it to the account of books, &c. which is in balance against me, deducting it accordingly. So that the letters are yours, if you like them, at this rate; and he and I are going to hunt for more Lady Montague letters, which he thinks of finding. I write in haste. Thanks for the article, and believe me

"Yours," &c.

To the charge brought against Lord Byron by some English travellers of being, in general, repulsive and inhospitable to his own countrymen, I have already made allusion; and shall now add to the testimony then cited in disproof of such a charge some particulars, communicated to me by Captain Basil Hall, which exhibit the courtesy and kindliness of the noble poet's disposition in their true, natural light.

"On the last day of August, 1818 (says this distinguished writer and traveller), I was taken ill with an ague at Venice, and having heard enough of the low state of the medical art in that country, I was not a little anxious as to the advice I should take. I was not acquainted with any person in Venice to whom I could refer, and had only one letter of introduction, which was to Lord Byron; but as there were many stories floating about of his Lordship's unwillingness to be pestered with tourists, I had felt unwilling, before this moment, to intrude myself in that shape. Now, however, that I was seriously unwell, I felt sure that this offensive character would merge in that of a countryman in distress, and I sent the letter by one of my travelling companions to

Lord Byron's lodgings, with a note, excusing the liberty I was taking, explaining that I was in want of medical assistance, and saying I should not send to any one till I heard the name of the person who, in his Lordship's opinion, was the best practitioner in Venice.

"Unfortunately for me, Lord Byron was still in bed, though it was near noon, and still more unfortunately, the bearer of my message scrupled to awake him, without first coming back to consult me. By this time I was in all the agonies of a cold ague fit, and, therefore, not at all in a condition to be consulted upon any thing—so I replied pettishly, 'Oh, by no means disturb Lord Byron on my account—ring for the landlord, and send for any one he recommends.' This absurd injunction being forthwith and literally attended to, in the course of an hour I was under the discipline of mine host's friend, whose skill and success it is no part of my present purpose to descant upon:—it is sufficient to mention that I was irrevocably in his hands long before the following most kind note was brought to me, in great haste, by Lord Byron's servant.

"'Venice, August 31. 1818.

"'Dear Sir,

"'Dr. Aglietti is the best physician, not only in Venice, but in Italy: his residence is on the Grand Canal, and easily found; I forget the number, but am probably the only person in Venice who don't know it. There is no comparison between him and any of the other medical people here. I regret very much to hear of your indisposition, and shall do myself the honour of waiting upon you the moment I am up. I write this in bed, and have only just received the letter and note. I beg you to believe that nothing but the extreme lateness of my hours could have prevented me from replying immediately, or coming in person. I have not been called a minute.—I have the honour to be, very truly,

"'Your most obedient servant,

"'BYRON.'

"His Lordship soon followed this note, and I heard his voice in the next room; but although he waited more than an hour, I could not see him, being under the inexorable hands of the doctor. In the course of the same evening he again called, but I was asleep. When I awoke I found his Lordship's valet sitting by my bedside. 'He had his master's orders,' he said, 'to remain with me while I was unwell, and was instructed to say, that whatever his Lordship had, or could procure, was at my service, and that he would come to me and sit with me, or do whatever I liked, if I would only let him know in what way he could be useful.'

"Accordingly, on the next day, I sent for some book, which was brought, with a list of his library. I forget what it was which prevented my seeing Lord Byron on this day, though he called more than once; and on the next, I was too ill with fever to talk to any one.

"The moment I could get out, I took a gondola and went to pay my respects, and to thank his Lordship for his attentions. It was then nearly three o'clock, but he was not yet up; and when I went again on the following day at five, I had the mortification to learn that he had gone, at the same hour, to call upon me, so that we had crossed each other on the canal; and, to my deep and lasting regret, I was obliged to leave Venice without seeing him."

LETTER 322. TO MR. MOORE.

"Venice, September 19. 1818.

"An English newspaper here would be a prodigy, and an opposition one a monster; and except some ex tracts from extracts in the vile, garbled Paris gazettes, nothing of the kind reaches the Veneto-Lombard public, who are, perhaps, the most oppressed in Europe. My correspondences with England are mostly on business, and chiefly with my * * *, who has no very exalted notion, or extensive conception, of an author's attributes; for he once took up an Edinburgh Review, and, looking at it a minute, said to me, 'So, I see you have got into the magazine,'—which is the only sentence I ever heard him utter upon literary matters, or the men thereof.

"My first news of your Irish Apotheosis has, consequently, been from yourself. But, as it will not be forgotten in a hurry, either by your friends or your enemies, I hope to have it more in detail from some of the former, and, in the mean time, I wish you joy with all my heart. Such a moment must have been a good deal better than Westminster-abbey,—besides being an assurance of that one day (many years hence, I trust,) into the bargain.

"I am sorry to perceive, however, by the close of your letter, that even you have not escaped the 'surgit amari,' &c. and that your damned deputy has been gathering such 'dew from the still vext Bermoothes'—or rather vexatious. Pray, give me some items of the affair, as you say it is a serious one; and, if it grows more so, you should make a trip over here for a few months, to see how things turn out. I suppose you are a violent admirer of England by your staying so long in it. For my own part, I have passed, between the age of one-and-twenty and thirty, half the intervenient years out of it without regretting any thing, except that I ever returned to it at all, and the gloomy prospect before me of business and parentage obliging me, one day, to return to it again,—at least, for the transaction of affairs, the signing of papers, and inspecting of children.

"I have here my natural daughter, by name Allegra,—a pretty little girl enough, and reckoned like papa. Her mamma is English,—but it is a long story, and—there's an end. She is about twenty months old.

"I have finished the first Canto (a long one, of about 180 octaves) of a poem in the style and manner of 'Beppo', encouraged by the good success of the same. It is called 'Don Juan', and is meant to be a little quietly facetious upon every thing. But I doubt whether it is not—at least, as far as it has yet gone—too free for these very modest days. However, I shall try the experiment, anonymously, and if it don't take, it will be discontinued. It is dedicated to S * * in good, simple, savage verse, upon the * * * *'s politics, and the way he got them. But the bore of copying it out is intolerable; and if I had an amanuensis he would be of no use, as my writing is so difficult to decipher.

> "My poem's Epic, and is meant to be
> Divided in twelve books, each book containing
> With love and war, a heavy gale at sea—
> A list of ships, and captains, and kings reigning—
> New characters, &c. &c.

The above are two stanzas, which I send you as a brick of my Babel, and by which you can judge of the texture of the structure.

"In writing the Life of Sheridan, never mind the angry lies of the humbug Whigs. Recollect that he was an Irishman and a clever fellow, and that we have had some very pleasant days with him. Don't forget that he was at school at Harrow, where, in my time, we used to show his name—R.B. Sheridan, 1765,—as an honour to the walls. Remember * *. Depend upon it that there were worse folks going, of that gang, than ever Sheridan was.

"What did Parr mean by 'haughtiness and coldness?' I listened to him with admiring ignorance, and respectful silence. What more could a talker for fame have?—they don't like to be answered. It was at Payne Knight's I met him, where he gave me more Greek than I could carry away. But I certainly meant to (and did) treat him with the most respectful deference.

"I wish you a good night, with a Venetian benediction, 'Benedetto te, e la terra che ti fara!'—'May you be blessed, and the earth which you will make!'—is it not pretty? You would think it still prettier if you had heard it, as I did two hours ago, from the lips of a Venetian girl, with large black eyes, a face like Faustina's, and the figure of a Juno—tall and energetic as a Pythoness, with eyes flashing, and her dark hair streaming in the moonlight—one of those women who may be made any thing. I am sure if I put a poniard into the hand of this one, she would plunge it where I told her,—and into me, if I offended her. I like this kind of animal, and am sure that I should have preferred Medea to any woman that ever breathed. You may, perhaps, wonder that I don't in that case. I could have forgiven the dagger or the bowl, any thing, but the deliberate desolation piled upon me, when I stood alone upon my hearth, with my household gods shivered around me * * Do you suppose I have forgotten or forgiven it? It has comparatively swallowed up in me every other feeling, and I am only a spectator upon earth, till a tenfold opportunity offers. It may come yet. There are others more to be blamed than * * * *, and it is on these that my eyes are fixed unceasingly."

LETTER 323. TO MR. MURRAY.

"Venice, September 24. 1818.

"In the one hundredth and thirty-second stanza of Canto fourth, the stanza runs in the manuscript—

> "And thou, who never yet of human wrong
> Left the unbalanced scale, great Nemesis!

and not 'lost,' which is nonsense, as what losing a scale means, I know not; but leaving an unbalanced scale, or a scale unbalanced, is intelligible. Correct this, I pray,—not for the public, or the poetry, but I do not choose to have blunders made in addressing any of the deities so seriously as this is addressed.

"Yours, &c.

"P.S. In the translation from the Spanish, alter

> "In increasing squadrons flew,

to—

> To a mighty squadron grew.

"What does 'thy waters wasted them' mean (in the Canto)? That is not me. Consult the MS. always.

"I have written the first Canto (180 octave stanzas) of a poem in the style of Beppo, and have Mazeppa to finish besides.

"In referring to the mistake in stanza 132. I take the opportunity to desire that in future, in all parts of my writings referring to religion, you will be more careful, and not forget that it is possible that in addressing the Deity a blunder may become a blasphemy; and I do not choose to suffer such infamous perversions of my words or of my intentions.

"I saw the Canto by accident."

LETTER 324. TO MR. MURRAY.

"Venice, January 20. 1819.

"The opinions which I have asked of Mr. H. and others were with regard to the poetical merit, and not as to what they may think due to the cant of the day, which still reads the Bath Guide, Little's Poems, Prior, and Chaucer, to say nothing of Fielding and Smollet. If published, publish entire, with the above-mentioned exceptions; or you may publish anonymously, or not at all. In the latter event, print 50 on my account, for private distribution.

"Yours, &c.

"I have written to Messrs. K. and H. to desire that they will not erase more than I have stated.

"The second Canto of Don Juan is finished in 206 stanzas."

LETTER 325. TO MR. MURRAY.

"Venice, January 25. 1819.

"You will do me the favour to print privately (for private distribution) fifty copies of 'Don Juan.' The list of the men to whom I wish it to be presented, I will send hereafter. The other two poems had best be added to the collective edition: I do not approve of their being published separately. Print Don Juan entire, omitting, of course, the lines on Castlereagh, as I am not on the spot to meet him. I have a second Canto ready, which will be sent by and by. By this post, I have written to Mr. Hobhouse, addressed to your care.

"Yours, &c.

"P.S. I have acquiesced in the request and representation; and having done so, it is idle to detail my arguments in favour of my own self-love and 'Poeshie;' but I protest. If the poem has poetry, it would stand; if not, fall; the rest is 'leather and prunello,' and has never yet affected any human production 'pro or con.' Dulness is the only annihilator in such cases. As to the cant of the day, I despise it, as I have ever done all its other finical fashions, which become you as paint became the ancient Britons. If you admit this prudery, you must omit half Ariosto, La Fontaine, Shakspeare, Beaumont, Fletcher, Massinger, Ford, all the Charles Second writers; in short, something of most who have written before Pope and are worth reading, and much of Pope himself. Read him—most of you don't—but do—and I will forgive you; though the inevitable consequence would be that you would burn all I have ever written, and all your other wretched Claudians of the day (except Scott and Crabbe) into the bargain. I wrong Claudian, who was a poet, by naming him with such fellows; but he was the 'ultimus Romanorum,' the tail of the comet, and these persons are the tail of an old gown cut into a waistcoat for Jackey; but being both tails, I have compared the one with the other, though very unlike, like all similes. I write in a passion and a sirocco, and I was up till six this morning at the Carnival: but I protest, as I did in my former letter."

LETTER 326. TO MR. MURRAY.

"Venice, February 1. 1819.

"After one of the concluding stanzas of the first Canto of 'Don Juan,' which ends with (I forget the number)—

<blockquote>
"To have ...
... when the original is dust,
A book, a d——d bad picture, and worse bust,
</blockquote>

insert the following stanza:—

<blockquote>
"What are the hopes of man, &c.
</blockquote>

"I have written to you several letters, some with additions, and some upon the subject of the poem itself, which my cursed puritanical committee have protested against publishing. But we will circumvent them on that point. I have not yet begun to copy out the second Canto, which is finished, from natural laziness, and the discouragement of the milk and water they have thrown upon the first. I say all this to them as to you, that is, for you to say to them, for I will have nothing underhand. If they had told me the poetry was bad, I would have acquiesced; but they say the contrary, and then talk to me about morality—the first time I ever heard the word from any body who was not a rascal that used it for a purpose. I maintain that it is the most moral of poems; but if people won't discover the moral, that is their fault, not mine. I have already written to beg that in any case you will print fifty for private distribution. I will send you the list of persons to whom it is to be sent afterwards.

"Within this last fortnight I have been rather indisposed with a rebellion of stomach, which would retain nothing, (liver, I suppose,) and an inability, or fantasy, not to be able to eat of any thing with relish but a kind of Adriatic fish called 'scampi,' which happens to be the most indigestible of marine viands. However, within these last two days, I am better, and very truly yours."

LETTER 327. TO MR. MURRAY.

"Venice, April 6. 1819.

"The second Canto of Don Juan was sent, on Saturday last, by post, in four packets, two of four, and two of three sheets each, containing in all two hundred and seventeen stanzas, octave measure. But I will permit no curtailments, except those mentioned about Castlereagh and * * * *. You sha'n't make canticles of my cantos. The poem will please, if it is lively; if it is stupid, it will fail: but I will have none of your damned cutting and slashing. If you please, you may publish anonymously; it will perhaps be better; but I will battle my way against them all, like a porcupine.

"So you and Mr. Foscolo, &c. want me to undertake what you call a 'great work?' an Epic

Poem, I suppose, or some such pyramid. I'll try no such thing; I hate tasks. And then 'seven or eight years!' God send us all well this day three months, let alone years. If one's years can't be better employed than in sweating poesy, a man had better be a ditcher. And works, too!—is Childe Harold nothing? You have so many 'divine poems,' is it nothing to have written a human one? without any of your worn-out machinery. Why, man, I could have spun the thoughts of the four Cantos of that poem into twenty, had I wanted to book-make, and its passion into as many modern tragedies. Since you want length, you shall have enough of Juan, for I'll make fifty Cantos.

"And Foscolo, too! Why does he not do something more than the Letters of Ortis, and a tragedy, and pamphlets? He has good fifteen years more at his command than I have: what has he done all that time?—proved his genius, doubtless, but not fixed its fame, nor done his utmost.

"Besides, I mean to write my best work in Italian, and it will take me nine years more thoroughly to master the language; and then if my fancy exist, and I exist too, I will try what I can do really. As to the estimation of the English which you talk of, let them calculate what it is worth, before they insult me with their insolent condescension.

"I have not written for their pleasure. If they are pleased, it is that they chose to be so; I have never flattered their opinions, nor their pride; nor will I. Neither will I make 'Ladies' books 'al dilettar le femine e la plebe.' I have written from the fulness of my mind, from passion, from impulse, from many motives, but not for their 'sweet voices.'

"I know the precise worth of popular applause, for few scribblers have had more of it; and if I chose to swerve into their paths, I could retain it, or resume it. But I neither love ye, nor fear ye; and though I buy with ye and sell with ye, I will neither eat with ye, drink with ye, nor pray with ye. They made me, without any search, a species of popular idol; they, without reason or judgment, beyond the caprice of their good pleasure, threw down the image from its pedestal; it was not broken with the fall, and they would, it seems, again replace it,—but they shall not.

"You ask about my health: about the beginning of the year I was in a state of great exhaustion, attended by such debility of stomach that nothing remained upon it; and I was obliged to reform my 'way of life,' which was conducting me from the 'yellow leaf' to the ground, with all deliberate speed. I am better in health and morals, and very much yours, &c.

"P.S. I have read Hodgson's 'Friends.' He is right in defending Pope against the bastard pelicans of the poetical winter day, who add insult to their parricide, by sucking the blood of the parent of English real poetry,—poetry without fault,—and then spurning the bosom which fed them."

It was about the time when the foregoing letter was written, and when, as we perceive, like the first return of reason after intoxication, a full consciousness of some of the evils of his late libertine course of life had broken upon him, that an attachment differing altogether, both in duration and devotion, from any of those that, since the dream of his boyhood, had inspired him, gained an influence over his mind which lasted through his few remaining years; and, undeniably wrong and immoral (even allowing for the Italian estimate of such frailties) as was the nature of the connection to which this attachment led, we can hardly perhaps,—taking into account the far worse wrong from which it rescued and preserved him,—consider it otherwise than as an event fortunate both for his reputation and happiness.

The fair object of this last, and (with one signal exception) only real love of his whole life, was a young Romagnese lady, the daughter of Count Gamba, of Ravenna, and married, but a short time before Lord Byron first met with her, to an old and wealthy widower, of the same city, Count Guiccioli. Her husband had in early life been the friend of Alfieri, and had distinguished himself by his zeal in promoting the establishment of a National Theatre, in which the talents of Alfieri and his own wealth were to be combined. Notwithstanding his age, and a character, as it appears, by no means reputable, his great opulence rendered him an object of ambition among the mothers of Ravenna, who, according to the too frequent maternal practice, were seen vying with each other in attracting so rich a purchaser for their daughters, and the young Teresa Gamba, not yet sixteen, and just emancipated from a convent, was the selected victim.

The first time Lord Byron had ever seen this lady was in the autumn of 1818, when she made her appearance, three days after her marriage, at the house of the Countess Albrizzi, in all the gaiety of bridal array, and the first delight of exchanging a convent for the world. At this time, however, no acquaintance ensued between them;—it was not till the spring of the present year that, at an evening party of Madame Benzoni's, they were introduced to each other. The love that sprung out of this meeting was instantaneous and mutual, though with the usual disproportion of sacrifice between the parties; such an event being, to the man, but one of the many scenes of life, while, with woman, it generally constitutes the whole drama. The young Italian found herself suddenly inspired with a passion of which, till that moment, her mind could not have formed the least idea;—she had thought of love but as an amusement, and now became its slave. If at the outset, too, less slow to be won than an Englishwoman, no sooner did she begin to understand the full despotism of the passion than her heart shrunk from it as something terrible, and she would have escaped, but that the chain was already around her.

No words, however, can describe so simply and feelingly as her own, the strong impression which their first meeting left upon her mind:—

"I became acquainted (says Madame Guiccioli) with Lord Byron in the April of 1819:—he was introduced to me at Venice, by the Countess Benzoni, at one of that lady's parties. This introduction, which had so much influence over the lives of us both, took place contrary to our wishes, and had been permitted by us only from courtesy. For myself, more fatigued than usual that evening on account of the late hours they keep at Venice, I went with great repugnance to this party, and purely in obedience to Count Guiccioli. Lord Byron, too, who was averse to forming new acquaintances,—alleging that he had entirely renounced all attachments, and was unwilling any more to expose himself to their consequences,—on being requested by the countess Benzoni to allow himself to be presented to me, refused, and, at last, only assented from a desire to oblige her.

"His noble and exquisitely beautiful countenance, the tone of his voice, his manners, the thousand enchantments that surrounded him, rendered him so different and so superior a being to any whom I had hitherto seen, that it was impossible he should not have left the most profound impression upon me. From that evening, during the whole of my subsequent stay at Venice, we met every day."

LETTER 328. TO MR. MURRAY.

"Venice, May 15. 1819.

"I have got your extract, and the 'Vampire.' I need not say it is not mine. There is a rule to go by: you are my publisher (till we quarrel), and what is not published by you is not written by me.

"Next week I set out for Romagna—at least, in all probability. You had better go on with the publications, without waiting to hear farther, for I have other things in my head. 'Mazeppa' and the 'Ode' separate?—what think you? Juan anonymous, without the Dedication; for I won't be shabby, and attack Southey under cloud of night.

"Yours," &c.

In another letter on the subject of the Vampire, I find the following interesting particulars:—

"TO MR. ———.

"The story of Shelley's agitation is true. I can't tell what seized him, for he don't want courage. He was once with me in a gale of wind, in a small boat, right under the rocks between Meillerie and St. Gingo. We were five in the boat—a servant, two boatmen, and ourselves. The sail was mismanaged, and the boat was filling fast. He can't swim. I stripped off my coat, made him strip off his, and take hold of an oar, telling him that I thought (being myself an expert swimmer) I could save him, if he would not struggle when I took hold of him—unless we got smashed against the rocks, which were high and sharp, with an awkward surf on them at that minute. We were then about a hundred yards from shore, and the boat in peril. He answered me with the greatest coolness, 'that he had no notion of being saved, and that I would have enough to do to save myself, and begged not to trouble me.' Luckily, the boat righted, and, bailing, we got round a point into St. Gingo, where the inhabitants came down and embraced the boatmen on their escape, the wind having been high enough to tear up some huge trees from the Alps above us, as we saw next day.

"And yet the same Shelley, who was as cool as it was possible to be in such circumstances, (of which I am no judge myself, as the chance of swimming naturally gives self-possession when near shore,) certainly had the fit of phantasy which Polidori describes, though not exactly as he describes it.

"The story of the agreement to write the ghost-books is true; but the ladies are not sisters. Mary Godwin (now Mrs. Shelley) wrote Frankenstein, which you have reviewed, thinking it Shelley's. Methinks it is a wonderful book for a girl of nineteen,—not nineteen, indeed, at that time. I enclose you the beginning of mine, by which you will see how far it resembles Mr. Colburn's publication. If you choose to publish it, you may, stating why, and with such explanatory proem as you please. I never went on with it, as you will perceive by the date. I began it in an old account-book of Miss Milbanke's, which I kept because it contains the word 'Household,' written by her twice on the inside blank page of the covers, being the only two scraps I have in the world in her writing, except her name to the Deed of Separation. Her letters I sent back except those of the quarrelling correspondence, and those, being documents, are placed in the hands of a third person, with copies of several of my own; so that I have no kind of memorial whatever of her, but these two words,—and her actions. I have torn the leaves containing the part of the Tale out of the book, and enclose them with this sheet.

"What do you mean? First you seem hurt by my letter, and then, in your next, you talk of its 'power,' and so forth. 'This is a d——d blind story, Jack; but never mind, go on.' You may be sure I said nothing on purpose to plague you; but if you will put me 'in a frenzy, I will never call you Jack again.' I remember nothing of the epistle at present.

"What do you mean by Polidori's Diary? Why, I defy him to say any thing about me, but he is welcome. I have nothing to reproach me with on his score, and I am much mistaken if that is not his own opinion. But why publish the names of the two girls? and in such a manner?—what a blundering piece of exculpation! He asked Pictet, &c. to dinner, and of course was left to entertain them. I went into society solely to present him (as I told him), that he might return into good company if he chose; it was the best thing for his youth and circumstances: for myself, I had done with society, and, having presented him, withdrew to my own 'way of life.' It is true that I returned without entering Lady Dalrymple Hamilton's, because I saw it full. It is true that Mrs. Hervey (she writes novels) fainted at my entrance into Coppet, and then came back again. On her fainting, the Duchess de Broglie exclaimed, 'This is too much—at sixty-five years of age!'—I never gave 'the English' an opportunity of avoiding me; but I trust that, if ever I do, they will seize it. With regard to Mazeppa and the Ode, you may join or separate them, as you please, from the two Cantos.

"Don't suppose I want to put you out of humour. I have a great respect for your good and gentlemanly qualities, and return your personal friendship towards me; and although I think you a little spoilt by 'villanous company,'—wits, persons of honour about town, authors, and fashionables, together with your 'I am just going to call at Carlton House, are you walking that way?'—I say, notwithstanding 'pictures, taste, Shakspeare, and the musical glasses,' you deserve and possess the esteem of those whose esteem is worth having, and of none more (however useless it may be) than yours very truly, &c.

"P.S. Make my respects to Mr. Gifford. I am perfectly aware that 'Don Juan' must set us all by the ears, but that is my concern, and my beginning. There will be the 'Edinburgh,' and all, too, against it, so that, like 'Rob Roy,' I shall have my hands full."

LETTER 329. TO MR. MURRAY.

"Venice, May 25. 1819.

"I have received no proofs by the last post, and shall probably have quitted Venice before the arrival of the next. There wanted a few stanzas to the termination of Canto first in the last proof; the next will, I presume, contain them, and the whole or a portion of Canto second; but it will be idle to wait for further answers from me, as I have directed that my letters wait for my return (perhaps in a month, and probably so); therefore do not wait for further advice from me. You may as well talk to the wind, and better—for it will at least convey your accents a little further than they would otherwise have gone; whereas I shall neither echo nor acquiesce in your 'exquisite reasons.' You may omit the note of reference to Hobhouse's travels, in Canto second, and you will put as motto to the whole—

'Difficile est proprie communia dicere.'—HORACE.

"A few days ago I sent you all I know of Polidori's Vampire. He may do, say, or write, what he pleases, but I wish he would not attribute to me his own compositions. If he has any thing of mine in his possession, the MS. will put it beyond controversy; but I scarcely think that any one who knows me would believe the thing in the Magazine to be mine, even if they saw it in my own hieroglyphics.

"I write to you in the agonies of a sirocco, which annihilates me; and I have been fool enough to do four things since dinner, which are as well omitted in very hot weather: 1stly, * * * *; 2dly, to play at billiards from 10 to 12, under the influence of lighted lamps, that doubled the heat; 3dly, to go afterwards into a red-hot conversazione of the Countess Benzoni's; and, 4thly, to begin this letter at three in the morning: but being begun, it must be finished.

"Ever very truly and affectionately yours,
"B.

"P.S. I petition for tooth-brushes, powder, magnesia, Macassar oil (or Russia), the sashes, and Sir Nl. Wraxall's Memoirs of his own Times. I want, besides, a bull-dog, a terrier, and two Newfoundland dogs; and I want (is it Buck's?) a life of Richard 3d, advertised by Longman long, long, long ago; I asked for it at least three years since. See Longman's advertisements."

About the middle of April, Madame Guiccioli had been obliged to quit Venice with her husband. Having several houses on the road from Venice to Ravenna, it was his habit to stop at these mansions, one after the other, in his journeys between the two cities; and from all these places the enamoured young Countess now wrote to Lord Byron, expressing, in the most passionate and pathetic terms, her despair at leaving him. So utterly, indeed, did this feeling overpower her, that three times, in the course of her first day's journey, she was seized with fainting fits. In one of her letters, which I saw when at Venice, dated, if I recollect right, from "Cà Zen, Cavanelle di Po," she tells him that the solitude of this place, which she had before found irksome, was, now that one sole idea occupied her mind, become dear and welcome to her, and promises that, as soon as she arrives at Ravenna, "she will, according to his wish, avoid all general society, and devote herself to reading, music, domestic occupations, riding on horseback,—every thing, in short, that she knew he would most like." What a change for a young and simple girl, who, but a few weeks before, had thought only of society and the world, but who now saw no other happiness but in the hope of making herself worthy, by seclusion and self-instruction, of the illustrious object of her devotion!

On leaving this place, she was attacked with a dangerous illness on the road, and arrived half dead at Ravenna; nor was it found possible to revive or comfort her till an assurance was received from Lord Byron, expressed with all the fervour of real passion, that, in the course of the ensuing month, he would pay her a visit. Symptoms of consumption, brought on by her state of mind, had already shown themselves; and, in addition to the pain which this separation had caused her, she was also suffering much grief from the loss of her mother, who, at this time, died in giving birth to her fourteenth child. Towards the latter end of May she wrote to acquaint Lord Byron that, having prepared all her relatives and friends to expect him, he might now, she thought, venture to make his appearance at Ravenna. Though, on the lady's account, hesitating as to the prudence of such a step, he, in obedience to her wishes, on the 2d of June, set out from La Mira (at which place he had again taken a villa for the summer), and proceeded towards Romagna.

From Padua he addressed a letter to Mr. Hoppner, chiefly occupied with matters of household concern which that gentleman had undertaken to manage for him at Venice, but, on the immediate object of his journey, expressing himself in a tone so light and jesting, as it would be difficult for those not versed in his character to conceive that he could ever bring himself, while under the influence of a passion so sincere, to assume. But such is ever the wantonness of the mocking spirit, from which nothing,—not even love,—remains sacred; and which, at last, for want of other food, turns upon himself. The same horror, too, of hypocrisy that led Lord Byron to exaggerate his own errors, led him also to disguise, under a seemingly heartless ridicule, all those natural and kindly qualities by which they were redeemed.

This letter from Padua concludes thus:—

"A journey in an Italian June is a conscription; and if I was not the most constant of men, I should now be swimming from the Lido, instead of smoking in the dust of Padua. Should there be letters from England, let them wait my return. And do look at my house and (not lands, but) waters, and scold;—and deal out the monies to Edgecombe with an air of reluctance and a shake of the head—and put queer questions to him—and turn up your nose when he answers.

"Make my respect to the Consules—and to the Chevalier—and to Scotin—and to all the counts and countesses of our acquaintance.

"And believe me ever

"Your disconsolate and affectionate," &c.

As a contrast to the strange levity of this letter, as well as in justice to the real earnestness of the passion, however censurable in all other respects, that now engrossed him, I shall here transcribe some stanzas which he wrote in the course of this journey to Romagna, and which, though already published, are not comprised in the regular collection of his works.

"River, that rollest by the ancient walls, Where dwells the lady of my love, when she Walks by thy brink, and there perchance recalls A faint and fleeting memory of me;

"What if thy deep and ample stream should be A mirror of my heart, where she may read The thousand thoughts I now betray to thee, Wild as thy wave, and headlong as thy speed!

"What do I say—a mirror of my heart? Are not thy waters sweeping, dark, and strong? Such as my feelings were and are, thou art; And such as thou art were my passions long.

"Time may have somewhat tamed them,—not for ever; Thou overflow'st thy banks, and not for aye Thy bosom overboils, congenial river! Thy floods subside, and mine have sunk away,

"But left long wrecks behind, and now again, Borne in our old unchanged career, we move; Thou tendest wildly onwards to the main, And I—to loving one I should not love.

"The current I behold will sweep beneath Her native walls and murmur at her feet; Her eyes will look on thee, when she shall breathe The twilight air, unharm'd by summer's heat.

"She will look on thee,—I have look'd on thee, Full of that thought; and, from that moment,

ne'er Thy waters could I dream of, name, or see, Without the inseparable sigh for her!
"Her bright eyes will be imaged in thy stream,— Yes! they will meet the wave I gaze on now: Mine cannot witness, even in a dream, That happy wave repass me in its flow!
"The wave that bears my tears returns no more: Will she return by whom that wave shall sweep?— Both tread thy banks, both wander on thy shore, I by thy source, she by the dark-blue deep.
"But that which keepeth us apart is not Distance, nor depth of wave, nor space of earth. But the distraction of a various lot, As various as the climates of our birth.
"A stranger loves the lady of the land, Born far beyond the mountains, but his blood Is all meridian, as if never fann'd By the black wind that chills the polar flood.
"My blood is all meridian; were it not, I had not left my clime, nor should I be, In spite of tortures, ne'er to be forgot, A slave again of love,—at least of thee.
"'Tis vain to struggle—let me perish young— Live as I lived, and love as I have loved; To dust if I return, from dust I sprung, And then, at least, my heart can ne'er be moved."

On arriving at Bologna and receiving no further intelligence from the Contessa, he began to be of opinion, as we shall perceive in the annexed interesting letters, that he should act most prudently, for all parties, by returning to Venice.

LETTER 330. TO MR. HOPPNER.

"Bologna, June 6. 1819.

"I am at length joined to Bologna, where I am settled like a sausage, and shall be broiled like one, if this weather continues. Will you thank Mengaldo on my part for the Ferrara acquaintance, which was a very agreeable one. I stayed two days at Ferrara, and was much pleased with the Count Mosti, and the little the shortness of the time permitted me to see of his family. I went to his conversazione, which is very far superior to any thing of the kind at Venice—the women almost all young—several pretty—and the men courteous and cleanly. The lady of the mansion, who is young, lately married, and with child, appeared very pretty by candlelight (I did not see her by day), pleasing in her manners, and very lady-like, or thorough-bred, as we call it in England,—a kind of thing which reminds one of a racer, an antelope, or an Italian greyhound. She seems very fond of her husband, who is amiable and accomplished; he has been in England two or three times, and is young. The sister, a Countess somebody—I forget what—(they are both Maffei by birth, and Veronese of course)—is a lady of more display; she sings and plays divinely; but I thought she was a d———d long time about it. Her likeness to Madame Flahaut (Miss Mercer that was) is something quite extraordinary.

"I had but a bird's eye view of these people, and shall not probably see them again; but I am very much obliged to Mengaldo for letting me see them at all. Whenever I meet with any thing agreeable in this world, it surprises me so much, and pleases me so much (when my passions are not interested one way or the other), that I go on wondering for a week to come. I feel, too, in great admiration of the Cardinal Legate's red stockings.

"I found, too, such a pretty epitaph in the Certosa cemetery, or rather two: one was

'Martini Luigi

Implora pace;'

the other,

'Lucrezia Picini
Implora eterna quiete.'

That was all; but it appears to me that these two and three words comprise and compress all that can be said on the subject,—and then, in Italian, they are absolute music. They contain doubt, hope, and humility; nothing can be more pathetic than the 'implora' and the modesty of the request;—they have had enough of life—they want nothing but rest—they implore it, and 'eterna quiete.' It is like a Greek inscription in some good old heathen 'City of the Dead.' Pray, if I am shovelled into the Lido churchyard in your time, let me have the 'implora pace,' and nothing else, for my epitaph. I never met with any, ancient or modern, that pleased me a tenth part so much.

"In about a day or two after you receive this letter, I will thank you to desire Edgecombe to prepare for my return. I shall go back to Venice before I village on the Brenta. I shall stay but a few days in Bologna. I am just going out to see sights, but shall not present my introductory letters for a day or two, till I have run over again the place and pictures; nor perhaps at all, if I find that I have books and sights enough to do without the inhabitants. After that, I shall return to Venice, where you may expect me about the eleventh, or perhaps sooner. Pray make my thanks acceptable to Mengaldo: my respects to the Consuless, and to Mr. Scott. I hope my daughter is well.

"Ever yours, and truly.

"P.S. I went over the Ariosto MS. &c. &c. again at Ferrara, with the castle, and cell, and house, &c. &c.

"One of the Ferrarese asked me if I knew 'Lord Byron,' an acquaintance of his, now at Naples. I told him 'No!' which was true both ways; for I knew not the impostor, and in the other, no one knows himself. He stared when told that I was 'the real Simon Pure.' Another asked me if I had not translated 'Tasso.' You see what fame is! how accurate! how boundless! I don't know how others feel, but I am always the lighter and the better looked on when I have got rid of mine; it sits on me like armour on the Lord Mayor's champion; and I got rid of all the husk of literature, and the attendant babble, by answering, that I had not translated Tasso, but a namesake had; and by the blessing of Heaven, I looked so little like a poet, that every body believed me."

LETTER 331. TO MR. MURRAY.

"Bologna, June 7. 1819.

"Tell Mr. Hobhouse that I wrote to him a few days ago from Ferrara. It will therefore be idle in him or you to wait for any further answers or returns of proofs from Venice, as I have directed that no English letters be sent after me. The publication can be proceeded in without, and I am already sick of your remarks, to which I think not the least attention ought to be paid.

"Tell Mr. Hobhouse that, since I wrote to him, I had availed myself of my Ferrara letters, and found the society much younger and better there than at Venice. I am very much pleased with the little the shortness of my stay permitted me to see of the Gonfaloniere Count Mosti, and his family and friends in general.

"I have been picture-gazing this morning at the famous Domenichino and Guido, both of which are superlative. I afterwards went to the beautiful cemetery of Bologna, beyond the walls, and found, besides the superb burial-ground, an original of a Custode, who reminded one of the grave-digger in Hamlet. He has a collection of capuchins' skulls, labelled on the forehead, and taking down one of them, said, 'This was Brother Desiderio Berro, who died at forty—one of my best friends. I begged his head of his brethren after his decease, and they gave it me. I put it in lime, and then boiled it. Here it is, teeth and all, in excellent preservation. He was the merriest, cleverest fellow I ever knew. Wherever he went, he brought joy; and whenever any one was melancholy, the sight of him was enough to make him cheerful again. He walked so actively, you might have taken him for a dancer—he joked—he laughed—oh! he was such a Frate as I never saw before, nor ever shall again!'

"He told me that he had himself planted all the cypresses in the cemetery; that he had the greatest attachment to them and to his dead people; that since 1801 they had buried fifty-three thousand persons. In showing some older monuments, there was that of a Roman girl of twenty, with a bust by Bernini. She was a princess Bartorini, dead two centuries ago: he said that, on opening her grave, they had found her hair complete, and 'as yellow as gold.' Some of the epitaphs at Ferrara pleased me more than the more splendid monuments at Bologna; for instance:—

"Martini Luigi
Implora pace;

Can any thing be more full of pathos? Those few words say all that can be said or sought: the dead had had enough of life; all they wanted was rest, and this they implore! There is all the helplessness, and humble hope, and deathlike prayer, that can arise from the grave—'implora pace.' I hope, whoever may survive me, and shall see me put in the foreigners' burying-ground at the Lido, within the fortress by the Adriatic, will see those two words, and no more, put over me. I trust they won't think of 'pickling, and bringing me home to Clod or Blunderbuss Hall.' I am sure my bones would not rest in an English grave, or my clay mix with the earth of that country. I believe the thought would drive me mad on my deathbed, could I suppose that any of my friends would be base enough to convey my carcass back to your soil. I would not even feed your worms, if I could help it.

"So, as Shakspeare says of Mowbray, the banished Duke of Norfolk, who died at Venice (see Richard II.) that he, after fighting

"'Against black Pagans, Turks, and Saracens,
And toiled with works of war, retired himself
To Italy, and there, at Venice, gave
His body to that pleasant country's earth,
And his pure soul unto his captain, Christ,

Under whose colours he had fought so long.'

"Before I left Venice, I had returned to you your late, and Mr. Hobhouse's sheets of Juan. Don't wait for further answers from me, but address yours to Venice, as usual. I know nothing of my own movements; I may return there in a few days, or not for some time. All this depends on circumstances. I left Mr. Hoppner very well. My daughter Allegra was well too, and is growing pretty; her hair is growing darker, and her eyes are blue. Her temper and her ways, Mr. Hoppner says, are like mine, as well as her features: she will make, in that case, a manageable young lady.

"I have never heard any thing of Ada, the little Electra of Mycenae. But there will come a day of reckoning, even if I should not live to see it. What a long letter I have scribbled! Yours, &c.

"P.S. Here, as in Greece, they strew flowers on the tombs. I saw a quantity of rose-leaves, and entire roses, scattered over the graves at Ferrara. It has the most pleasing effect you can imagine."

While he was thus lingering irresolute at Bologna, the Countess Guiccioli had been attacked with an intermittent fever, the violence of which, combining with the absence of a confidential person to whom she had been in the habit of intrusting her letters, prevented her from communicating with him. At length, anxious to spare him the disappointment of finding her so ill on his arrival, she had begun a letter, requesting that he would remain at Bologna till the visit to which she looked forward should bring her there also; and was in the act of writing, when a friend came in to announce the arrival of an English lord in Ravenna. She could not doubt for an instant that it was her noble friend; and he had, in fact, notwithstanding his declaration to Mr. Hoppner that it was his intention to return to Venice immediately, wholly altered this resolution before the letter announcing it was despatched,—the following words being written on the outside cover:—"I am just setting off for Ravenna, June 8. 1819.—I changed my mind this morning, and decided to go on."

The reader, however, shall have Madame Guiccioli's own account of these events, which, fortunately for the interest of my narration, I am enabled to communicate.

"On my departure from Venice, he had promised to come and see me at Ravenna. Dante's tomb, the classical pine wood, the relics of antiquity which are to be found in that place, afforded a sufficient pretext for me to invite him to come, and for him to accept my invitation. He came, in fact, in the month of June, arriving at Ravenna on the day of the festival of the Corpus Domini; while I, attacked by a consumptive complaint, which had its origin from the moment of my quitting Venice, appeared on the point of death. The arrival of a distinguished foreigner at Ravenna, a town so remote from the routes ordinarily followed by travellers, was an event which gave rise to a good deal of conversation. His motives for such a visit became the subject of discussion, and these he himself afterwards involuntarily divulged; for having made some enquiries with a view to paying me a visit, and being told that it was unlikely that he would ever see me again, as I was at the point of death, he replied, if such were the case, he hoped that he should die also; which circumstance, being repeated, revealed the object of his journey. Count Guiccioli, having been acquainted with Lord Byron at Venice, went to visit him now, and in the hope that his presence might amuse, and be of some use to me in the state in which I then found myself, invited him to call upon me. He came the day following. It is impossible to describe the anxiety he showed,—the delicate attentions that he paid me. For a long time he had perpetually medical books in his hands; and not trusting my physicians, he obtained permission from Count Guiccioli to send for a very clever physician, a friend of his, in whom he placed great confidence. The attentions of Professor Aglietti (for so this celebrated Italian was called), together with tranquillity, and the inexpressible happiness which I experienced in Lord Byron's society, had so good an effect on my health, that only two months afterwards I was able to accompany my husband in a tour he was obliged to make to visit his various estates."

LETTER 332. TO MR. HOPPNER.

"Ravenna, June 20. 1819.

"I wrote to you from Padua, and from Bologna, and since from Ravenna. I find my situation very agreeable, but want my horses very much, there being good riding in the environs. I can fix no time for my return to Venice—it may be soon or late—or not at all—it all depends on the Donna, whom I found very seriously in bed with a cough and spitting of blood, &c. all of which has subsided. I found all the people here firmly persuaded that she would never recover;—they were mistaken, however.

"My letters were useful as far as I employed them; and I like both the place and people, though I don't trouble the latter more than I can help She manages very well—but if I come away with a stiletto in my gizzard some fine afternoon, I shall not be astonished. I can't make him out at all—he visits me frequently, and takes me out (like Whittington, the Lord Mayor) in a coach and six horses. The fact appears to be, that he is completely governed by her—for that matter, so am I. The people here don't know what to make of us, as he had the character of jealousy with all his wives—this is the third. He is the richest of the Ravennese, by their own account, but is not popular among them. Now do, pray, send off Augustine, and carriage and cattle, to Bologna, without fail or delay, or I shall lose my remaining shred of senses. Don't forget this. My coming, going, and every thing, depend upon HER entirely, just as Mrs. Hoppner (to whom I remit my reverences) said in the true spirit of female prophecy.

"You are but a shabby fellow not to have written before. And I am truly yours," &c.

LETTER 333. TO MR. MURRAY.

"Ravenna, June 29. 1819.

"The letters have been forwarded from Venice, but I trust that you will not have waited for further alterations—I will make none.

"I have no time to return you the proofs—publish without them. I am glad you think the poesy good; and as to 'thinking of the effect,' think you of the sale, and leave me to pluck the porcupines who may point their quills at you.

"I have been here (at Ravenna) these four weeks, having left Venice a month ago;—I came to see my 'Amica,' the Countess Guiccioli, who has been, and still continues, very unwell. * * She is only in her seventeenth, but not of a strong constitution. She has a perpetual cough and an intermittent fever, but bears up most gallantly in every sense of the word. Her husband (this is his third wife) is the richest noble of Ravenna, and almost of Romagna; he is also not the youngest, being upwards of three-score, but in good preservation. All this will appear strange to you, who do not understand the meridian morality, nor our way of life in such respects, and I cannot at present expound the difference;—but you would find it much the same in these parts. At Faenza there is Lord * * * * with an opera girl; and at the inn in the same town is a Neapolitan Prince, who serves the wife of the Gonfaloniere of that city. I am on duty here—so you see 'Così fan tutti e tutte.'

"I have my horses here, saddle as well as carriage, and ride or drive every day in the forest, the Pineta, the scene of Boccaccio's novel, and Dryden's fable of Honoria, &c. &c.; and I see my Dama every day; but I feel seriously uneasy about her health, which seems very precarious. In losing her, I should lose a being who has run great risks on my account, and whom I have every reason to love—but I must not think this possible. I do not know what I should do if she died, but I ought to blow my brains out—and I hope that I should. Her husband is a very polite personage, but I wish he would not carry me out in his coach and six, like Whittington and his cat.

"You ask me if I mean to continue D.J. &c. How should I know? What encouragement do you give me, all of you, with your nonsensical prudery? publish the two Cantos, and then you will see. I desired Mr. Kinnaird to speak to you on a little matter of business; either he has not spoken, or you have not answered. You are a pretty pair, but I will be even with you both. I perceive that Mr. Hobhouse has been challenged by Major Cartwright—Is the Major 'so cunning of fence?'—why did not they fight?—they ought.

"Yours," &c.

LETTER 334. TO MR. HOPPNER.

"Ravenna, July 2. 1819.

"Thanks for your letter and for Madame's. I will answer it directly. Will you recollect whether I did not consign to you one or two receipts of Madame Mocenigo's for house-rent—(I am not sure of this, but think I did—if not, they will be in my drawers)—and will you desire Mr. Dorville to have the goodness to see if Edgecombe has receipts to all payments hitherto made by him on my account, and that there are no debts at Venice? On your answer, I shall send order of further remittance to carry on my household expenses, as my present return to Venice is very problematical; and it may happen—but I can say nothing positive—every thing with me being indecisive and undecided, except the disgust which Venice excites when fairly compared with any other city in this part of Italy. When I say Venice, I mean the Venetians—the city itself is superb as its history—but the people are what I never thought them till they taught me to think so.

"The best way will be to leave Allegra with Antonio's spouse till I can decide something about her and myself—but I thought that you would have had an answer from Mrs. V——r. You have had bore enough with me and mine already.

"I greatly fear that the Guiccioli is going into a consumption, to which her constitution tends. Thus it is with every thing and every body for whom I feel any thing like a real attachment;—'War, death, or discord, doth lay siege to them.' I never even could keep alive a dog that I liked or

[Handwritten annotation: Two doctors (Ravenna) 2nd line]

that liked me. Her symptoms are obstinate cough of the lungs, and occasional fever, &c. &c. and there are latent causes of an eruption in the skin, which she foolishly repelled into the system two years ago: but I have made them send her case to Aglietti; and have begged him to come—if only for a day or two—to consult upon her state.

"If it would not bore Mr. Dorville, I wish he would keep an eye on E—— and on my other ragamuffins. I might have more to say, but I am absorbed about La Gui. and her illness. I cannot tell you the effect it has upon me.

"The horses came, &c. &c. and I have been galloping through the pine forest daily.

"Believe me, &c.

"P.S. My benediction on Mrs. Hoppner, a pleasant journey among the Bernese tyrants, and safe return. You ought to bring back a Platonic Bernese for my reformation. If any thing happens to my present Amica, I have done with the passion for ever—it is my last love. As to libertinism, I have sickened myself of that, as was natural in the way I went on, and I have at least derived that advantage from vice, to love in the better sense of the word. This will be my last adventure—I can hope no more to inspire attachment, and I trust never again to feel it."

The impression which, I think, cannot but be entertained, from some passages of these letters, of the real fervour and sincerity of his attachment to Madame Guiccioli, would be still further confirmed by the perusal of his letters to that lady herself, both from Venice and during his present stay at Ravenna—all bearing, throughout, the true marks both of affection and passion. Such effusions, however, are but little suited to the general eye. It is the tendency of all strong feeling, from dwelling constantly on the same idea, to be monotonous; and those often-repeated vows and verbal endearments, which make the charm of true love-letters to the parties concerned in them, must for ever render even the best of them cloying to others. Those of Lord Byron to Madame Guiccioli, which are for the most part in Italian, and written with a degree of ease and correctness attained rarely by foreigners, refer chiefly to the difficulties thrown in the way of their meetings,—not so much by the husband himself, who appears to have liked and courted Lord Byron's society, as by the watchfulness of other relatives, and the apprehension felt by themselves lest their intimacy should give uneasiness to the father of the lady, Count Gamba, a gentleman to whose good nature and amiableness of character all who know him bear testimony.

In the near approaching departure of the young Countess for Bologna, Lord Byron foresaw a risk of their being again separated; and under the impatience of this prospect, though through the whole of his preceding letters the fear of committing her by any imprudence seems to have been his ruling thought, he now, with that wilfulness of the moment which has so often sealed the destiny of years, proposed that she should, at once, abandon her husband and fly with him:—"c'è uno solo rimedio efficace," he says,—"cioè d' andar vià insieme." To an Italian wife, almost every thing but this is permissible. The same system which so indulgently allows her a friend, as one of the regular appendages of her matrimonial establishment, takes care also to guard against all unseemly consequences of this privilege; and in return for such convenient facilities of wrong exacts rigidly an observance of all the appearances of right. Accordingly, the open step of deserting the husband for the lover instead of being considered, as in England, but a sign and sequel of transgression, takes rank, in Italian morality, as the main transgression itself; and being an offence, too, rendered wholly unnecessary by the latitude otherwise enjoyed, becomes, from its rare occurrence, no less monstrous than odious.

The proposition, therefore, of her noble friend seemed to the young Contessa little less than sacrilege, and the agitation of her mind, between the horrors of such a step, and her eager readiness to give up all and every thing for him she adored, was depicted most strongly in her answer to the proposal. In a subsequent letter, too, the romantic girl even proposed, as a means of escaping the ignominy of an elopement, that she should, like another Juliet, "pass for dead,"—assuring him that there were many easy ways of effecting such a deception.

LETTER 335. TO MR. MURRAY.

"Ravenna, August 1. 1819.

[Address your Answer to Venice, however.]

"Don't be alarmed. You will see me defend myself gaily—that is, if I happen to be in spirits; and by spirits, I don't mean your meaning of the word, but the spirit of a bull-dog when pinched, or a bull when pinned; it is then that they make best sport; and as my sensations under an attack are probably a happy compound of the united energies of these amiable animals, you may perhaps see what Marrall calls 'rare sport,' and some good tossing and goring, in the course of the controversy. But I must be in the right cue first, and I doubt I am almost too far off to be in a sufficient fury for the purpose. And then I have effeminated and enervated myself with love and the summer in these last two months.

"I wrote to Mr. Hobhouse, the other day, and foretold that Juan would either fall entirely or succeed completely; there will be no medium. Appearances are not favourable; but as you write the day after publication, it can hardly be decided what opinion will predominate. You seem in a fright, and doubtless with cause. Come what may I never will flatter the million's canting in any shape. Circumstances may or may not have placed me at times in a situation to lead the public opinion, but the public opinion never led, nor ever shall lead, me. I will not sit on a degraded throne; so pray put Messrs. * * or * *, or Tom Moore, or * * * upon it; they will all of them be transported with their coronation.

"P.S. The Countess Guiccioli is much better than she was. I sent you, before leaving Venice, the real original sketch which gave rise to the 'Vampire,' &c.—Did you get it?"

This letter was, of course (like most of those he addressed to England at this time), intended to be shown; and having been, among others, permitted to see it, I took occasion, in my very next communication to Lord Byron, to twit him a little with the passage in it relating to myself,—the only one, as far as I can learn, that ever fell from my noble friend's pen during our intimacy, in which he has spoken of me otherwise than in terms of kindness and the most undeserved praise. Transcribing his own words, as well as I could recollect them, at the top of my letter, I added, underneath, "Is this the way you speak of your friends?" Not long after, too, when visiting him at Venice, I remember making the same harmless little sneer a subject of raillery with him; but he declared boldly that he had no recollection of having ever written such words, and that, if they existed, "he must have been half asleep when he wrote them."

I have mentioned the circumstance merely for the purpose of remarking, that with a sensibility vulnerable at so many points as his was, and acted upon by an imagination so long practised in self-tormenting, it is only wonderful that, thinking constantly, as his letters prove him to have been, of distant friends, and receiving from few or none equal proofs of thoughtfulness in return, he should not more frequently have broken out into such sallies against the absent and "unreplying." For myself, I can only say that, from the moment I began to unravel his character, the most slighting and even acrimonious expressions that I could have heard he had, in a fit of spleen, uttered against me, would have no more altered my opinion of his disposition, nor disturbed my affection for him, than the momentary clouding over of a bright sky could leave an impression on the mind of gloom, after its shadow had passed away.

LETTER 336. TO MR. MURRAY.

"Ravenna, August 9. 1819.

"Talking of blunders reminds me of Ireland—Ireland of Moore. What is this I see in Galignani about 'Bermuda—agent—deputy—appeal—attachment,' &c.? What is the matter? Is it any thing in which his friends can be of use to him? Pray inform me.

"Of Don Juan I hear nothing further from you; * * *, but the papers don't seem so fierce as the letter you sent me seemed to anticipate, by their extracts at least in Galignani's Messenger. I never saw such a set of fellows as you are! And then the pains taken to exculpate the modest publisher—he remonstrated, forsooth! I will write a preface that shall exculpate you and * * *, &c. completely, on that point; but, at the same time, I will cut you up, like gourds. You have no more soul than the Count de Caylus, (who assured his friends, on his death-bed, that he had none, and that he must know better than they whether he had one or no,) and no more blood than a water-melon! And I see there hath been asterisks, and what Perry used to called 'domned cutting and slashing'—but, never mind.

"I write in haste. To-morrow I set off for Bologna. I write to you with thunder, lightning, &c. and all the winds of heaven whistling through my hair, and the racket of preparation to boot. 'My mistress dear, who hath fed my heart upon smiles and wine' for the last two months, set off with her husband for Bologna this morning, and it seems that I follow him at three to-morrow morning. I cannot tell how our romance will end, but it hath gone on hitherto most erotically. Such perils and escapes! Juan's are as child's play in comparison. The fools think that all my poeshie is always allusive to my own adventures: I have had at one time or another better and more extraordinary and perilous and pleasant than these, every day of the week, if I might tell them; but that must never be.

"I hope Mrs. M. has accouched.

"Yours ever."

LETTER 337. TO MR. MURRAY.

"Bologna, August 12. 1819.

"I do not know how far I may be able to reply to your letter, for I am not very well to-day. Last night I went to the representation of Alfieri's Mirra, the two last acts of which threw me into convulsions. I do not mean by that word a lady's hysterics, but the agony of reluctant tears, and the choking shudder, which I do not often undergo for fiction. This is but the second time for any thing under reality: the first was on seeing Kean's Sir Giles Overreach. The worst was, that the 'Dama' in whose box I was, went off in the same way, I really believe more from fright than any other sympathy—at least with the players: but she has been ill, and I have been ill, and we are all languid and pathetic this morning, with great expenditure of sal volatile. But, to return to your letter of the 23d of July.

"You are right, Gifford is right, Crabbe is right, Hobhouse is right—you are all right, and I am all wrong; but do, pray, let me have that pleasure. Cut me up root and branch; quarter me in the Quarterly; send round my 'disjecti membra poetæ,' like those of the Levite's concubine; make me, if you will, a spectacle to men and angels; but don't ask me to alter, for I won't:—I am obstinate and lazy—and there's the truth.

"But, nevertheless, I will answer your friend P * *, who objects to the quick succession of fun and gravity, as if in that case the gravity did not (in intention, at least) heighten the fun. His metaphor is, that 'we are never scorched and drenched at the same time.' Blessings on his experience! Ask him these questions about 'scorching and drenching.' Did he never play at cricket, or walk a mile in hot weather? Did he never spill a dish of tea over himself in handing the cup to his charmer, to the great shame of his nankeen breeches? Did he never swim in the sea at noonday with the sun in his eyes and on his head, which all the foam of ocean could not cool? Did he never draw his foot out of too hot water, d——ning his eyes and his valet's? Did he never tumble into a river or lake, fishing, and sit in his wet clothes in the boat, or on the bank, afterwards 'scorched and drenched,' like a true sportsman? 'Oh for breath to utter!'—but make him my compliments; he is a clever fellow for all that—a very clever fellow.

"You ask me for the plan of Donny Johnny: I have no plan; I had no plan; but I had or have materials; though if, like Tony Lumpkin, 'I am to be snubbed so when I am in spirits,' the poem will be naught, and the poet turn serious again. If it don't take, I will leave it off where it is, with all due respect to the public; but if continued, it must be in my own way. You might as well make Hamlet (or Diggory) 'act mad' in a strait waistcoat as trammel my buffoonery, if I am to be a buffoon; their gestures and my thoughts would only be pitiably absurd and ludicrously constrained. Why, man, the soul of such writing is its licence; at least the liberty of that licence, if one likes—not that one should abuse it. It is like Trial by Jury and Peerage and the Habeas Corpus—a very fine thing, but chiefly in the reversion; because no one wishes to be tried for the mere pleasure of proving his possession of the privilege.

"But a truce with these reflections. You are too earnest and eager about a work never intended to be serious. Do you suppose that I could have any intention but to giggle and make giggle?—a playful satire, with as little poetry as could be helped, was what I meant. And as to the indecency, do, pray, read in Boswell what Johnson, the sullen moralist, says of Prior and Paulo Purgante.

"Will you get a favour done for me? You can, by your government friends, Croker, Canning, or my old schoolfellow Peel, and I can't. Here it is. Will you ask them to appoint (without salary or emolument) a noble Italian (whom I will name afterwards) consul or vice-consul for Ravenna?

He is a man of very large property,—noble, too; but he wishes to have a British protection, in case of changes. Ravenna is near the sea. He wants no emolument whatever. That his office might be useful, I know; as I lately sent off from Ravenna to Trieste a poor devil of an English sailor, who had remained there sick, sorry, and pennyless (having been set ashore in 1814), from the want of any accredited agent able or willing to help him homewards. Will you get this done? If you do, I will then send his name and condition, subject, of course, to rejection, if not approved when known.

"I know that in the Levant you make consuls and vice-consuls, perpetually, of foreigners. This man is a patrician, and has twelve thousand a year. His motive is a British protection in case of new invasions. Don't you think Croker would do it for us? To be sure, my interest is rare!! but, perhaps, a brother wit in the Tory line might do a good turn at the request of so harmless and long absent a Whig, particularly as there is no salary or burden of any sort to be annexed to the office.

"I can assure you, I should look upon it as a great obligation; but, alas! that very circumstance may, very probably, operate to the contrary—indeed, it ought; but I have, at least, been an honest and an open enemy. Amongst your many splendid government connections, could not you, think you, get our Bibulus made a Consul? or make me one, that I may make him my Vice. You may be assured that, in case of accidents in Italy, he would be no feeble adjunct—as you would think, if you knew his patrimony.

"What is all this about Tom Moore? but why do I ask? since the state of my own affairs would not permit me to be of use to him, though they are greatly improved since 1816, and may, with some more luck and a little prudence, become quite clear. It seems his claimants are American merchants? There goes Nemesis! Moore abused America. It is always thus in the long run:—Time, the Avenger. You have seen every trampler down, in turn, from Buonaparte to the simplest individuals. You saw how some were avenged even upon my insignificance, and how in turn * * * paid for his atrocity. It is an odd world; but the watch has its mainspring, after all.

"So the Prince has been repealing Lord Edward Fitzgerald's forfeiture? Ecco un' sonetto!

"To be the father of the fatherless,
To stretch the hand from the throne's height, and raise
His offspring, who expired in other days
To make thy sire's sway by a kingdom less,—
This is to be a monarch, and repress
Envy into unutterable praise.
Dismiss thy guard, and trust thee to such traits,
For who would lift a hand, except to bless?
Were it not easy, sir, and is't not sweet
To make thyself beloved? and to be
Omnipotent by Mercy's means? for thus
Thy sovereignty would grow but more complete,
A despot thou, and yet thy people free,

And by the heart, not hand, enslaving us.

"There, you dogs! there's a sonnet for you: you won't have such as that in a hurry from Mr. Fitzgerald. You may publish it with my name, an' ye wool. He deserves all praise, bad and good; it was a very noble piece of principality. Would you like an epigram—a translation?
"If for silver, or for gold,
You could melt ten thousand pimples
Into half a dozen dimples,
Then your face we might behold,
Looking, doubtless, much more snugly,
Yet ev'n then 'twould be d——d ugly.

"This was written on some Frenchwoman, by Rulhieres, I believe. Yours."
LETTER 338. TO MR. MURRAY.
"Bologna, August 23. 1819.
"I send you a letter to R * *ts, signed Wortley Clutterbuck, which you may publish in what form you please, in answer to his article. I have had many proofs of men's absurdity, but he beats all in folly. Why, the wolf in sheep's clothing has tumbled into the very trap! We'll strip him. The letter is written in great haste, and amidst a thousand vexations. Your letter only came yesterday, so that there is no time to polish: the post goes out to-morrow. The date is 'Little Piddlington.' Let * * * * correct the press: he knows and can read the handwriting. Continue to keep the anonymous about 'Juan;' it helps us to fight against overwhelming numbers. I have a thousand distractions at present; so excuse haste, and wonder I can act or write at all. Answer by post, as usual.
"Yours.
"P.S. If I had had time, and been quieter and nearer, I would have cut him to hash; but as it is, you can judge for yourselves."
The letter to the Reviewer, here mentioned, had its origin in rather an amusing circumstance. In the first Canto of Don Juan appeared the following passage:—
"For fear some prudish readers should grow skittish, I've bribed My Grandmother's Review,— the British!
"I sent it in a letter to the editor, Who thank'd me duly by return of post— I'm for a handsome article his creditor; Yet if my gentle Muse he please to roast, And break a promise after having made it her, Denying the receipt of what it cost, And smear his page with gall instead of honey,
All I can say is—that he had the money."
On the appearance of the poem, the learned editor of the Review in question allowed himself to be decoyed into the ineffable absurdity of taking the charge as serious, and, in his succeeding number, came forth with an indignant contradiction of it. To this tempting subject the letter, written so hastily off at Bologna, related; but, though printed for Mr. Murray, in a pamphlet consisting of twenty-three pages, it was never published by him. Being valuable, however, as one

of the best specimens we have of Lord Byron's simple and thoroughly English prose, I shall here preserve some extracts from it.

"TO THE EDITOR OF THE BRITISH REVIEW.

"My dear R——ts,

"As a believer in the Church of England—to say nothing of the State—I have been an occasional reader, and great admirer, though not a subscriber, to your Review. But I do not know that any article of its contents ever gave me much surprise till the eleventh of your late twenty-seventh number made its appearance. You have there most manfully refuted a calumnious accusation of bribery and corruption, the credence of which in the public mind might not only have damaged your reputation as a clergyman and an editor, but, what would have been still worse, have injured the circulation of your journal; which, I regret to hear, is not so extensive as the 'purity (as you well observe) of its, &c. &c.' and the present taste for propriety, would induce us to expect. The charge itself is of a solemn nature; and, although in verse, is couched in terms of such circumstantial gravity as to induce a belief little short of that generally accorded to the thirty-nine articles, to which you so generously subscribed on taking your degrees. It is a charge the most revolting to the heart of man from its frequent occurrence; to the mind of a statesman from its occasional truth; and to the soul of an editor from its moral impossibility. You are charged then in the last line of one octave stanza, and the whole eight lines of the next, viz. 209th and 210th of the first Canto of that 'pestilent poem,' Don Juan, with receiving, and still more foolishly acknowledging, the receipt of certain moneys to eulogise the unknown author, who by this account must be known to you, if to nobody else. An impeachment of this nature, so seriously made, there is but one way of refuting; and it is my firm persuasion, that whether you did or did not (and I believe that you did not) receive the said moneys, of which I wish that he had specified the sum, you are quite right in denying all knowledge of the transaction. If charges of this nefarious description are to go forth, sanctioned by all the solemnity of circumstance, and guaranteed by the veracity of verse (as Counsellor Phillips would say), what is to become of readers hitherto implicitly confident in the not less veracious prose of our critical journals? what is to become of the reviews; and, if the reviews fail, what is to become of the editors? It is common cause, and you have done well to sound the alarm. I myself, in my humble sphere, will be one of your echoes. In the words of the tragedian Liston, 'I love a row,' and you seem justly determined to make one.

"It is barely possible, certainly improbable, that the writer might have been in jest; but this only aggravates his crime. A joke, the proverb says, 'breaks no bones;' but it may break a bookseller, or it may be the cause of bones being broken. The jest is but a bad one at the best for the author, and might have been a still worse one for you, if your copious contradiction did not certify to all whom it may concern your own indignant innocence, and the immaculate purity of the British Review. I do not doubt your word, my dear R——ts, yet I cannot help wishing that, in a case of such vital importance, it had assumed the more substantial shape of an affidavit sworn before the Lord Mayor Atkins, who readily receives any deposition; and doubtless would have brought it in some way as evidence of the designs of the Reformers to set fire to London, at the same time that

Response to a bad review

he himself meditates the same good office towards the river Thames.

"I recollect hearing, soon after the publication, this subject discussed at the tea-table of Mr. * * * the poet,—and Mrs. and the Misses * * * * * being in a corner of the room perusing the proof sheets of Mr. * * *'s poems, the male part of the conversazione were at liberty to make some observations on the poem and passage in question, and there was a difference of opinion. Some thought the allusion was to the 'British Critic;' others, that by the expression 'My Grandmother's Review,' it was intimated that 'my grandmother' was not the reader of the review, but actually the writer; thereby insinuating, my dear Mr. R———ts, that you were an old woman; because, as people often say, 'Jeffrey's Review," 'Gifford's Review,' in lieu of Edinburgh and Quarterly, so 'My Grandmother's Review' and R———ts's might be also synonymous. Now, whatever colour this insinuation might derive from the circumstance of your wearing a gown, as well as from your time of life, your general style, and various passages of your writings,—I will take upon myself to exculpate you from all suspicion of the kind, and assert, without calling Mrs. R———ts in testimony, that if ever you should be chosen Pope, you will pass through all the previous ceremonies with as much credit as any pontiff since the parturition of Joan. It is very unfair to judge of sex from writings, particularly from those of the British Review. We are all liable to be deceived, and it is an indisputable fact that many of the best articles in your journal, which were attributed to a veteran female, were actually written by you yourself, and yet to this day there are people who could never find out the difference. But let us return to the more immediate question.

"I agree with you that it is impossible Lord B. should be the author, not only because, as a British peer and a British poet, it would be impracticable for him to have recourse to such facetious fiction, but for some other reasons which you have omitted to state. In the first place, his Lordship has no grandmother. Now the author—and we may believe him in this—doth expressly state that the 'British' is his 'Grandmother's Review;' and if, as I think I have distinctly proved, this was not a mere figurative allusion to your supposed intellectual age and sex, my dear friend, it follows, whether you be she or no, that there is such an elderly lady still extant.

"Shall I give you what I think a prudent opinion? I don't mean to insinuate, God forbid! but if, by any accident, there should have been such a correspondence between you and the unknown author, whoever he may be, send him back his money; I dare say he will be very glad to have it again; it can't be much, considering the value of the article and the circulation of the journal; and you are too modest to rate your praise beyond its real worth:—don't be angry, I know you won't, at this appraisement of your powers of eulogy: for on the other hand, my dear fellow, depend upon it your abuse is worth, not its own weight, that's a feather, but your weight in gold. So don't spare it; if he has bargained for that, give it handsomely, and depend upon your doing him a friendly office.

"What the motives of this writer may have been for (as you magnificently translate his quizzing you) 'stating, with the particularity which belongs to fact, the forgery of a groundless fiction,' (do, pray, my dear R., talk a little less 'in King Cambyses' vein,') I cannot pretend to say; perhaps to laugh at you, but that is no reason for your benevolently making all the world laugh also. I approve of your being angry, I tell you I am angry too, but you should not have shown it so outrageously. Your solemn 'if somebody personating the Editor of the, &c. &c. has received from Lord B. or from any other person,' reminds me of Charley Incledon's usual exordium when people came into the tavern to hear him sing without paying their share of the reckoning—'if a maun, or ony maun, or ony other maun,' &c. &c.; you have both the same redundant eloquence. But why should you think any body would personate you? Nobody would dream of such a prank who ever read your compositions, and perhaps not many who have heard your conversation. But I have been inoculated with a little of your prolixity. The fact is, my dear R——ts, that somebody has tried to make a fool of you, and what he did not succeed in doing, you have done for him and for yourself."

Towards the latter end of August, Count Guiccioli, accompanied by his lady, went for a short time to visit some of his Romagnese estates, while Lord Byron remained at Bologna alone. And here, with a heart softened and excited by the new feeling that had taken possession of him, he appears to have given himself up, during this interval of solitude, to a train of melancholy and impassioned thought, such as, for a time, brought back all the romance of his youthful days. That spring of natural tenderness within his soul, which neither the world's efforts nor his own had been able to chill or choke up, was now, with something of its first freshness, set flowing once more. He again knew what it was to love and be loved,—too late, it is true, for happiness, and too wrongly for peace, but with devotion enough, on the part of the woman, to satisfy even his thirst for affection, and with a sad earnestness, on his own, a foreboding fidelity, which made him cling but the more passionately to this attachment from feeling that it would be his last.

A circumstance which he himself used to mention as having occurred at this period will show how over-powering, at times, was the rush of melancholy over his heart. It was his fancy, during Madame Guiccioli's absence from Bologna, to go daily to her house at his usual hour of visiting her, and there, causing her apartments to be opened, to sit turning over her books, and writing in them. He would then descend into her garden, where he passed hours in musing; and it was on an occasion of this kind, as he stood looking, in a state of unconscious reverie, into one of those fountains so common in the gardens of Italy, that there came suddenly into his mind such desolate fancies, such bodings of the misery he might bring on her he loved, by that doom which (as he has himself written) "makes it fatal to be loved," that, overwhelmed with his own thoughts, he burst into an agony of tears.

During the same few days it was that he wrote in the last page of Madame Guiccioli's copy of "Corinne" the following remarkable note:—

"My dearest Teresa,—I have read this book in your garden;—my love, you were absent, or else I could not have read it. It is a favourite book of yours, and the writer was a friend of mine. You will not understand these English words, and others will not understand them—which is the reason I have not scrawled them in Italian. But you will recognise the hand-writing of him who passionately loved you, and you will divine that, over a book which was yours, he could only think of love. In that word, beautiful in all languages, but most so in yours—Amor mio—is comprised my existence here and hereafter. I feel I exist here, and I fear that I shall exist hereafter,—to what purpose you will decide; my destiny rests with you, and you are a woman, seventeen years of age, and two out of a convent. I wish that you had stayed there, with all my heart,—or, at least, that I had never met you in your married state.

"But all this is too late. I love you, and you love me,—at least, you say so, and act as if you did so, which last is a great consolation in all events. But I more than love you, and cannot cease to love you.

"Think of me, sometimes, when the Alps and the ocean divide us,—but they never will, unless you wish it. BYRON.

"Bologna, August 25. 1819."

LETTER 339. TO MR. MURRAY.

"Bologna, August 24. 1819.

"I wrote to you by last post, enclosing a buffooning letter for publication, addressed to the buffoon R——ts, who has thought proper to tie a canister to his own tail. It was written off-hand, and in the midst of circumstances not very favourable to facetiousness, so that there may, perhaps, be more bitterness than enough for that sort of small acid punch:—you will tell me.

"Keep the anonymous, in any case: it helps what fun there may be. But if the matter grow serious about Don Juan, and you feel yourself in a scrape, or me either, own that I am the author. I will never shrink; and if you do, I can always answer you in the question of Guatimozin to his minister—each being on his own coals.

"I wish that I had been in better spirits; but I am out of sorts, out of nerves, and now and then (I begin to fear) out of my senses. All this Italy has done for me, and not England: I defy all you, and your climate to boot, to make me mad. But if ever I do really become a bedlamite, and wear a strait waistcoat, let me be brought back among you; your people will then be proper company.

"I assure you what I here say and feel has nothing to do with England, either in a literary or personal point of view. All my present pleasures or plagues are as Italian as the opera. And after all, they are but trifles; for all this arises from my 'Dama's' being in the country for three days (at Capo-fiume). But as I could never live but for one human being at a time, (and, I assure you, that one has never been myself, as you may know by the consequences, for the selfish are successful in life,) I feel alone and unhappy.

"I have sent for my daughter from Venice, and I ride daily, and walk in a garden, under a purple canopy of grapes, and sit by a fountain, and talk with the gardener of his tools, which seem greater than Adam's, and with his wife, and with his son's wife, who is the youngest of the party, and, I think, talks best of the three. Then I revisit the Campo Santo, and my old friend, the sexton, has two—but one the prettiest daughter imaginable; and I amuse myself with contrasting her beautiful and innocent face of fifteen with the skulls with which he has peopled several cells, and particularly with that of one skull dated 1766, which was once covered (the tradition goes) by the most lovely features of Bologna—noble and rich. When I look at these, and at this girl—when I think of what they were, and what she must be—why, then, my dear Murray, I won't shock you by saying what I think. It is little matter what becomes of us 'bearded men,' but I don't like the notion of a beautiful woman's lasting less than a beautiful tree—than her own picture—her own shadow, which won't change so to the sun as her face to the mirror. I must leave off, for my head aches consumedly. I have never been quite well since the night of the representation of Alfieri's Mirra, a fortnight ago. Yours ever."

LETTER 340. TO MR. MURRAY.

"Bologna, August 29. 1819.

"I have been in a rage these two days, and am still bilious therefrom. You shall hear. A captain of dragoons, * *, Hanoverian by birth, in the Papal troops at present, whom I had obliged by a loan when nobody would lend him a paul, recommended a horse to me, on sale by a Lieutenant * *, an officer who unites the sale of cattle to the purchase of men. I bought it. The next day, on shoeing the horse, we discovered the thrush,—the animal being warranted sound. I sent to reclaim the contract and the money. The lieutenant desired to speak with me in person. I consented. He came. It was his own particular request. He began a story. I asked him if he would return the money. He said no—but he would exchange. He asked an exorbitant price for his other horses. I told him that he was a thief. He said he was an officer and a man of honour, and pulled out a Parmesan passport signed by General Count Neifperg. I answered, that as he was an officer, I would treat him as such; and that as to his being a gentleman, he might prove it by returning the money: as for his Parmesan passport, I should have valued it more if it had been a Parmesan cheese. He answered in high terms, and said that if it were the morning (it was about eight o'clock in the evening) he would have satisfaction. I then lost my temper: 'As for THAT,' I replied, 'you shall have it directly,—it will be mutual satisfaction, I can assure you. You are a thief, and, as you say, an officer; my pistols are in the next room loaded; take one of the candles, examine, and make your choice of weapons.' He replied, that pistols were English weapons; he always fought with the sword. I told him that I was able to accommodate him, having three regimental swords in a drawer near us: and he might take the longest and put himself on guard.

"All this passed in presence of a third person. He then said No; but to-morrow morning he would give me the meeting at any time or place. I answered that it was not usual to appoint meetings in the presence of witnesses, and that we had best speak man to man, and appoint time and instruments. But as the man present was leaving the room, the Lieutenant * *, before he could shut the door after him, ran out roaring 'Help and murder' most lustily, and fell into a sort of hysteric in the arms of about fifty people, who all saw that I had no weapon of any sort or kind about me, and followed him, asking him what the devil was the matter with him. Nothing would do: he ran away without his hat, and went to bed, ill of the fright. He then tried his complaint at the police, which dismissed it as frivolous. He is, I believe, gone away, or going.

"The horse was warranted, but, I believe, so worded that the villain will not be obliged to refund, according to law. He endeavoured to raise up an indictment of assault and battery, but as it was in a public inn, in a frequented street, there were too many witnesses to the contrary; and, as a military man, he has not cut a martial figure, even in the opinion of the priests. He ran off in such a hurry that he left his hat, and never missed it till he got to his hostel or inn. The facts are as I tell you, I can assure you. He began by 'coming Captain Grand over me,' or I should never have thought of trying his 'cunning in fence.' But what could I do? He talked of 'honour, and satisfaction, and his commission;' he produced a military passport; there are severe punishments

T on B's death

for regular duels on the Continent, and trifling ones for rencontres, so that it is best to fight it out directly; he had robbed, and then wanted to insult me;—what could I do? My patience was gone, and the weapons at hand, fair and equal. Besides, it was just after dinner, when my digestion was bad, and I don't like to be disturbed. His friend * * is at Forli; we shall meet on my way back to Ravenna. The Hanoverian seems the greater rogue of the two; and if my valour does not ooze away like Acres's—'Odds flints and triggers!' if it should be a rainy morning, and my stomach in disorder, there may be something for the obituary.

"Now pray, 'Sir Lucius, do not you look upon me as a very ill-used gentleman?' I send my Lieutenant to match Mr. Hobhouse's Major Cartwright: and so 'good morrow to you, good master Lieutenant.' With regard to other things I will write soon, but I have been quarrelling and fooling till I can scribble no more."

In the month of September, Count Guiccioli, being called away by business to Ravenna, left his young Countess and her lover to the free enjoyment of each other's society at Bologna. The lady's ill health, which had been the cause of her thus remaining behind, was thought, soon after, to require the still further advantage of a removal to Venice; and the Count her husband, being written to on the subject, consented, with the most complaisant readiness, that she should proceed thither in company with Lord Byron. "Some business" (says the lady's own Memoir) "having called Count Guiccioli to Ravenna, I was obliged, by the state of my health, instead of accompanying him, to return to Venice, and he consented that Lord Byron should be the companion of my journey. We left Bologna on the fifteenth of September: we visited the Euganean Hills and Arquà, and wrote our names in the book which is presented to those who make this pilgrimage. But I cannot linger over these recollections of happiness;—the contrast with the present is too dreadful. If a blessed spirit, while in the full enjoyment of heavenly happiness, were sent down to this earth to suffer all its miseries, the contrast could not be more dreadful between the past and the present, than what I have endured from the moment when that terrible word reached my ears, and I for ever lost the hope of again beholding him, one look from whom I valued beyond earth's all happiness. When I arrived at Venice, the physicians ordered that I should try the country air, and Lord Byron, having a villa at La Mira, gave it up to me, and came to reside there with me. At this place we passed the autumn, and there I had the pleasure of forming your acquaintance."

It was my good fortune, at this period, in the course of a short and hasty tour through the north of Italy, to pass five or six days with Lord Byron at Venice. I had written to him on my way thither to announce my coming, and to say how happy it would make me could I tempt him to accompany me as far as Rome.

During my stay at Geneva, an opportunity had been afforded me of observing the exceeding readiness with which even persons the least disposed to be prejudiced gave an ear to any story relating to Lord Byron, in which the proper portions of odium and romance were but plausibly mingled. In the course of conversation, one day, with the late amiable and enlightened Monsieur D * *, that gentleman related, with much feeling, to my fellow-traveller and myself, the details of a late act of seduction of which Lord Byron had, he said, been guilty, and which was made to

Moore in Switzerland
Geneva

comprise within itself all the worst features of such unmanly frauds upon innocence;—the victim, a young unmarried lady, of one of the first families of Venice, whom the noble seducer had lured from her father's house to his own, and, after a few weeks, most inhumanly turned her out of doors. In vain, said the relator, did she entreat to become his servant, his slave;—in vain did she ask to remain in some dark corner of his mansion, from which she might be able to catch a glimpse of his form as he passed. Her betrayer was obdurate, and the unfortunate young lady, in despair at being thus abandoned by him, threw herself into the canal, from which she was taken out but to be consigned to a mad-house. Though convinced that there must be considerable exaggeration in this story, it was only on my arrival at Venice I ascertained that the whole was a romance; and that out of the circumstances (already laid before the reader) connected with Lord Byron's fantastic and, it must be owned, discreditable fancy for the Fornarina, this pathetic tale, so implicitly believed at Geneva, was fabricated.

Having parted at Milan, with Lord John Russell, whom I had accompanied from England, and whom I was to rejoin, after a short visit to Rome, at Genoa, I made purchase of a small and (as it soon proved) crazy travelling carriage, and proceeded alone on my way to Venice. My time being limited, I stopped no longer at the intervening places than was sufficient to hurry over their respective wonders, and, leaving Padua at noon on the 8th of October, I found myself, about two o'clock, at the door of my friend's villa, at La Mira. He was but just up, and in his bath; but the servant having announced my arrival, he returned a message that, if I would wait till he was dressed, he would accompany me to Venice. The interval I employed in conversing with my old acquaintance, Fletcher, and in viewing, under his guidance, some of the apartments of the villa.

It was not long before Lord Byron himself made his appearance; and the delight I felt in meeting him once more, after a separation of so many years, was not a little heightened by observing that his pleasure was, to the full, as great, while it was rendered doubly touching by the evident rarity of such meetings to him of late, and the frank outbreak of cordiality and gaiety with which he gave way to his feelings. It would be impossible, indeed, to convey to those who have not, at some time or other, felt the charm of his manner, any idea of what it could be when under the influence of such pleasurable excitement as it was most flatteringly evident he experienced at this moment.

I was a good deal struck, however, by the alteration that had taken place in his personal appearance. He had grown fatter both in person and face, and the latter had most suffered by the change,—having lost, by the enlargement of the features, some of that refined and spiritualised look that had, in other times, distinguished it. The addition of whiskers, too, which he had not long before been induced to adopt, from hearing that some one had said he had a "faccia di musico," as well as the length to which his hair grew down on his neck, and the rather foreign air of his coat and cap,—all combined to produce that dissimilarity to his former self I had observed in him. He was still, however, eminently handsome; and, in exchange for whatever his features might have lost of their high, romantic character, they had become more fitted for the expression of that arch, waggish wisdom, that Epicurean play of humour, which he had shown to be equally inherent in his various and prodigally gifted nature; while, by the somewhat increased roundness of the contours, the resemblance of his finely formed mouth and chin to those of the Belvedere Apollo had become still more striking.

His breakfast, which I found he rarely took before three or four o'clock in the afternoon, was speedily despatched,—his habit being to eat it standing, and the meal in general consisting of one or two raw eggs, a cup of tea without either milk or sugar, and a bit of dry biscuit. Before we took our departure, he presented me to the Countess Guiccioli, who was at this time, as my readers already know, living under the same roof with him at La Mira; and who, with a style of beauty singular in an Italian, as being fair-complexioned and delicate, left an impression upon my mind, during this our first short interview, of intelligence and amiableness such as all that I have since known or heard of her has but served to confirm.

We now started together, Lord Byron and myself, in my little Milanese vehicle, for Fusina,—his portly gondolier Tita, in a rich livery and most redundant mustachios, having seated himself on the front of the carriage, to the no small trial of its strength, which had already once given way, even under my own weight, between Verona and Vicenza. On our arrival at Fusina, my noble friend, from his familiarity with all the details of the place, had it in his power to save me both trouble and expense in the different arrangements relative to the custom-house, remise, &c.; and the good-natured assiduity with which he bustled about in despatching these matters, gave me an opportunity of observing, in his use of the infirm limb, a much greater degree of activity than I had ever before, except in sparring, witnessed.

As we proceeded across the Lagoon in his gondola, the sun was just setting, and it was an evening such as Romance would have chosen for a first sight of Venice, rising "with her tiara of bright towers" above the wave; while, to complete, as might be imagined, the solemn interest of the scene, I beheld it in company with him who had lately given a new life to its glories, and sung of that fair City of the Sea thus grandly:—

> "I stood in Venice on the Bridge of Sighs; A palace and a prison on each hand: I saw from out the wave her structures rise As from the stroke of the enchanter's wand: A thousand years their cloudy wings expand Around me, and a dying glory smiles O'er the far times, when many a subject land Look'd to the winged lion's marble piles, Where Venice sat in state, throned in her hundred isles."

But, whatever emotions the first sight of such a scene might, under other circumstances, have inspired me with, the mood of mind in which I now viewed it was altogether the very reverse of what might have been expected. The exuberant gaiety of my companion, and the recollections,—any thing but romantic,—into which our conversation wandered, put at once completely to flight all poetical and historical associations; and our course was, I am almost ashamed to say, one of uninterrupted merriment and laughter till we found ourselves at the steps of my friend's palazzo on the Grand Canal. All that had ever happened, of gay or ridiculous, during our London life together,—his scrapes and my lecturings,—our joint adventures with the Bores and Blues, the two great enemies, as he always called them, of London happiness,—our joyous nights together at Watier's, Kinnaird's, &c. and "that d——d supper of Rancliffe's which ought to have been a dinner,"—all was passed rapidly in review between us, and with a flow of humour and hilarity, on his side, of which it would have been difficult, even for persons far graver than I can pretend to be, not to have caught the contagion.

He had all along expressed his determination that I should not go to any hotel, but fix my quarters at his house during the period of my stay; and, had he been residing there himself, such an arrangement would have been all that I most desired. But, this not being the case, a common hotel was, I thought, a far readier resource; and I therefore entreated that he would allow me to order an apartment at the Gran Bretagna, which had the reputation, I understood, of being a comfortable hotel. This, however, he would not hear of; and, as an inducement for me to agree to his plan, said that, as long as I chose to stay, though he should be obliged to return to La Mira in the evenings, he would make it a point to come to Venice every day and dine with me. As we now turned into the dismal canal, and stopped before his damp-looking mansion, my predilection for the Gran Bretagna returned in full force; and I again ventured to hint that it would save an abundance of trouble to let me proceed thither. But "No—no," he answered,—"I see you think you'll be very uncomfortable here; but you'll find that it is not quite so bad as you expect."

As I groped my way after him through the dark hall, he cried out, "Keep clear of the dog;" and before we had proceeded many paces farther, "Take care, or that monkey will fly at you;"—a curious proof, among many others, of his fidelity to all the tastes of his youth, as it agrees perfectly with the description of his life at Newstead, in 1809, and of the sort of menagerie which his visitors had then to encounter in their progress through his hall. Having escaped these dangers, I followed him up the staircase to the apartment destined for me. All this time he had been despatching servants in various directions,—one, to procure me a laquais de place; another to go in quest of Mr. Alexander Scott, to whom he wished to give me in charge; while a third was sent to order his Segretario to come to him. "So, then, you keep a Secretary?" I said. "Yes," he answered, "a fellow who can't write—but such are the names these pompous people give to things."

When we had reached the door of the apartment it was discovered to be locked, and, to all appearance, had been so for some time, as the key could not be found;—a circumstance which, to my English apprehension, naturally connected itself with notions of damp and desolation, and I again sighed inwardly for the Gran Bretagna. Impatient at the delay of the key, my noble host, with one of his humorous maledictions, gave a vigorous kick to the door and burst it open; on which we at once entered into an apartment not only spacious and elegant, but wearing an aspect of comfort and habitableness which to a traveller's eye is as welcome as it is rare. "Here," he said, in a voice whose every tone spoke kindness and hospitality,—"these are the rooms I use myself, and here I mean to establish you."

He had ordered dinner from some Tratteria, and while waiting its arrival—as well as that of Mr. Alexander Scott, whom he had invited to join us—we stood out on the balcony, in order that, before the daylight was quite gone, I might have some glimpses of the scene which the Canal presented. Happening to remark, in looking up at the clouds, which were still bright in the west, that "what had struck me in Italian sunsets was that peculiar rosy hue—" I had hardly pronounced the word "rosy," when Lord Byron, clapping his hand on my mouth, said, with a laugh, "Come, d——n it, Tom, don't be poetical." Among the few gondolas passing at the time, there was one at some distance, in which sat two gentlemen, who had the appearance of being English; and, observing them to look our way, Lord Byron putting his arms a-kimbo, said with a sort of comic swagger, "Ah! if you, John Bulls, knew who the two fellows are, now standing up here, I think you would stare!"—I risk mentioning these things, though aware how they may be turned against myself, for the sake of the otherwise indescribable traits of manner and character which they convey. After a very agreeable dinner, through which the jest, the story, and the laugh were almost uninterruptedly carried on, our noble host took leave of us to return to La Mira, while Mr. Scott and I went to one of the theatres, to see the Ottavia of Alfieri.

The ensuing evenings, during my stay, were passed much in the same manner,—my mornings being devoted, under the kind superintendence of Mr. Scott, to a hasty, and, I fear, unprofitable view of the treasures of art with which Venice abounds. On the subjects of painting and sculpture Lord Byron has, in several of his letters, expressed strongly and, as to most persons will appear, heretically his opinions. In his want, however, of a due appreciation of these arts, he but resembled some of his great precursors in the field of poetry;—both Tasso and Milton, for example, having evinced so little tendency to such tastes, that, throughout the whole of their pages, there is not, I fear, one single allusion to any of those great masters of the pencil and chisel, whose works, nevertheless, both had seen. That Lord Byron, though despising the imposture and jargon with which the worship of the Arts is, like other worships, clogged and mystified, felt deeply, more especially in sculpture, whatever imaged forth true grace and energy, appears from passages of his poetry, which are in every body's memory, and not a line of which but thrills alive with a sense of grandeur and beauty such as it never entered into the capacity of a mere connoisseur even to conceive.

In reference to this subject, as we were conversing one day after dinner about the various collections I had visited that morning, on my saying that fearful as I was, at all times, of praising any picture, lest I should draw upon myself the connoisseur's sneer for my pains, I would yet, to him, venture to own that I had seen a picture at Milan which—"The Hagar!" he exclaimed, eagerly interrupting me; and it was in fact this very picture I was about to mention as having wakened in me, by the truth of its expression, more real emotion than any I had yet seen among the chefs-d'oeuvre of Venice. It was with no small degree of pride and pleasure I now discovered that my noble friend had felt equally with myself the affecting mixture of sorrow and reproach with which the woman's eyes tell the whole story in that picture.

On the second evening of my stay, Lord Byron having, as before, left us for La Mira, I most willingly accepted the offer of Mr. Scott to introduce me to the conversazioni of the two celebrated ladies, with whose names, as leaders of Venetian fashion, the tourists to Italy have made every body acquainted. To the Countess A * *'s parties Lord Byron had chiefly confined himself during the first winter he passed at Venice; but the tone of conversation at these small meetings being much too learned for his tastes, he was induced, the following year, to discontinue his attendance at them, and chose, in preference, the less erudite, but more easy, society of the Countess B * *. Of the sort of learning sometimes displayed by the "blue" visitants at Madame A * *'s, a circumstance mentioned by the noble poet himself may afford some idea. The conversation happening to turn, one evening, upon the statue of Washington, by Canova, which had been just shipped off for the United States, Madame A * *, who was then engaged in compiling a Description Raisonnée of Canova's works, and was anxious for information respecting the subject of this statue, requested that some of her learned guests would detail to her all they knew of him. This task a Signor * * (author of a book on Geography and Statistics) undertook to perform, and, after some other equally sage and authentic details, concluded by informing her that "Washington was killed in a duel by Burke."—"What," exclaimed Lord Byron, as he stood biting his lips with impatience during this conversation, "what, in the name of folly, are you all thinking of?"—for he now recollected the famous duel between Hamilton and Colonel Burr, whom, it was evident, this learned worthy had confounded with Washington and Burke!

In addition to the motives easily conceivable for exchanging such a society for one that offered, at least, repose from such erudite efforts, there was also another cause more immediately leading to the discontinuance of his visits to Madame A * *. This lady, who has been sometimes honoured with the title of "The De Staël of Italy," had written a book called "Portraits," containing sketches of the characters of various persons of note; and it being her intention to introduce Lord Byron into this assemblage, she had it intimated to his Lordship that an article in which his portraiture had been attempted was to appear in a new edition she was about to publish of her work. It was expected, of course, that this intimation would awaken in him some desire to see the sketch; but, on the contrary, he was provoking enough not to manifest the least symptoms of curiosity. Again and again was the same hint, with as little success, conveyed; till, at length, on finding that no impression could be produced in this manner, a direct offer was made, in Madame A * *'s own name, to submit the article to his perusal. He could now contain himself no longer. With more sincerity than politeness, he returned for answer to the lady, that he was by no means ambitious of appearing in her work; that, from the shortness, as well as the distant nature of their acquaintance, it was impossible she could have qualified herself to be his portrait-painter, and that, in short, she could not oblige him more than by committing the article to the flames.

Whether the tribute thus unceremoniously treated ever met the eyes of Lord Byron, I know not; but he could hardly, I think, had he seen it, have escaped a slight touch of remorse at having thus spurned from him a portrait drawn in no unfriendly spirit, and, though affectedly expressed, seizing some of the less obvious features of his character,—as, for instance, that diffidence so little to be expected from a career like his, with the discriminating niceness of a female hand. The following are extracts from this Portrait:—

"'Toi, dont le monde encore ignore le vrai nom, Esprit mystérieux, Mortel, Ange, ou Démon, Qui que tu sois, Byron, bon ou fatal génie, J'aime de tes conceits la sauvage harmonie.'
LAMARTINE.

"It would be to little purpose to dwell upon the mere beauty of a countenance in which the expression of an extraordinary mind was so conspicuous. What serenity was seated on the forehead, adorned with the finest chestnut hair, light, curling, and disposed with such art, that the art was hidden in the imitation of most pleasing nature! What varied expression in his eyes! They were of the azure colour of the heavens, from which they seemed to derive their origin. His teeth, in form, in colour, in transparency, resembled pearls; but his cheeks were too delicately tinged with the hue of the pale rose. His neck, which he was in the habit of keeping uncovered as much as the usages of society permitted, seemed to have been formed in a mould, and was very white. His hands were as beautiful as if they had been the works of art. His figure left nothing to be desired, particularly by those who found rather a grace than a defect in a certain light and gentle undulation of the person when he entered a room, and of which you hardly felt tempted to enquire the cause. Indeed it was scarcely perceptible,—the clothes he wore were so long.

"He was never seen to walk through the streets of Venice, nor along the pleasant banks of the Brenta, where he spent some weeks of the summer; and there are some who assert that he has never seen, excepting from a window, the wonders of the 'Piazza di San Marco;'—so powerful in him was the desire of not showing himself to be deformed in any part of his person. I, however, believe that he has often gazed on those wonders, but in the late and solitary hour, when the stupendous edifices which surrounded him, illuminated by the soft and placid light of the moon, appeared a thousand times more lovely.

"His face appeared tranquil like the ocean on a fine spring morning; but, like it, in an instant became changed into the tempestuous and terrible, if a passion, (a passion did I say?) a thought, a word, occurred to disturb his mind. His eyes then lost all their sweetness, and sparkled so that it became difficult to look on them. So rapid a change would not have been thought possible; but it was impossible to avoid acknowledging that the natural state of his mind was the tempestuous.

"What delighted him greatly one day annoyed him the next; and whenever he appeared constant in the practice of any habits, it arose merely from the indifference, not to say contempt, in which he held them all: whatever they might be, they were not worthy that he should occupy his thoughts with them. His heart was highly sensitive, and suffered itself to be governed in an extraordinary degree by sympathy; but his imagination carried him away, and spoiled every thing. He believed in presages, and delighted in the recollection that he held this belief in common with Napoleon. It appeared that, in proportion as his intellectual education was cultivated, his moral education was neglected, and that he never suffered himself to know or observe other restraints than those imposed by his inclinations. Nevertheless, who could believe that he had a constant, and almost infantine timidity, of which the evidences were so apparent as to render its existence indisputable, notwithstanding the difficulty experienced in associating with Lord Byron a sentiment which had the appearance of modesty? Conscious as he was that, wherever he presented himself, all eyes were fixed on him, and all lips, particularly those of the women, were opened to say, 'There he is, that is Lord Byron,'—he necessarily found himself in the situation of an actor obliged to sustain a character, and to render an account, not to others (for about them he gave himself no concern), but to himself, of his every action and word. This occasioned him a feeling of uneasiness which was obvious to every one.

"He remarked on a certain subject (which in 1814 was the topic of universal discourse) that 'the world was worth neither the trouble taken in its conquest, nor the regret felt at its loss,' which saying (if the worth of an expression could ever equal that of many and great actions) would almost show the thoughts and feelings of Lord Byron to be more stupendous and unmeasured than those of him respecting whom he spoke.

"His gymnastic exercises were sometimes violent, and at others almost nothing. His body, like his spirit, readily accommodated itself to all his inclinations. During an entire winter, he went out every morning alone to row himself to the island of Armenians, (a small island situated in the midst of a tranquil lake, and distant from Venice about half a league,) to enjoy the society of those learned and hospitable monks, and to learn their difficult language; and, in the evening, entering again into his gondola, he went, but only for a couple of hours, into company. A second winter, whenever the water of the lake was violently agitated, he was observed to cross it, and landing on the nearest terra firma, to fatigue at least two horses with riding.

"No one ever heard him utter a word of French, although he was perfectly conversant with that language. He hated the nation and its modern literature; in like manner, he held the modern Italian literature in contempt, and said it possessed but one living author,—a restriction which I know not whether to term ridiculous, or false and injurious. His voice was sufficiently sweet and flexible. He spoke with much suavity, if not contradicted, but rather addressed himself to his neighbour than to the entire company.

"Very little food sufficed him; and he preferred fish to flesh for this extraordinary reason, that the latter, he said, rendered him ferocious. He disliked seeing women eat; and the cause of this extraordinary antipathy must be sought in the dread he always had, that the notion he loved to cherish of their perfection and almost divine nature might be disturbed. Having always been governed by them, it would seem that his very self-love was pleased to take refuge in the idea of their excellence,—a sentiment which he knew how (God knows how) to reconcile with the contempt in which, shortly afterwards, almost with the appearance of satisfaction, he seemed to hold them. But contradictions ought not to surprise us in characters like Lord Byron's; and then, who does not know that the slave holds in detestation his ruler?

"Lord Byron disliked his countrymen, but only because he knew that his morals were held in contempt by them. The English, themselves rigid observers of family duties, could not pardon him the neglect of his, nor his trampling on principles; therefore neither did he like being presented to them, nor did they, especially when they had their wives with them, like to cultivate his acquaintance. Still there was a strong desire in all of them to see him, and the women in particular, who did not dare to look at him but by stealth, said in an under voice, 'What a pity it is!' If, however, any of his compatriots of exalted rank and of high reputation came forward to treat him with courtesy, he showed himself obviously flattered by it, and was greatly pleased with such association. It seemed that to the wound which remained always open in his ulcerated heart such soothing attentions were as drops of healing balm, which comforted him.

"Speaking of his marriage,—a delicate subject, but one still agreeable to him, if it was treated in a friendly voice,—he was greatly moved, and said it had been the innocent cause of all his errors and all his griefs. Of his wife he spoke with much respect and affection. He said she was an illustrious lady, distinguished for the qualities of her heart and understanding, and that all the fault of their cruel separation lay with himself. Now, was such language dictated by justice or by vanity? Does it not bring to mind the saying of Julius, that the wife of Caesar must not even be suspected? What vanity in that saying of Caesar! In fact, if it had not been from vanity, Lord Byron would have admitted this to no one. Of his young daughter, his dear Ada, he spoke with great tenderness, and seemed to be pleased at the great sacrifice he had made in leaving her to comfort her mother. The intense hatred he bore his mother-in-law, and a sort of Euryclea of Lady Byron, two women to whose influence he, in a great measure, attributed her estrangement from him,—demonstrated clearly how painful the separation was to him, notwithstanding some bitter pleasantries which occasionally occur in his writings against her also, dictated rather by rancour than by indifference."

From the time of his misunderstanding with Madame A * * *, the visits of the noble poet were transferred to the house of the other great rallying point of Venetian society, Madame B * * *,—a lady in whose manners, though she had long ceased to be young, there still lingered much of that attaching charm, which a youth passed in successful efforts to please seldom fails to leave behind. That those powers of pleasing, too, were not yet gone, the fidelity of, at least, one devoted admirer testified; nor is she supposed to have thought it impossible that Lord Byron himself might yet be linked on at the end of that long chain of lovers, which had, through so many years, graced the triumphs of her beauty. If, however, there could have been, in any case, the slightest chance of such a conquest, she had herself completely frustrated it by introducing her distinguished visitor to Madame Guiccioli,—a step by which she at last lost, too, even the ornament of his presence at her parties, as in consequence of some slighting conduct, on her part, towards his "Dama," he discontinued his attendance at her evening assemblies, and at the time of my visit to Venice had given up society altogether.

I could soon collect, from the tone held respecting his conduct at Madame B * * *'s, how subversive of all the morality of intrigue they considered the late step of which he had been guilty in withdrawing his acknowledged "Amica" from the protection of her husband, and placing her, at once, under the same roof with himself. "You must really (said the hostess herself to me) scold your friend;—till this unfortunate affair, he conducted himself so well!"—a eulogy on his previous moral conduct which, when I reported it the following day to my noble host, provoked at once a smile and sigh from his lips.

The chief subject of our conversation, when alone, was his marriage, and the load of obloquy which it had brought upon him. He was most anxious to know the worst that had been alleged of his conduct; and as this was our first opportunity of speaking together on the subject, I did not hesitate to put his candour most searchingly to the proof, not only by enumerating the various charges I had heard brought against him by others, but by specifying such portions of these charges as I had been inclined to think not incredible myself. To all this he listened with patience, and answered with the most unhesitating frankness, laughing to scorn the tales of unmanly outrage related of him, but, at the same time, acknowledging that there had been in his conduct but too much to blame and regret, and stating one or two occasions, during his domestic life, when he had been irritated into letting "the breath of bitter words" escape him,—words, rather those of the unquiet spirit that possessed him than his own, and which he now evidently remembered with a degree of remorse and pain which might well have entitled them to be forgotten by others.

It was, at the same time, manifest, that, whatever admissions he might be inclined to make respecting his own delinquencies, the inordinate measure of the punishment dealt out to him had sunk deeply into his mind, and, with the usual effect of such injustice, drove him also to be unjust himself;—so much so, indeed, as to impute to the quarter, to which he now traced all his ill fate, a feeling of fixed hostility to himself, which would not rest, he thought, even at his grave, but continue to persecute his memory as it was now embittering his life. So strong was this impression upon him, that during one of our few intervals of seriousness, he conjured me, by our friendship, if, as he both felt and hoped, I should survive him, not to let unmerited censure settle upon his name, but, while I surrendered him up to condemnation, where he deserved it, to vindicate him where aspersed.

How groundless and wrongful were these apprehensions, the early death which he so often predicted and sighed for has enabled us, unfortunately but too soon, to testify. So far from having to defend him against any such assailants, an unworthy voice or two, from persons more injurious as friends than as enemies, is all that I find raised in hostility to his name; while by none, I am inclined to think, would a generous amnesty over his grave be more readily and cordially concurred in than by her, among whose numerous virtues a forgiving charity towards himself was the only one to which she had not yet taught him to render justice.

I have already had occasion to remark, in another part of this work, that with persons who, like Lord Byron, live centred in their own tremulous web of sensitiveness, those friends of whom they see least, and who, therefore, least frequently come in collision with them in those every-day realities from which such natures shrink so morbidly, have proportionately a greater chance of retaining a hold on their affections. There is, however, in long absence from persons of this temperament, another description of risk hardly less, perhaps, to be dreaded. If the station a friend holds in their hearts is, in near intercourse with them, in danger from their sensitiveness, it is almost equally, perhaps, at the mercy of their too active imaginations during absence. On this very point, I recollect once expressing my apprehensions to Lord Byron, in a passage of a letter addressed to him but a short time before his death, of which the following is, as nearly as I can recall it, the substance:—"When with you, I feel sure of you; but, at a distance, one is often a little afraid of being made the victim, all of a sudden, of some of those fanciful suspicions, which, like meteoric stones, generate themselves (God knows how) in the upper regions of your imagination, and come clattering down upon our heads, some fine sunny day, when we are least expecting such an invasion."

In writing thus to him, I had more particularly in recollection a fancy of this kind respecting myself, which he had, not long before my present visit to him at Venice, taken into his head. In a ludicrous, and now, perhaps, forgotten publication of mine, giving an account of the adventures of an English family in Paris, there had occurred the following description of the chief hero of the tale:—

"A fine, sallow, sublime sort of Werter-faced man, With mustachios which gave (what we read of so oft) The dear Corsair expression, half savage, half soft,— As hyænas in love may be fancied to look, or A something between Abelard and old Blucher."

On seeing this doggrel, my noble friend,—as I might, indeed, with a little more thought, have anticipated,—conceived the notion that I meant to throw ridicule on his whole race of poetic heroes, and accordingly, as I learned from persons then in frequent intercourse with him, flew out into one of his fits of half humorous rage against me. This he now confessed himself, and, in laughing over the circumstance with me, owned that he had even gone so far as, in his first moments of wrath, to contemplate some little retaliation for this perfidious hit at his heroes. "But when I recollected," said he, "what pleasure it would give the whole tribe of blockheads and blues to see you and me turning out against each other, I gave up the idea." He was, indeed, a striking instance of what may be almost invariably observed, that they who best know how to wield the weapon of ridicule themselves, are the most alive to its power in the hands of others. I remember, one day,—in the year 1813, I think,—as we were conversing together about critics and their influence on the public. "For my part," he exclaimed, "I don't care what they say of me, so they don't quiz me."—"Oh, you need not fear that,"—I answered, with something, perhaps, of a half suppressed smile on my features,—"nobody could quiz you"—"You could, you villain!" he replied, clenching his hand at me, and looking, at the same time, with comic earnestness into my face.

Before I proceed any farther with my own recollections, I shall here take the opportunity of extracting some curious particulars respecting the habits and mode of life of my friend while at Venice, from an account obligingly furnished me by a gentleman who long resided in that city, and who, during the greater part of Lord Byron's stay, lived on terms of the most friendly intimacy with him.

"I have often lamented that I kept no notes of his observations during our rides and aquatic excursions. Nothing could exceed the vivacity and variety of his conversation, or the cheerfulness of his manner. His remarks on the surrounding objects were always original: and most particularly striking was the quickness with which he availed himself of every circumstance, however trifling in itself, and such as would have escaped the notice of almost any other person, to carry his point in such arguments as we might chance to be engaged in. He was feelingly alive to the beauties of nature, and took great interest in any observations, which, as a dabbler in the arts, I ventured to make upon the effects of light and shadow, or the changes produced in the colour of objects by every variation in the atmosphere.

"The spot where we usually mounted our horses had been a Jewish cemetery; but the French, during their occupation of Venice, had thrown down the enclosures, and levelled all the tombstones with the ground, in order that they might not interfere with the fortifications upon the Lido, under the guns of which it was situated. To this place, as it was known to be that where he alighted from his gondola and met his horses, the curious amongst our country people, who were anxious to obtain a glimpse of him, used to resort; and it was amusing in the extreme to witness the excessive coolness with which ladies, as well as gentlemen, would advance within a very few paces of him, eyeing him, some with their glasses, as they would have done a statue in a museum, or the wild beasts at Exeter 'Change. However flattering this might be to a man's vanity, Lord Byron, though he bore it very patiently, expressed himself, as I believe he really was, excessively annoyed at it.

"I have said that our usual ride was along the sea-shore, and that the spot where we took horse, and of course dismounted, had been a cemetery. It will readily be believed, that some caution was necessary in riding over the broken tombstones, and that it was altogether an awkward place for horses to pass. As the length of our ride was not very great, scarcely more than six miles in all, we seldom rode fast, that we might at least prolong its duration; and enjoy as much as possible the refreshing air of the Adriatic. One day, as we were leisurely returning homewards, Lord Byron, all at once, and without saying any thing to me, set spurs to his horse and started off at full gallop, making the greatest haste he could to get to his gondola. I could not conceive what fit had seized him, and had some difficulty in keeping even within a reasonable distance of him, while I looked around me to discover, if I were able, what could be the cause of his unusual precipitation. At length I perceived at some distance two or three gentlemen, who were running along the opposite side of the island nearest the Lagoon, parallel with him, towards his gondola, hoping to get there in time to see him alight; and a race actually took place between them, he endeavouring to outstrip them. In this he, in fact, succeeded, and, throwing himself quickly from his horse, leapt into his gondola, of which he hastily closed the blinds, ensconcing himself in a corner so as not to be seen. For my own part, not choosing to risk my neck over the ground I have spoken of, I followed more leisurely as soon as I came amongst the gravestones, but got to the place of embarkation just at the same moment with my curious countrymen, and in time to witness their disappointment at having had their run for nothing. I found him exulting in his success in outstripping them. He expressed in strong terms his annoyance at what he called their impertinence, whilst I could not but laugh at his impatience, as well as at the mortification of the unfortunate pedestrians, whose eagerness to see him, I said, was, in my opinion, highly flattering to him. That, he replied, depended on the feeling with which they came; and he had not the vanity to believe that they were influenced by any admiration of his character or of his abilities, but that they were impelled merely by idle curiosity. Whether it was so or not, I cannot help thinking that if they had been of the other sex, he would not have been so eager to escape from their observation, as in that case he would have repaid them glance for glance.

"The curiosity that was expressed by all classes of travellers to see him, and the eagerness with which they endeavoured to pick up any anecdotes of his mode of life, were carried to a length which will hardly be credited. It formed the chief subject of their enquiries of the gondoliers who conveyed them from terra firma to the floating city; and these people, who are generally loquacious, were not at all backward in administering to the taste and humours of their passengers, relating to them the most extravagant and often unfounded stories. They took care to point out the house where he lived, and to give such hints of his movements as might afford them an opportunity of seeing him. Many of the English visitors, under pretext of seeing his house, in which there were no paintings of any consequence, nor, besides himself, any thing worthy of notice, contrived to obtain admittance through the cupidity of his servants, and with the most barefaced impudence forced their way even into his bedroom, in the hopes of seeing him. Hence arose, in a great measure, his bitterness towards them, which he has expressed in a note to one of his poems, on the occasion of some unfounded remark made upon him by an anonymous traveller in Italy; and it certainly appears well calculated to foster that cynicism which prevails in his latter works more particularly, and which, as well as the misanthropical expressions that occur in those which first raised his reputation, I do not believe to have been his natural feeling. Of this I am certain, that I never witnessed greater kindness than in Lord Byron.

"The inmates of his family were all extremely attached to him, and would have endured any thing on his account. He was indeed culpably lenient to them; for even when instances occurred of their neglecting their duty, or taking an undue advantage of his good-nature, he rather bantered than spoke seriously to them upon it, and could not bring himself to discharge them, even when he had threatened to do so. An instance occurred within my knowledge of his unwillingness to act harshly towards a tradesman whom he had materially assisted, not only by lending him money, but by forwarding his interest in every way that he could. Notwithstanding repeated acts of kindness on Lord Byron's part, this man robbed and cheated him in the most barefaced manner; and when at length Lord Byron was induced to sue him at law for the recovery of his money, the only punishment he inflicted upon him, when sentence against him was passed, was to put him in prison for one week, and then to let him out again, although his debtor had subjected him to a considerable additional expense, by dragging him into all the different courts of appeal, and that he never at last recovered one halfpenny of the money owed to him. Upon this subject he writes to me from Ravenna, 'If * * is in (prison), let him out; if out, put him in for a week, merely for a lesson, and give him a good lecture.'

"He was also ever ready to assist the distressed, and he was most unostentatious in his charities: for besides considerable sums which he gave away to applicants at his own house, he contributed largely by weekly and monthly allowances to persons whom he had never seen, and who, as the money reached them by other hands, did not even know who was their benefactor. One or two instances might be adduced where his charity certainly bore an appearance of ostentation; one particularly, when he sent fifty louis d'or to a poor printer whose house had been burnt to the ground, and all his property destroyed; but even this was not unattended with advantage; for it in a manner compelled the Austrian authorities to do something for the poor sufferer, which I have no hesitation in saying they would not have done otherwise; and I attribute it entirely to the publicity of his donation, that they allowed the man the use of an unoccupied house belonging to the government until he could rebuild his own, or re-establish his business elsewhere. Other instances might be perhaps discovered where his liberalities proceeded from selfish, and not very worthy motives; but these are rare, and it would be unjust in the extreme to assume them as proofs of his character."

It has been already mentioned that, in writing to my noble friend to announce my coming, I had expressed a hope that he would be able to go on with me to Rome; and I had the gratification of finding, on my arrival, that he was fully prepared to enter into this plan. On becoming acquainted, however, with all the details of his present situation, I so far sacrificed my own wishes and pleasure as to advise strongly that he should remain at La Mira. In the first place, I saw reason to apprehend that his leaving Madame Guiccioli at this crisis might be the means of drawing upon him the suspicion of neglecting, if not actually deserting, a young person who had just sacrificed so much to her devotion for him, and whose position, at this moment, between the Count and Lord Byron, it required all the generous prudence of the latter to shield from shame or fall. There had just occurred too, as it appeared to me, a most favourable opening for the retrieval of, at least, the imprudent part of the transaction, by replacing the lady instantly under her husband's protection, and thus enabling her still to retain that station in society which, in such society, nothing but such imprudence could have endangered.

This latter hope had been suggested by a letter he one day showed me, (as we were dining together alone, at the well-known Pellegrino,) which had that morning been received by the Contessa from her husband, and the chief object of which was—not to express any censure of her conduct, but to suggest that she should prevail upon her noble admirer to transfer into his keeping a sum of 1000l., which was then lying, if I remember right, in the hands of Lord Byron's banker at Ravenna, but which the worthy Count professed to think would be more advantageously placed in his own. Security, the writer added, would be given, and five per cent. interest allowed; as to accept of the sum on any other terms he should hold to be an "avvilimento" to him. Though, as regarded the lady herself, who has since proved, by a most noble sacrifice, how perfectly disinterested were her feelings throughout, this trait of so wholly opposite a character in her lord must have still further increased her disgust at returning to him, yet so important did it seem, as well for her friend's sake as her own, to retrace, while there was yet time, their last imprudent step, that even the sacrifice of this sum, which I saw would materially facilitate such an arrangement, did not appear to me by any means too high a price to pay for it. On this point, however, my noble friend entirely differed with me; and nothing could be more humorous and amusing than the manner in which, in his newly assumed character of a lover of money, he dilated on the many virtues of a thousand pounds, and his determination not to part with a single one of them to Count Guiccioli. Of his confidence, too, in his own power of extricating himself from this difficulty he spoke with equal gaiety and humour; and Mr. Scott, who joined our party after dinner, having taken the same view of the subject as I did, he laid a wager of two sequins with that gentleman, that, without any such disbursement, he would yet bring all right again, and "save the lady and the money too."

It is indeed, certain, that he had at this time taken up the whim (for it hardly deserves a more serious name) of minute and constant watchfulness over his expenditure; and, as most usually happens, it was with the increase of his means that this increased sense of the value of money came. The first symptom I saw of this new fancy of his was the exceeding joy which he manifested on my presenting to him a rouleau of twenty Napoleons, which Lord K * *d, to whom he had, on some occasion, lent that sum, had intrusted me with, at Milan, to deliver into his hands. With the most joyous and diverting eagerness, he tore open the paper, and, in counting over the sum, stopped frequently to congratulate himself on the recovery of it.

Of his household frugalities I speak but on the authority of others; but it is not difficult to conceive that, with a restless spirit like his, which delighted always in having something to contend with, and which, but a short time before, "for want," as he said, "of something craggy to break upon," had tortured itself with the study of the Armenian language, he should, in default of all better excitement, find a sort of stir and amusement in the task of contesting, inch by inch, every encroachment of expense, and endeavouring to suppress what he himself calls

"That climax of all earthly ills, The inflammation of our weekly bills."

In truth, his constant recurrence to the praise of avarice in Don Juan, and the humorous zest with which he delights to dwell on it, shows how new-fangled, as well as how far from serious, was his adoption of this "good old-gentlemanly vice." In the same spirit he had, a short time before my arrival at Venice, established a hoarding-box, with a slit in the lid, into which he occasionally put sequins, and, at stated periods, opened it to contemplate his treasures. His own ascetic style of living enabled him, as far as himself was concerned, to gratify this taste for economy in no ordinary degree,—his daily bill of fare, when the Margarita was his companion, consisting, I have been assured, of but four beccafichi, of which the Fornarina eat three, leaving even him hungry.

That his parsimony, however (if this new phasis of his ever-shifting character is to be called by such a name), was very far from being of that kind which Bacon condemns, as "withholding men from works of liberality," is apparent from all that is known of his munificence, at this very period,—some particulars of which, from a most authentic source, have just been cited, proving amply that while, for the indulgence of a whim, he kept one hand closed, he gave free course to his generous nature by dispensing lavishly from the other. It should be remembered, too, that as long as money shall continue to be one of the great sources of power, so long will they who seek influence over their fellow-men attach value to it as an instrument; and the more lowly they are inclined to estimate the disinterestedness of the human heart, the more available and precious will they consider the talisman that gives such power over it. Hence, certainly, it is not among those who have thought highest of mankind that the disposition to avarice has most generally displayed itself. In Swift the love of money was strong and avowed; and to Voltaire the same propensity was also frequently imputed,—on about as sufficient grounds, perhaps, as to Lord Byron.

On the day preceding that of my departure from Venice, my noble host, on arriving from La Mira to dinner, told me, with all the glee of a schoolboy who had been just granted a holiday, that, as this was my last evening, the Contessa had given him leave to "make a night of it," and that accordingly he would not only accompany me to the opera, but we should sup together at some cafe (as in the old times) afterwards. Observing a volume in his gondola, with a number of paper marks between the leaves, I enquired of him what it was?—"Only a book," he answered, "from which I am trying to crib, as I do wherever I can;—and that's the way I get the character of an original poet." On taking it up and looking into it, I exclaimed, "Ah, my old friend, Agathon!"—"What!" he cried, archly, "you have been beforehand with me there, have you?"

Though in imputing to himself premeditated plagiarism, he was, of course, but jesting, it was, I am inclined to think, his practice, when engaged in the composition of any work, to excite thus his vein by the perusal of others, on the same subject or plan, from which the slightest hint caught by his imagination, as he read, was sufficient to kindle there such a train of thought as, but for that spark, had never been awakened, and of which he himself soon forgot the source. In the present instance, the inspiration he sought was of no very elevating nature,—the anti-spiritual doctrines of the Sophist in this Romance being what chiefly, I suspect, attracted his attention to its pages, as not unlikely to supply him with fresh argument and sarcasm for those depreciating views of human nature and its destiny, which he was now, with all the wantonness of unbounded genius, enforcing in Don Juan.

Of this work he was, at the time of my visit to him, writing the third Canto, and before dinner, one day, read me two or three hundred lines of it;—beginning with the stanzas "Oh Wellington," &c. which at that time formed the opening of this third Canto, but were afterwards reserved for the commencement of the ninth. My opinion of the poem, both as regarded its talent and its mischief, he had already been made acquainted with, from my having been one of those,—his Committee, as he called us,—to whom, at his own desire, the manuscript of the two first Cantos had been submitted, and who, as the reader has seen, angered him not a little by deprecating the publication of it. In a letter which I, at that time, wrote to him on the subject, after praising the exquisite beauty of the scenes between Juan and Haidée, I ventured to say, "Is it not odd that the same licence which, in your early Satire, you blamed me for being guilty of on the borders of my twentieth year, you are now yourself (with infinitely greater power, and therefore infinitely greater mischief) indulging in after thirty!"

Though I now found him, in full defiance of such remonstrances, proceeding with this work, he had yet, as his own letters prove, been so far influenced by the general outcry against his poem, as to feel the zeal and zest with which he had commenced it considerably abated,—so much so, as to render, ultimately, in his own opinion, the third and fourth Cantos much inferior in spirit to the two first. So sensitive, indeed,—in addition to his usual abundance of this quality,—did he, at length, grow on the subject, that when Mr. W. Bankes, who succeeded me, as his visiter, happened to tell him, one day, that he had heard a Mr. Saunders (or some such name), then resident at Venice, declare that, in his opinion, "Don Juan was all Grub Street," such an effect had this disparaging speech upon his mind, (though coming from a person who, as he himself would have it, was "nothing but a d——d salt-fish seller,") that, for some time after, by his own confession to Mr. Bankes, he could not bring himself to write another line of the poem; and, one morning, opening a drawer where the neglected manuscript lay, he said to his friend, "Look here—this is all Mr. Saunders's 'Grub Street.'"

To return, however, to the details of our last evening together at Venice. After a dinner with Mr. Scott at the Pellegrino, we all went, rather late, to the opera, where the principal part in the Baccanali di Roma was represented by a female singer, whose chief claim to reputation, according to Lord Byron, lay in her having stilettoed one of her favourite lovers. In the intervals between the singing he pointed out to me different persons among the audience, to whom celebrity of various sorts, but, for the most part, disreputable, attached; and of one lady who sat

Venice at night

near us, he related an anecdote, which, whether new or old, may, as creditable to Venetian facetiousness, be worth, perhaps, repeating. This lady had, it seems, been pronounced by Napoleon the finest woman in Venice; but the Venetians, not quite agreeing with this opinion of the great man, contented themselves with calling her "La Bella per Decréto,"—adding (as the Decrees always begin with the word "Considerando"), "Ma senza il Considerando."

From the opera, in pursuance of our agreement to "make a night of it," we betook ourselves to a sort of cabaret in the Place of St. Mark, and there, within a few yards of the Palace of the Doges, sat drinking hot brandy punch, and laughing over old times, till the clock of St. Mark struck the second hour of the morning. Lord Byron then took me in his gondola, and, the moon being in its fullest splendour, he made the gondoliers row us to such points of view as might enable me to see Venice, at that hour, to advantage. Nothing could be more solemnly beautiful than the whole scene around, and I had, for the first time, the Venice of my dreams before me. All those meaner details which so offend the eye by day were now softened down by the moonlight into a sort of visionary indistinctness; and the effect of that silent city of palaces, sleeping, as it were, upon the waters, in the bright stillness of the night, was such as could not but affect deeply even the least susceptible imagination. My companion saw that I was moved by it, and though familiar with the scene himself, seemed to give way, for the moment, to the same strain of feeling; and, as we exchanged a few remarks suggested by that wreck of human glory before us, his voice, habitually so cheerful, sunk into a tone of mournful sweetness, such as I had rarely before heard from him, and shall not easily forget. This mood, however, was but of the moment; some quick turn of ridicule soon carried him off into a totally different vein, and at about three o'clock in the morning, at the door of his own palazzo, we parted, laughing, as we had met;—an agreement having been first made that I should take an early dinner with him next day at his villa, on my road to Ferrara.

Having employed the morning of the following day in completing my round of sights at Venice,—taking care to visit specially "that picture by Giorgione," to which the poet's exclamation, "such a woman!" will long continue to attract all votaries of beauty,—I took my departure from Venice, and, at about three o'clock, arrived at La Mira. I found my noble host waiting to receive me, and, in passing with him through the hall, saw his little Allegra, who, with her nursery maid, was standing there as if just returned from a walk. To the perverse fancy he had for falsifying his own character, and even imputing to himself faults the most alien to his nature, I have already frequently adverted, and had, on this occasion, a striking instance of it. After I had spoken a little, in passing, to the child, and made some remark on its beauty, he said to me,—"Have you any notion—but I suppose you have—of what they call the parental feeling? For myself, I have not the least." And yet, when that child died, in a year or two afterwards, he who now uttered this artificial speech was so overwhelmed by the event, that those who were about him at the time actually trembled for his reason!

A short time before dinner he left the room, and in a minute or two returned, carrying in his hand a white leather bag. "Look here," he said, holding it up—"this would be worth something to Murray, though you, I dare say, would not give sixpence for it."—"What is it?" I asked.—"My

Life and Adventures," he answered. On hearing this, I raised my hands in a gesture of wonder. "It is not a thing," he continued, "that can be published during my lifetime, but you may have it—if you like—there, do whatever you please with it." In taking the bag, and thanking him most warmly, I added, "This will make a nice legacy for my little Tom, who shall astonish the latter days of the nineteenth century with it." He then added, "You may show it to any of our friends you think worthy of it:"—and this is, nearly word for word, the whole of what passed between us on the subject.

At dinner we were favoured with the presence of Madame Guiccioli, who was so obliging as to furnish me, at Lord Byron's suggestion, with a letter of introduction to her brother, Count Gamba, whom it was probable, they both thought, I should meet at Rome. This letter I never had an opportunity of presenting; and as it was left open for me to read, and was, the greater part of it, I have little doubt, dictated by my noble friend, I may venture, without impropriety, to give an extract from it here;—premising that the allusion to the "Castle," &c. refers to some tales respecting the cruelty of Lord Byron to his wife, which the young Count had heard, and, at this time, implicitly believed. After a few sentences of compliment to the bearer, the letter proceeds:—"He is on his way to see the wonders of Rome, and there is no one, I am sure, more qualified to enjoy them. I shall be gratified and obliged by your acting, as far as you can, as his guide. He is a friend of Lord Byron's, and much more accurately acquainted with his history than those who have related it to you. He will accordingly describe to you, if you ask him, the shape, the dimensions, and whatever else you may please to require, of that Castle in which he keeps imprisoned a young and innocent wife, &c. &c. My dear Pietro, whenever you feel inclined to laugh, do send two lines of answer to your sister, who loves and ever will love you with the greatest tenderness.—Teresa Guiccioli."

After expressing his regret that I had not been able to prolong my stay at Venice, my noble friend said, "At least, I think, you might spare a day or two to go with me to Arquà. I should like," he continued, thoughtfully, "to visit that tomb with you:"—then, breaking off into his usual gay tone; "a pair of poetical pilgrims—eh, Tom, what say you?"—That I should have declined this offer, and thus lost the opportunity of an excursion which would have been remembered, as a bright dream, through all my after-life, is a circumstance I never can think of without wonder and self-reproach. But the main design on which I had then set my mind of reaching Rome, and, if possible, Naples, within the limited period which circumstances allowed, rendered me far less alive than I ought to have been to the preciousness of the episode thus offered to me.

When it was time for me to depart, he expressed his intention to accompany me a few miles; and, ordering his horses to follow, proceeded with me in the carriage as far as Strà, where for the last time—how little thinking it was to be the last!—I bade my kind and admirable friend farewell.

LETTER 341. TO MR. HOPPNER.

"October 22. 1819.

"I am glad to hear of your return, but I do not know how to congratulate you—unless you think differently of Venice from what I think now, and you thought always. I am, besides, about to renew your troubles by requesting you to be judge between Mr. E * * * and myself in a small matter of imputed peculation and irregular accounts on the part of that phoenix of secretaries. As I knew that you had not parted friends, at the same time that I refused for my own part any judgment but yours, I offered him his choice of any person, the least scoundrel native to be found in Venice, as his own umpire; but he expressed himself so convinced of your impartiality, that he declined any but you. This is in his favour.—The paper within will explain to you the default in his accounts. You will hear his explanation, and decide if it so please you. I shall not appeal from the decision.

"As he complained that his salary was insufficient, I determined to have his accounts examined, and the enclosed was the result.—It is all in black and white with documents, and I have despatched Fletcher to explain (or rather to perplex) the matter.

"I have had much civility and kindness from Mr. Dorville during your journey, and I thank him accordingly.

"Your letter reached me at your departure, and displeased me very much:—not that it might not be true in its statement and kind in its intention, but you have lived long enough to know how useless all such representations ever are and must be in cases where the passions are concerned. To reason with men in such a situation is like reasoning with a drunkard in his cups—the only answer you will get from him is, that he is sober, and you are drunk.

"Upon that subject we will (if you like) be silent. You might only say what would distress me without answering any purpose whatever; and I have too many obligations to you to answer you in the same style. So that you should recollect that you have also that advantage over me. I hope to see you soon.

"I suppose you know that they said at Venice, that I was arrested at Bologna as a Carbonaro—story about as true as their usual conversation. Moore has been here—I lodged him in my house at Venice, and went to see him daily; but I could not at that time quit La Mira entirely. You and I were not very far from meeting in Switzerland. With my best respects to Mrs. Hoppner, believe me ever and truly, &c.

"P.S. Allegra is here in good health and spirits—I shall keep her with me till I go to England, which will perhaps be in the spring. It has just occurred to me that you may not perhaps like to undertake the office of judge between Mr. E. and your humble servant.—Of course, as Mr. Liston (the comedian, not the ambassador) says, 'it is all hoptional;' but I have no other resource. I do not wish to find him a rascal, if it can be avoided, and would rather think him guilty of carelessness than cheating. The case is this—can I, or not, give him a character for honesty?—It is not my intention to continue him in my service."

LETTER 342. TO MR. HOPPNER.

"October 25. 1819.

"You need not have made any excuses about the letter: I never said but that you might, could, should, or would have reason. I merely described my own state of inaptitude to listen to it at that time, and in those circumstances. Besides, you did not speak from your own authority—but from what you said you had heard. Now my blood boils to hear an Italian speaking ill of another

Italian, because, though they lie in particular, they speak truth in general by speaking ill at all;—and although they know that they are trying and wishing to lie, they do not succeed, merely because they can say nothing so bad of each other, that it may not, and must not be true, from the atrocity of their long debased national character.

"With regard to E., you will perceive a most irregular, extravagant account, without proper documents to support it. He demanded an increase of salary, which made me suspect him; he supported an outrageous extravagance of expenditure, and did not like the dismission of the cook; he never complained of him—as in duty bound—at the time of his robberies. I can only say, that the house expense is now under one half of what it then was, as he himself admits. He charged for a comb eighteen francs,—the real price was eight. He charged a passage from Fusina for a person named Iambelli, who paid it herself, as she will prove if necessary. He fancies, or asserts himself, the victim of a domestic complot against him;—accounts are accounts—prices are prices;—let him make out a fair detail. I am not prejudiced against him—on the contrary, I supported him against the complaints of his wife, and of his former master, at a time when I could have crushed him like an earwig; and if he is a scoundrel, he is the greatest of scoundrels, an ungrateful one. The truth is, probably, that he thought I was leaving Venice, and determined to make the most of it. At present he keeps bringing in account after account, though he had always money in hand—as I believe you know my system was never to allow longer than a week's bills to run. Pray read him this letter—I desire nothing to be concealed against which he may defend himself.

"Pray how is your little boy? and how are you?—I shall be up in Venice very soon, and we will be bilious together. I hate the place and all that it inherits.

"Yours," &c.

LETTER 343. TO MR. HOPPNER.

"October 28. 1819.

"I have to thank you for your letter, and your compliment to Don Juan. I said nothing to you about it, understanding that it is a sore subject with the moral reader, and has been the cause of a great row; but I am glad you like it. I will say nothing about the shipwreck, except that I hope you think it is as nautical and technical as verse could admit in the octave measure.

"The poem has not sold well, so Murray says—'but the best judges, &c. say, &c.' so says that worthy man. I have never seen it in print. The third Canto is in advance about one hundred stanzas; but the failure of the two first has weakened my estro, and it will neither be so good as the two former, nor completed, unless I get a little more riscaldato in its behalf. I understand the outcry was beyond every thing.—Pretty cant for people who read Tom Jones, and Roderick Random, and the Bath Guide, and Ariosto, and Dryden, and Pope—to say nothing of Little's Poems! Of course I refer to the morality of these works, and not to any pretension of mine to compete with them in any thing but decency. I hope yours is the Paris edition, and that you did not pay the London price. I have seen neither except in the newspapers.

"Pray make my respects to Mrs. H., and take care of your little boy. All my household have the fever and ague, except Fletcher, Allegra, and mysen (as we used to say in Nottinghamshire), and

To Murray about Memoirs

the horses, and Mutz, and Moretto. In the beginning of November, perhaps sooner, I expect to have the pleasure of seeing you. To-day I got drenched by a thunder-storm, and my horse and groom too, and his horse all bemired up to the middle in a cross-road. It was summer at noon, and at five we were bewintered; but the lightning was sent perhaps to let us know that the summer was not yet over. It is queer weather for the 27th October.

"Yours," &c.

LETTER 344. TO MR. MURRAY.

"Venice, October 29. 1819.

"Yours of the 15th came yesterday. I am sorry that you do not mention a large letter addressed to your care for Lady Byron, from me, at Bologna, two months ago. Pray tell me, was this letter received and forwarded?

"You say nothing of the vice-consulate for the Ravenna patrician, from which it is to be inferred that the thing will not be done.

"I had written about a hundred stanzas of a third Canto to Don Juan, but the reception of the two first is no encouragement to you nor me to proceed.

"I had also written about 600 lines of a poem, the Vision (or Prophecy) of Dante, the subject a view of Italy in the ages down to the present—supposing Dante to speak in his own person, previous to his death, and embracing all topics in the way of prophecy, like Lycophron's Cassandra; but this and the other are both at a stand-still for the present.

"I gave Moore, who is gone to Rome, my Life in MS., in seventy-eight folio sheets, brought down to 1816. But this I put into his hands for his care, as he has some other MSS. of mine—a Journal kept in 1814, &c. Neither are for publication during my life; but when I am cold you may do what you please. In the mean time, if you like to read them you may, and show them to anybody you like—I care not.

"The Life is Memoranda, and not Confessions I have left out all my loves (except in a general way), and many other of the most important things (because I must not compromise other people), so that it is like the play of Hamlet—'the part of Hamlet omitted by particular desire.' But you will find many opinions, and some fun, with a detailed account of my marriage, and its consequences, as true as a party concerned can make such account, for I suppose we are all prejudiced.

"I have never read over this Life since it was written, so that I know not exactly what it may repeat or contain. Moore and I passed some merry days together.

"I probably must return for business, or in my way to America. Pray, did you get a letter for Hobhouse, who will have told you the contents? I understand that the Venezuelan commissioners had orders to treat with emigrants; now I want to go there. I should not make a bad South-American planter, and I should take my natural daughter, Allegra, with me, and settle. I wrote, at length, to Hobhouse, to get information from Perry, who, I suppose, is the best topographer and trumpeter of the new republicans. Pray write.

"Yours ever.

"P.S. Moore and I did nothing but laugh. He will tell you of 'my whereabouts,' and all my proceedings at this present; they are as usual. You should not let those fellows publish false 'Don Juans;' but do not put my name, because I mean to cut R——ts up like a gourd, in the preface, if I continue the poem."

LETTER 345. TO MR. HOPPNER.

"October 29. 1819.

"The Ferrara story is of a piece with all the rest of the Venetian manufacture,—you may judge. I only changed horses there since I wrote to you, after my visit in June last. 'Convent' and 'carry off', quotha! and 'girl.' I should like to know who has been carried off, except poor dear me. I have been more ravished myself than anybody since the Trojan war; but as to the arrest and its causes, one is as true as the other, and I can account for the invention of neither. I suppose it is some confusion of the tale of the F * * and of Me. Guiccioli, and half a dozen more; but it is useless to unravel the web, when one has only to brush it away. I shall settle with Master E. who looks very blue at your in-decision, and swears that he is the best arithmetician in Europe; and so I think also, for he makes out two and two to be five.

"You may see me next week. I have a horse or two more (five in all), and I shall repossess myself of Lido, and I will rise earlier, and we will go and shake our livers over the beach, as heretofore, if you like—and we will make the Adriatic roar again with our hatred of that now empty oyster-shell, without its pearl, the city of Venice.

"Murray sent me a letter yesterday: the impostors have published two new third Cantos of Don Juan;—the devil take the impudence of some blackguard bookseller or other therefor! Perhaps I did not make myself understood; he told me the sale had been great, 1200 out of 1500 quarto, I believe (which is nothing after selling 13,000 of the Corsair in one day); but that the 'best judges,' &c. had said it was very fine, and clever, and particularly good English, and poetry, and all those consolatory things, which are not, however, worth a single copy to a bookseller: and as to the author, of course I am in a d——ned passion at the bad taste of the times, and swear there is nothing like posterity, who, of course, must know more of the matter than their grandfathers. There has been an eleventh commandment to the women not to read it, and, what is still more extraordinary, they seem not to have broken it. But that can be of little import to them, poor things, for the reading or non-reading a book will never * * * *.

"Count G. comes to Venice next week, and I am requested to consign his wife to him, which shall be done. What you say of the long evenings at the Mira, or Venice, reminds me of what Curran said to Moore:—'So I hear you have married a pretty woman, and a very good creature, too—an excellent creature. Pray—um! how do you pass your evenings?' It is a devil of a question that, and perhaps as easy to answer with a wife as with a mistress.

"If you go to Milan, pray leave at least a Vice-Consul—the only vice that will ever be wanting in Venice. D'Orville is a good fellow. But you shall go to England in the spring with me, and plant Mrs. Hoppner at Berne with her relations for a few months. I wish you had been here (at Venice, I mean, not the Mira) when Moore was here—we were very merry and tipsy. He hated Venice, by the way, and swore it was a sad place.

"So Madame Albrizzi's death is in danger—poor woman! Moore told me that at Geneva they had made a devil of a story of the Fornaretta:—'Young lady seduced!—subsequent abandonment!—leap into the Grand Canal!'—and her being in the 'hospital of fous in consequence!' I should like to know who was nearest being made 'fou,' and be d——d to them I Don't you think me in the interesting character of a very ill used gentleman? I hope your little boy is well. Allegrina is flourishing like a pomegranate blossom. Yours," &c.

LETTER 346. TO MR. MURRAY.

"Venice, November 8. 1819.

"Mr. Hoppner has lent me a copy of 'Don Juan,' Paris edition, which he tells me is read in Switzerland by clergymen and ladies with considerable approbation. In the second Canto, you must alter the 49th stanza to

"'Twas twilight, and the sunless day went down
Over the waste of waters, like a veil
Which if withdrawn would but disclose the frown
Of one whose hate is mask'd but to assail;
Thus to their hopeless eyes the night was shown,
And grimly darkled o'er their faces pale
And the dim desolate deep; twelve days had Fear
Been their familiar, and now Death was here.

"I have been ill these eight days with a tertian fever, caught in the country on horseback in a thunderstorm. Yesterday I had the fourth attack: the two last were very smart, the first day as well as the last being preceded by vomiting. It is the fever of the place and the season. I feel weakened, but not unwell, in the intervals, except headach and lassitude.

"Count Guiccioli has arrived in Venice, and has presented his spouse (who had preceded him two months for her health and the prescriptions of Dr. Aglietti) with a paper of conditions, regulations of hours and conduct, and morals, &c. &c. &c. which he insists on her accepting, and she persists in refusing. I am expressly, it should seem, excluded by this treaty, as an indispensable preliminary; so that they are in high dissension, and what the result may be I know not, particularly as they are consulting friends.

"To-night, as Countess Guiccioli observed me poring over 'Don Juan,' she stumbled by mere chance on the 137th stanza of the first Canto, and asked me what it meant. I told her, 'Nothing—but "your husband is coming."' As I said this in Italian, with some emphasis, she started up in a fright, and said, 'Oh, my God, is he coming?' thinking it was her own, who either was or ought to have been at the theatre. You may suppose we laughed when she found out the mistake. You will be amused, as I was;—it happened not three hours ago.

"I wrote to you last week, but have added nothing to the third Canto since my fever, nor to 'The Prophecy of Dante.' Of the former there are about 100 octaves done; of the latter about 500 lines—perhaps more. Moore saw the third Juan, as far as it then went. I do not know if my fever will let me go on with either, and the tertian lasts, they say, a good while. I had it in Malta on my way home, and the malaria fever in Greece the year before that. The Venetian is not very fierce,

Fever in Venice

but I was delirious one of the nights with it, for an hour or two, and, on my senses coming back, found Fletcher sobbing on one side of the bed, and La Contessa Guiccioli weeping on the other; so that I had no want of attendance. I have not yet taken any physician, because, though I think they may relieve in chronic disorders, such as gout and the like, &c. &c. &c. (though they can't cure them)—just as surgeons are necessary to set bones and tend wounds—yet I think fevers quite out of their reach, and remediable only by diet and nature.

"I don't like the taste of bark, but I suppose that I must take it soon.

"Tell Rose that somebody at Milan (an Austrian, Mr. Hoppner says) is answering his book. William Bankes is in quarantine at Trieste. I have not lately heard from you. Excuse this paper: it is long paper shortened for the occasion. What folly is this of Carlile's trial? why let him have the honours of a martyr? it will only advertise the books in question. Yours, &c.

"P.S. As I tell you that the Guiccioli business is on the eve of exploding in one way or the other, I will just add that, without attempting to influence the decision of the Contessa, a good deal depends upon it. If she and her husband make it up, you will, perhaps, see me in England sooner than you expect. If not, I shall retire with her to France or America, change my name, and lead a quiet provincial life. All this may seem odd, but I have got the poor girl into a scrape; and as neither her birth, nor her rank, nor her connections by birth or marriage are inferior to my own, I am in honour bound to support her through. Besides, she is a very pretty woman—ask Moore—and not yet one and twenty.

"If she gets over this and I get over my tertian, I will, perhaps, look in at Albemarle Street, some of these days, en passant to Bolivar."

LETTER 347. TO MR. BANKES.

"Venice, November 20. 1819.

"A tertian ague which has troubled me for some time, and the indisposition of my daughter, have prevented me from replying before to your welcome letter. I have not been ignorant of your progress nor of your discoveries, and I trust that you are no worse in health from your labours. You may rely upon finding every body in England eager to reap the fruits of them; and as you have done more than other men, I hope you will not limit yourself to saying less than may do justice to the talents and time you have bestowed on your perilous researches. The first sentence of my letter will have explained to you why I cannot join you at Trieste. I was on the point of setting out for England (before I knew of your arrival) when my child's illness has made her and me dependent on a Venetian Proto-Medico.

"It is now seven years since you and I met;—which time you have employed better for others and more honourably for yourself than I have done.

"In England you will find considerable changes, public and private,—you will see some of our old college contemporaries turned into lords of the Treasury, Admiralty, and the like,—others become reformers and orators,—many settled in life, as it is called,—and others settled in death; among the latter, (by the way, not our fellow collegians,) Sheridan, Curran, Lady Melbourne, Monk Lewis, Frederick Douglas, &c. &c. &c.; but you will still find Mr. * * living and all his family, as also * * * * *.

"Should you come up this way, and I am still here, you need not be assured how glad I shall be to see you; I long to hear some part from you, of that which I expect in no long time to see. At length you have had better fortune than any traveller of equal enterprise (except Humboldt), in returning safe; and after the fate of the Brownes, and the Parkes, and the Burckhardts, it is hardly less surprise than satisfaction to get you back again.

"Believe me ever

"And very affectionately yours,

"BYRON."

LETTER 348. TO MR. MURRAY.

"Venice, December 4. 1819.

"You may do as you please, but you are about a hopeless experiment. Eldon will decide against you, were it only that my name is in the record. You will also recollect that if the publication is pronounced against, on the grounds you mention, as indecent and blasphemous, that I lose all right in my daughter's guardianship and education, in short, all paternal authority, and every thing concerning her, except * * * * * * * * It was so decided in Shelley's case, because he had written Queen Mab, &c. &c. However, you can ask the lawyers, and do as you like: I do not inhibit you trying the question; I merely state one of the consequences to me. With regard to the copyright, it is hard that you should pay for a nonentity: I will therefore refund it, which I can very well do, not having spent it, nor begun upon it; and so we will be quits on that score. It lies at my banker's.

"Of the Chancellor's law I am no judge; but take up Tom Jones, and read his Mrs. Waters and Molly Seagrim; or Prior's Hans Carvel and Paulo Purganti: Smollett's Roderick Random, the chapter of Lord Strutwell, and many others; Peregrine Pickle, the scene of the Beggar Girl; Johnson's London, for coarse expressions; for instance, the words '* *,' and '* *;' Anstey's Bath Guide, the 'Hearken, Lady Betty, hearken;'—take up, in short, Pope, Prior, Congreve, Dryden, Fielding, Smollett, and let the counsel select passages, and what becomes of their copyright, if his Wat Tyler decision is to pass into a precedent? I have nothing more to say: you must judge for yourselves.

"I wrote to you some time ago. I have had a tertian ague; my daughter Allegra has been ill also, and I have been almost obliged to run away with a married woman; but with some difficulty, and many internal struggles, I reconciled the lady with her lord, and cured the fever of the child with bark, and my own with cold water. I think of setting out for England by the Tyrol in a few days, so that I could wish you to direct your next letter to Calais. Excuse my writing in great haste and late in the morning, or night, whichever you please to call it. The third Canto of 'Don Juan' is completed, in about two hundred stanzas; very decent, I believe, but do not know, and it is useless to discuss until it be ascertained if it may or may not be a property.

"My present determination to quit Italy was unlooked for; but I have explained the reasons in letters to my sister and Douglas Kinnaird, a week or two ago. My progress will depend upon the snows of the Tyrol, and the health of my child, who is at present quite recovered; but I hope to get on well, and am *letter to Teresa*

"Yours ever and truly.

"P.S. Many thanks for your letters, to which you are not to consider this as an answer, but as an acknowledgment."

The struggle which, at the time of my visit to him, I had found Lord Byron so well disposed to make towards averting, as far as now lay in his power, some of the mischievous consequences which, both to the object of his attachment and himself, were likely to result from their connection, had been brought, as the foregoing letters show, to a crisis soon after I left him. The Count Guiccioli, on his arrival at Venice, insisted, as we have seen, that his lady should return with him; and, after some conjugal negotiations, in which Lord Byron does not appear to have interfered, the young Contessa consented reluctantly to accompany her lord to Ravenna, it being first covenanted that, in future, all communication between her and her lover should cease.

"In a few days after this," says Mr. Hoppner, in some notices of his noble friend with which he has favoured me, "he returned to Venice, very much out of spirits, owing to Madame Guiccioli's departure, and out of humour with every body and every thing around him. We resumed our rides at the Lido; and I did my best not only to raise his spirits, but to make him forget his absent mistress, and to keep him to his purpose of returning to England. He went into no society; and having no longer any relish for his former occupation, his time, when he was not writing, hung heavy enough on hand."

The promise given by the lovers not to correspond was, as all parties must have foreseen, soon violated; and the letters Lord Byron addressed to the lady, at this time, though written in a language not his own, are rendered frequently even eloquent by the mere force of the feeling that governed him—a feeling which could not have owed its fuel to fancy alone, since now that reality had been so long substituted, it still burned on. From one of these letters, dated November 25th, I shall so far presume upon the discretionary power vested in me, as to lay a short extract or two before the reader—not merely as matters of curiosity, but on account of the strong evidence they afford of the struggle between passion and a sense of right that now agitated him.

"You are," he says, "and ever will be, my first thought. But, at this moment, I am in a state most dreadful, not knowing which way to decide;—on the one hand, fearing that I should compromise you for ever, by my return to Ravenna and the consequences of such a step, and, on the other, dreading that I shall lose both you and myself, and all that I have ever known or tasted of happiness, by never seeing you more. I pray of you, I implore you to be comforted, and to believe that I cannot cease to love you but with my life." In another part he says, "I go to save you, and leave a country insupportable to me without you. Your letters to F * * and myself do wrong to my motives—but you will yet see your injustice. It is not enough that I must leave you—from motives of which ere long you will be convinced—it is not enough that I must fly from Italy, with a heart deeply wounded, after having passed all my days in solitude since your departure, sick both in body and mind—but I must also have to endure your reproaches without answering and without deserving them. Farewell! in that one word is comprised the death of my happiness."

He had now arranged every thing for his departure for England, and had even fixed the day, when accounts reached him from Ravenna that the Contessa was alarmingly ill;—her sorrow at their separation having so much preyed upon her mind, that even her own family, fearful of the consequences, had withdrawn all opposition to her wishes, and now, with the sanction of Count Guiccioli himself, entreated her lover to hasten to Ravenna. What was he, in this dilemma, to do? Already had he announced his coming to different friends in England, and every dictate, he felt, of prudence and manly fortitude urged his departure. While thus balancing between duty and inclination, the day appointed for his setting out arrived; and the following picture, from the life, of his irresolution on the occasion, is from a letter written by a female friend of Madame Guiccioli, who was present at the scene:—"He was ready dressed for the journey, his gloves and cap on, and even his little cane in his hand. Nothing was now waited for but his coming down stairs,—his boxes being already all on board the gondola. At this moment, my Lord, by way of pretext, declares, that if it should strike one o'clock before every thing was in order (his arms being the only thing not yet quite ready), he would not go that day. The hour strikes, and he remains!"

 The writer adds, "it is evident he has not the heart to go;" and the result proved that she had not judged him wrongly. The very next day's tidings from Ravenna decided his fate, and he himself, in a letter to the Contessa, thus announces the triumph which she had achieved. "F * * * will already have told you, with her accustomed sublimity, that Love has gained the victory. I could not summon up resolution enough to leave the country where you are, without, at least, once more seeing you. On yourself, perhaps, it will depend, whether I ever again shall leave you. Of the rest we shall speak when we meet. You ought, by this time, to know which is most conducive to your welfare, my presence or my absence. For myself, I am a citizen of the world—all countries are alike to me. You have ever been, since our first acquaintance, the sole object of my thoughts. My opinion was, that the best course I could adopt, both for your peace and that of all your family, would have been to depart and go far, far away from you;—since to have been near and not approach you would have been, for me, impossible. You have however decided that I am to return to Ravenna. I shall accordingly return—and shall do—and be all that you wish. I cannot say more.

 On quitting Venice he took leave of Mr. Hoppner in a short but cordial letter, which I cannot better introduce than by prefixing to it the few words of comment with which this excellent friend of the noble poet has himself accompanied it:—"I need not say with what painful feeling I witnessed the departure of a person who, from the first day of our acquaintance, had treated me with unvaried kindness, reposing a confidence in me which it was beyond the power of my utmost efforts to deserve; admitting me to an intimacy which I had no right to claim, and listening with patience, and the greatest good temper, to the remonstrances I ventured to make upon his conduct."

LETTER 349. TO MR. HOPPNER.

"My dear Hoppner,

"Partings are but bitter work at best, so that I shall not venture on a second with you. Pray make my respects to Mrs. Hoppner, and assure her of my unalterable reverence for the singular goodness of her disposition, which is not without its reward even in this world—for those who are no great believers in human virtues would discover enough in her to give them a better opinion of their fellow-creatures and—what is still more difficult—of themselves, as being of the same species, however inferior in approaching its nobler models. Make, too, what excuses you can for my omission of the ceremony of leave-taking. If we all meet again, I will make my humblest apology; if not, recollect that I wished you all well; and, if you can, forget that I have given you a great deal of trouble.

"Yours," &c. &c.

LETTER 350. TO MR. MURRAY.

"Venice, December 10. 1819.

"Since I last wrote, I have changed my mind, and shall not come to England. The more I contemplate, the more I dislike the place and the prospect. You may, therefore, address to me as usual here, though I mean to go to another city. I have finished the third Canto of Don Juan, but the things I have read and heard discourage all further publication—at least for the present. You may try the copy question, but you'll lose it: the cry is up, and cant is up. I should have no objection to return the price of the copyright, and have written to Mr. Kinnaird by this post on the subject. Talk with him.

"I have not the patience, nor do I feel interest enough in the question, to contend with the fellows in their own slang; but I perceive Mr. Blackwood's Magazine and one or two others of your missives have been hyperbolical in their praise, and diabolical in their abuse. I like and admire W * *n, and he should not have indulged himself in such outrageous licence. It is overdone and defeats itself. What would he say to the grossness without passion and the misanthropy without feeling of Gulliver's Travels?—When he talks of Lady's Byron's business, he talks of what he knows nothing about; and you may tell him that no one can more desire a public investigation of that affair than I do.

"I sent home by Moore (for Moore only, who has my Journal also) my Memoir written up to 1816, and I gave him leave to show it to whom he pleased, but not to publish, on any account. You may read it, and you may let W * *n read it, if he likes—not for his public opinion, but his private; for I like the man, and care very little about his Magazine. And I could wish Lady B. herself to read it, that she may have it in her power to mark any thing mistaken or mis-stated; as it may probably appear after my extinction, and it would be but fair she should see it,—that is to say, herself willing.

"Perhaps I may take a journey to you in the spring; but I have been ill and am indolent and indecisive, because few things interest me. These fellows first abused me for being gloomy, and now they are wroth that I am, or attempted to be, facetious. I have got such a cold and headach that I can hardly see what I scrawl:—the winters here are as sharp as needles. Some time ago, I wrote to you rather fully about my Italian affairs; at present I can say no more except that you shall hear further by and by.

"Your Blackwood accuses me of treating women harshly: it may be so, but I have been their martyr; my whole life has been sacrificed to them and by them. I mean to leave Venice in a few days, but you will address your letters here as usual. When I fix elsewhere, you shall know."

Soon after this letter to Mr. Murray he set out for Ravenna, from which place we shall find his correspondence for the next year and a half dated. For a short time after his arrival, he took up his residence at an inn; but the Count Guiccioli having allowed him to hire a suite of apartments in the Palazzo Guiccioli itself, he was once more lodged under the same roof with the Countess Guiccioli.

LETTER 351. TO MR. HOPPNER.

"Ravenna, Dec. 31. 1819.

"I have been here this week, and was obliged to put on my armour and go the night after my arrival to the Marquis Cavalli's, where there were between two and three hundred of the best company I have seen in Italy,—more beauty, more youth, and more diamonds among the women than have been seen these fifty years in the Sea-Sodom. I never saw such a difference between two places of the same latitude, (or platitude, it is all one,)—music, dancing, and play, all in the same salle. The G.'s object appeared to be to parade her foreign friend as much as possible, and, faith, if she seemed to glory in so doing, it was not for me to be ashamed of it. Nobody seemed surprised;—all the women, on the contrary, were, as it were, delighted with the excellent example. The vice-legate, and all the other vices, were as polite as could be;—and I, who had acted on the reserve, was fairly obliged to take the lady under my arm, and look as much like a cicisbeo as I could on so short a notice,—to say nothing of the embarrassment of a cocked hat and sword, much more formidable to me than ever it will be to the enemy.

"I write in great haste—do you answer as hastily. I can understand nothing of all this; but it seems as if the G. had been presumed to be planted, and was determined to show that she was not,—plantation, in this hemisphere, being the greatest moral misfortune. But this is mere conjecture, for I know nothing about it—except that every body are very kind to her, and not discourteous to me. Fathers, and all relations, quite agreeable.

"Yours ever,

"B.

"P.S. Best respects to Mrs. H.

"I would send the compliments of the season; but the season itself is so complimentary with snow and rain that I wait for sunshine."

LETTER 352. TO MR. MOORE.

"January 2. 1320.

"My dear Moore,

"'To-day it is my wedding day;
And all the folks would stare,
If wife should dine at Edmonton,
And I should dine at Ware.'

Or thus:

"Here's a happy new year! but with reason,

Teresa ill i[n] Ravenna

> I beg you'll permit me to say—
> Wish me many returns of the season,
> But as few as you please of the day.

"My this present writing is to direct you that, if she chooses, she may see the MS. Memoir in your possession. I wish her to have fair play, in all cases, even though it will not be published till after my decease. For this purpose, it were but just that Lady B. should know what is there said of her and hers, that she may have full power to remark on or respond to any part or parts, as may seem fitting to herself. This is fair dealing, I presume, in all events.

"To change the subject, are you in England? I send you an epitaph for Castlereagh. * * * * * Another for Pitt:—

> "With death doom'd to grapple
> Beneath this cold slab, he
> Who lied in the Chapel
> Now lies in the Abbey.

"The gods seem to have made me poetical this day:—

> "In digging up your bones, Tom Paine,
> Will. Cobbett has done well:
> You visit him on earth again,
> He'll visit you in hell.

Or,

> "You come to him on earth again,
> He'll go with you to hell.

"Pray let not these versiculi go forth with my name, except among the initiated, because my friend H. has foamed into a reformer, and, I greatly fear, will subside into Newgate; since the Honourable House, according to Galignani's Reports of Parliamentary Debates, are menacing a prosecution to a pamphlet of his. I shall be very sorry to hear of any thing but good for him, particularly in these miserable squabbles; but these are the natural effects of taking a part in them.

"For my own part I had a sad scene since you went. Count Gu. came for his wife, and none of those consequences which Scott prophesied ensued. There was no damages, as in England, and so Scott lost his wager. But there was a great scene, for she would not, at first, go back with him—at least, she did go back with him; but he insisted, reasonably enough, that all communication should be broken off between her and me. So, finding Italy very dull, and having a fever tertian, I packed up my valise, and prepared to cross the Alps; but my daughter fell ill, and detained me.

"After her arrival at Ravenna, the Guiccioli fell ill again too; and at last, her father (who had,

Her reading (the) novel of M. de S[ta]

all along, opposed the liaison most violently till now) wrote to me to say that she was in such a state that he begged me to come and see her,—and that her husband had acquiesced, in consequence of her relapse, and that he (her father) would guarantee all this, and that there would be no farther scenes in consequence between them, and that I should not be compromised in any way. I set out soon after, and have been here ever since. I found her a good deal altered, but getting better:—all this comes of reading Corinna.

"The Carnival is about to begin, and I saw about two or three hundred people at the Marquis Cavalli's the other evening, with as much youth, beauty, and diamonds among the women, as ever averaged in the like number. My appearance in waiting on the Guiccioli was considered as a thing of course. The Marquis is her uncle, and naturally considered me as her relation.

"The paper is out, and so is the letter. Pray write. Address to Venice, whence the letters will be forwarded. Yours, &c. B."

LETTER 353. TO MR. HOPPNER.

"Ravenna, January 20. 1820.

"I have not decided any thing about remaining at Ravenna. I may stay a day, a week, a year, all my life; but all this depends upon what I can neither see nor foresee. I came because I was called, and will go the moment that I perceive what may render my departure proper. My attachment has neither the blindness of the beginning, nor the microscopic accuracy of the close to such liaisons; but 'time and the hour' must decide upon what I do. I can as yet say nothing, because I hardly know any thing beyond what I have told you.

"I wrote to you last post for my movables, as there is no getting a lodging with a chair or table here ready; and as I have already some things of the sort at Bologna which I had last summer there for my daughter, I have directed them to be moved; and wish the like to be done with those of Venice, that I may at least get out of the 'Albergo Imperiale,' which is imperial in all true sense of the epithet. Buffini may be paid for his poison. I forgot to thank you and Mrs. Hoppner for a whole treasure of toys for Allegra before our departure; it was very kind, and we are very grateful.

"Your account of the weeding of the Governor's party is very entertaining. If you do not understand the consular exceptions, I do; and it is right that a man of honour, and a woman of probity, should find it so, particularly in a place where there are not 'ten righteous.' As to nobility—in England none are strictly noble but peers, not even peers' sons, though titled by courtesy; nor knights of the garter, unless of the peerage, so that Castlereagh himself would hardly pass through a foreign herald's ordeal till the death of his father.

"The snow is a foot deep here. There is a theatre, and opera,—the Barber of Seville. Balls begin on Monday next. Pay the porter for never looking after the gate, and ship my chattels, and let me know, or let Castelli let me know, how my law-suits go on—but fee him only in proportion to his success. Perhaps we may meet in the spring yet, if you are for England. I see H * * has got into a scrape, which does not please me; he should not have gone so deep among those men without calculating the consequences. I used to think myself the most imprudent of all among my friends and acquaintances, but almost begin to doubt it.

"Yours," &c.
LETTER 354. TO MR. HOPPNER.
"Ravenna, January 31. 1820.

"You would hardly have been troubled with the removal of my furniture, but there is none to be had nearer than Bologna, and I have been fain to have that of the rooms which I fitted up for my daughter there in the summer removed here. The expense will be at least as great of the land carriage, so that you see it was necessity, and not choice. Here they get every thing from Bologna, except some lighter articles from Forli or Faenza.

"If Scott is returned, pray remember me to him, and plead laziness the whole and sole cause of my not replying:—dreadful is the exertion of letter-writing. The Carnival here is less boisterous, but we have balls and a theatre. I carried Bankes to both, and he carried away, I believe, a much more favourable impression of the society here than of that of Venice,—recollect that I speak of the native society only.

"I am drilling very hard to learn how to double a shawl, and should succeed to admiration if I did not always double it the wrong side out; and then I sometimes confuse and bring away two, so as to put all the Servanti out, besides keeping their Servite in the cold till every body can get back their property. But it is a dreadfully moral place, for you must not look at anybody's wife except your neighbour's,—if you go to the next door but one, you are scolded, and presumed to be perfidious. And then a relazione or an amicizia seems to be a regular affair of from five to fifteen years, at which period, if there occur a widowhood, it finishes by a sposalizio; and in the mean time it has so many rules of its own that it is not much better. A man actually becomes a piece of female property,—they won't let their Serventi marry until there is a vacancy for themselves. I know two instances of this in one family here.

"To-night there was a —— Lottery after the opera; it is an odd ceremony. Bankes and I took tickets of it, and buffooned together very merrily. He is gone to Firenze. Mrs. J * * should have sent you my postscript; there was no occasion to have bored you in person. I never interfere in anybody's squabbles,—she may scratch your face herself.

"The weather here has been dreadful—snow several feet—a fiume, broke down a bridge, and flooded heaven knows how many campi; then rain came—and it is still thawing—so that my saddle-horses have a sinecure till the roads become more practicable. Why did Lega give away the goat? a blockhead—I must have him again.

"Will you pay Missiaglia and the Buffo Buffini of the Gran Bretagna? I heard from Moore, who is at Paris; I had previously written to him in London, but he has not yet got my letter, apparently.

"Believe me," &c.
LETTER 355. TO MR. MURRAY.
"Ravenna, February 7. 1820.

"I have had no letter from you these two months; but since I came here in December, 1819, I sent you a letter for Moore, who is God knows where—in Paris or London, I presume. I have copied and cut the third Canto of Don Juan into two, because it was too long; and I tell you this

To Allegra

beforehand, because in case of any reckoning between you and me, these two are only to go for one, as this was the original form, and, in fact, the two together are not longer than one of the first: so remember that I have not made this division to double upon you; but merely to suppress some tediousness in the aspect of the thing. I should have served you a pretty trick if I had sent you, for example, cantos of 50 stanzas each.

"I am translating the first Canto of Pulci's Morgante Maggiore, and have half done it; but these last days of the Carnival confuse and interrupt every thing.

"I have not yet sent off the Cantos, and have some doubt whether they ought to be published, for they have not the spirit of the first. The outcry has not frightened but it has hurt me, and I have not written con amore this time. It is very decent, however, and as dull as 'the last new comedy.'

"I think my translations of Pulci will make you stare. It must be put by the original, stanza for stanza, and verse for verse; and you will see what was permitted in a Catholic country and a bigoted age to a churchman, on the score of religion;—and so tell those buffoons who accuse me of attacking the Liturgy.

"I write in the greatest haste, it being the hour of the Corso, and I must go and buffoon with the rest. My daughter Allegra is just gone with the Countess G. in Count G.'s coach and six to join the cavalcade, and I must follow with all the rest of the Ravenna world. Our old Cardinal is dead, and the new one not appointed yet; but the masquing goes on the same, the vice-legate being a good governor. We have had hideous frost and snow, but all is mild again.

"Yours," &c.

LETTER 356. TO MR. BANKES.
"Ravenna, February 19. 1820.

"I have room for you in the house here, as I had in Venice, if you think fit to make use of it; but do not expect to find the same gorgeous suite of tapestried halls. Neither dangers nor tropical heats have ever prevented your penetrating wherever you had a mind to it, and why should the snow now?—Italian snow—fie on it!—so pray come. Tita's heart yearns for you, and mayhap for your silver broad pieces; and your playfellow, the monkey, is alone and inconsolable.

"I forget whether you admire or tolerate red hair, so that I rather dread showing you all that I have about me and around me in this city. Come, nevertheless,—you can pay Dante a morning visit, and I will undertake that Theodore and Honoria will be most happy to see you in the forest hard by. We Goths, also, of Ravenna, hope you will not despise our arch-Goth, Theodoric. I must leave it to these worthies to entertain you all the fore part of the day, seeing that I have none at all myself—the lark that rouses me from my slumbers, being an afternoon bird. But, then, all your evenings, and as much as you can give me of your nights, will be mine. Ay! and you will find me eating flesh, too, like yourself or any other cannibal, except it be upon Fridays. Then, there are more Cantos (and be d——d to them) of what the courteous reader, Mr. S——, calls Grub Street, in my drawer, which I have a little scheme to commit to your charge for England; only I must first cut up (or cut down) two aforesaid Cantos into three, because I am grown base and mercenary, and it is an ill precedent to let my Mecænas, Murray, get too much for his money. I am busy, also, with Pulci—translating—servilely translating, stanza for stanza, and line for line—two octaves every night,—the same allowance as at Venice.

"Would you call at your banker's at Bologna, and ask him for some letters lying there for me, and burn them?—or I will—so do not burn them, but bring them,—and believe me ever and very affectionately Yours,

"BYRON.

"P.S. I have a particular wish to hear from yourself something about Cyprus, so pray recollect all that you can.—Good night."

LETTER 357. TO MR. MURRAY.

"Ravenna, February 21. 1820.

"The bull-dogs will be very agreeable. I have only those of this country, who, though good, have not the tenacity of tooth and stoicism in endurance of my canine fellow-citizens: then pray send them by the readiest conveyance—perhaps best by sea. Mr. Kinnaird will disburse for them, and deduct from the amount on your application or that of Captain Tyler.

"I see the good old King is gone to his place. One can't help being sorry, though blindness, and age, and insanity, are supposed to be drawbacks on human felicity; but I am not at all sure that the latter, at least, might not render him happier than any of his subjects.

"I have no thoughts of coming to the coronation, though I should like to see it, and though I have a right to be a puppet in it; but my division with Lady Byron, which has drawn an equinoctial line between me and mine in all other things, will operate in this also to prevent my being in the same procession.

"By Saturday's post I sent you four packets, containing Cantos third and fourth. Recollect that these two cantos reckon only as one with you and me, being, in fact, the third canto cut into two, because I found it too long. Remember this, and don't imagine that there could be any other motive. The whole is about 225 stanzas, more or less, and a lyric of 96 lines, so that they are no longer than the first single cantos: but the truth is, that I made the first too long, and should have cut those down also had I thought better. Instead of saying in future for so many cantos, say so many stanzas or pages: it was Jacob Tonson's way, and certainly the best; it prevents mistakes. I might have sent you a dozen cantos of 40 stanzas each,—those of 'The Minstrel' (Beattie's) are no longer,—and ruined you at once, if you don't suffer as it is. But recollect that you are not pinned down to any thing you say in a letter, and that, calculating even these two cantos as one only (which they were and are to be reckoned), you are not bound by your offer. Act as may seem fair to all parties.

"I have finished my translation of the first Canto of 'The Morgante Maggiore' of Pulci, which I will transcribe and send. It is the parent, not only of Whistlecraft, but of all jocose Italian poetry. You must print it side by side with the original Italian, because I wish the reader to judge of the fidelity: it is stanza for stanza, and often line for line, if not word for word.

"You ask me for a volume of manners, &c. on Italy. Perhaps I am in the case to know more of them than most Englishmen, because I have lived among the natives, and in parts of the country where Englishmen never resided before (I speak of Romagna and this place particularly); but *put in*

there are many reasons why I do not choose to treat in print on such a subject. I have lived in their houses and in the heart of their families, sometimes merely as 'amico di casa,' and sometimes as 'amico di cuore' of the Dama, and in neither case do I feel myself authorised in making a book of them. Their moral is not your moral; their life is not your life; you would not understand it; it is not English, nor French, nor German, which you would all understand. The conventual education, the cavalier servitude, the habits of thought and living are so entirely different, and the difference becomes so much more striking the more you live intimately with them, that I know not how to make you comprehend a people who are at once temperate and profligate, serious in their characters and buffoons in their amusements, capable of impressions and passions, which are at once sudden and durable (what you find in no other nation), and who actually have no society (what we would call so), as you may see by their comedies; they have no real comedy, not even in Goldoni, and that is because they have no society to draw it from.

"Their conversazioni are not society at all. They go to the theatre to talk, and into company to hold their tongues. The women sit in a circle, and the men gather into groups, or they play at dreary faro, or 'lotto reale,' for small sums. Their academic are concerts like our own, with better music and more form. Their best things are the carnival balls and masquerades, when every body runs mad for six weeks. After their dinners and suppers they make extempore verses and buffoon one another; but it is in a humour which you would not enter into, ye of the north.

"In their houses it is better. I should know something of the matter, having had a pretty general experience among their women, from the fisherman's wife up to the Nobil Dama, whom I serve. Their system has its rules, and its fitnesses, and its decorums, so as to be reduced to a kind of discipline or game at hearts, which admits few deviations, unless you wish to lose it. They are extremely tenacious, and jealous as furies, not permitting their lovers even to marry if they can help it, and keeping them always close to them in public as in private, whenever they can. In short, they transfer marriage to adultery, and strike the not out of that commandment. The reason is, that they marry for their parents, and love for themselves. They exact fidelity from a lover as a debt of honour, while they pay the husband as a tradesman, that is, not at all. You hear a person's character, male or female, canvassed not as depending on their conduct to their husbands or wives, but to their mistress or lover. If I wrote a quarto, I don't know that I could do more than amplify what I have here noted. It is to be observed that while they do all this, the greatest outward respect is to be paid to the husbands, not only by the ladies, but by their Serventi— particularly if the husband serves no one himself (which is not often the case, however); so that you would often suppose them relations—the Servente making the figure of one adopted into the family. Sometimes the ladies run a little restive and elope, or divide, or make a scene: but this is at starting, generally, when they know no better, or when they fall in love with a foreigner, or some such anomaly,—and is always reckoned unnecessary and extravagant.

"You enquire after Dante's Prophecy: I have not done more than six hundred lines, but will vaticinate at leisure.

"Of the bust I know nothing. No cameos or seals are to be cut here or elsewhere that I know of, in any good style. Hobhouse should write himself to Thorwaldsen: the bust was made and paid for three years ago.

"Pray tell Mrs. Leigh to request Lady Byron to urge forward the transfer from the funds. I wrote to Lady Byron on business this post, addressed to the care of Mr. D. Kinnaird."

LETTER 358. TO MR. BANKES.

"Ravenna, February 26. 1820.

"Pulci and I are waiting for you with impatience; but I suppose we must give way to the attraction of the Bolognese galleries for a time. I know nothing of pictures myself, and care almost as little: but to me there are none like the Venetian—above all, Giorgione. I remember well his Judgment of Solomon in the Mariscalchi in Bologna. The real mother is beautiful, exquisitely beautiful. Buy her, by all means, if you can, and take her home with you: put her in safety: for be assured there are troublous times brewing for Italy; and as I never could keep out of a row in my life, it will be my fate, I dare say, to be over head and ears in it; but no matter, these are the stronger reasons for coming to see me soon.

"I have more of Scott's novels (for surely they are Scott's) since we met, and am more and more delighted. I think that I even prefer them to his poetry, which (by the way) I redde for the first time in my life in your rooms in Trinity College.

"There are some curious commentaries on Dante preserved here, which you should see. Believe me ever, faithfully and most affectionately, yours," &c.

LETTER 359. TO MR. MURRAY.

"Ravenna, March 1. 1820.

"I sent you by last post the translation of the first Canto of the Morgante Maggiore, and wish you to ask Rose about the word 'sbergo,' i.e. 'usbergo,' which I have translated cuirass. I suspect that it means helmet also. Now, if so, which of the senses is best accordant with the text? I have adopted cuirass, but will be amenable to reasons. Of the natives, some say one, and some t'other: but they are no great Tuscans in Romagna. However, I will ask Sgricci (the famous improvisatore) to-morrow, who is a native of Arezzo. The Countess Guiccioli who is reckoned a very cultivated young lady, and the dictionary, say cuirass. I have written cuirass, but helmet runs in my head nevertheless—and will run in verse very well, whilk is the principal point. I will ask the Sposa Spina Spinelli, too, the Florentine bride of Count Gabriel Rusponi, just imported from Florence, and get the sense out of somebody.

"I have just been visiting the new Cardinal, who arrived the day before yesterday in his legation. He seems a good old gentleman, pious and simple, and not quite like his predecessor, who was a bon-vivant, in the worldly sense of the words.

"Enclosed is a letter which I received some time ago from Dallas. It will explain itself. I have not answered it. This comes of doing people good. At one time or another (including copyrights) this person has had about fourteen hundred pounds of my money, and he writes what he calls a posthumous work about me, and a scrubby letter accusing me of treating him ill, when I never did any such thing. It is true that I left off letter-writing, as I have done with almost everybody else; but I can't see how that was misusing him.

"I look upon his epistle as the consequence of my not sending him another hundred pounds, which he wrote to me for about two years ago, and which I thought proper to withhold, he having had his share, methought, of what I could dispone upon others.

"In your last you ask me after my articles of domestic wants; I believe they are as usual: the bull-dogs, magnesia, soda-powders, tooth-powders, brushes, and every thing of the kind which are here unattainable. You still ask me to return to England: alas! to what purpose? You do not know what you are requiring. Return I must, probably, some day or other (if I live), sooner or later; but it will not be for pleasure, nor can it end in good. You enquire after my health and SPIRITS in large letters: my health can't be very bad, for I cured myself of a sharp tertian ague, in three weeks, with cold water, which had held my stoutest gondolier for months, notwithstanding all the bark of the apothecary,—a circumstance which surprised Dr. Aglietti, who said it was a proof of great stamina, particularly in so epidemic a season. I did it out of dislike to the taste of bark (which I can't bear), and succeeded, contrary to the prophecies of every body, by simply taking nothing at all. As to spirits, they are unequal, now high, now low, like other people's I suppose, and depending upon circumstances.

"Pray send me W. Scott's new novels. What are their names and characters? I read some of his former ones, at least once a day, for an hour or so. The last are too hurried: he forgets Ravenswood's name, and calls him Edgar and then Norman; and Girder, the cooper, is styled now Gilbert, and now John; and he don't make enough of Montrose; but Dalgetty is excellent, and so is Lucy Ashton, and the b——h her mother. What is Ivanhoe? and what do you call his other? are there two? Pray make him write at least two a year: I like no reading so well.

"The editor of the Bologna Telegraph has sent me a paper with extracts from Mr. Mulock's (his name always reminds me of Muley Moloch of Morocco) 'Atheism answered,' in which there is a long eulogium of my poesy, and a great 'compatimento' for my misery. I never could understand what they mean by accusing me of irreligion. However, they may have it their own way. This gentleman seems to be my great admirer, so I take what he says in good part, as he evidently intends kindness, to which I can't accuse myself of being invincible.

"Yours," &c.

LETTER 360. TO MR. MURRAY.

"Ravenna, March 5. 1820.

"In case, in your country, you should not readily lay hands on the Morgante Maggiore, I send you the original text of the first Canto, to correspond with the translation which I sent you a few days ago. It is from the Naples edition in quarto of 1732,—dated Florence, however, by a trick of the trade, which you, as one of the allied sovereigns of the profession, will perfectly understand without any further spiegazione.

"It is strange that here nobody understands the real precise meaning of 'sbergo,' or 'usbergo,' an old Tuscan word, which I have rendered cuirass (but am not sure it is not helmet). I have asked at least twenty people, learned and ignorant, male and female, including poets, and officers civil and military. The dictionary says cuirass, but gives no authority; and a female friend of mine says positively cuirass, which makes me doubt the fact still more than before. Ginguené says 'bonnet de fer,' with the usual superficial decision of a Frenchman, so that I can't believe him:

and what between the dictionary, the Italian woman, and the Frenchman, there's no trusting to a word they say. The context, too, which should decide, admits equally of either meaning, as you will perceive. Ask Rose, Hobhouse, Merivale, and Foscolo, and vote with the majority. Is Frere a good Tuscan? if he be, bother him too. I have tried, you see, to be as accurate as I well could. This is my third or fourth letter, or packet, within the last twenty days."

LETTER 361. TO MR. MURRAY.

"Ravenna, March 14. 1820.

"Enclosed is Dante's Prophecy—Vision—or what not. Where I have left more than one reading (which I have done often), you may adopt that which Gifford, Frere, Rose, and Hobhouse, and others of your Utican Senate think the best or least bad. The preface will explain all that is explicable. These are but the four first cantos: if approved, I will go on.

"Pray mind in printing; and let some good Italian scholar correct the Italian quotations.

"Four days ago I was overturned in an open carriage between the river and a steep bank:—wheels dashed to pieces, slight bruises, narrow escape, and all that; but no harm done, though coachman, foot-man, horses, and vehicle, were all mixed together like macaroni. It was owing to bad driving, as I say; but the coachman swears to a start on the part of the horses. We went against a post on the verge of a steep bank, and capsized. I usually go out of the town in a carriage, and meet the saddle horses at the bridge; it was in going there that we boggled; but I got my ride, as usual, after the accident. They say here it was all owing to St. Antonio of Padua, (serious, I assure you,)—who does thirteen miracles a day,—that worse did not come of it. I have no objection to this being his fourteenth in the four-and-twenty-hours. He presides over overturns and all escapes therefrom, it seems: and they dedicate pictures, &c. to him, as the sailors once did to Neptune, after 'the high Roman fashion.'

"Yours, in haste."

LETTER 362. TO MR. MURRAY.

"Ravenna, March 20. 1820.

"Last post I sent you 'The Vision of Dante,'—four first Cantos. Enclosed you will find, line for line, in third rhyme (terza rima), of which your British blackguard reader as yet understands nothing, Fanny of Rimini. You know that she was born here, and married, and slain, from Gary, Boyd, and such people. I have done it into cramp English, line for line, and rhyme for rhyme, to try the possibility. You had best append it to the poems already sent by last three posts. I shall not allow you to play the tricks you did last year, with the prose you post-scribed to Mazeppa, which I sent to you not to be published, if not in a periodical paper,—and there you tacked it, without a word of explanation. If this is published, publish it with the original, and together with the Pulci translation, or the Dante imitation. I suppose you have both by now, and the Juan long before.

"FRANCESCA OF RIMINI.

"Translation from the Inferno of Dante, Canto 5th.

"'The land where I was born sits by the seas,
Upon that shore to which the Po descends,

>   With all his followers, in search of peace.
>   Love, which the gentle heart soon apprehends,
>   Seized him for the fair person which was ta'en
>   From me, and me even yet the mode offends.
>   Love, who to none beloved to love again
>   Remits, seized me with wish to please, so strong,
>   That, as thou seest, yet, yet it doth remain.
>   Love to one death conducted us along,
>   But Caina waits for him our life who ended:'
>   These were the accents utter'd by her tongue,—
>   Since first I listen'd to these souls offended,
>   I bow'd my visage and so kept it till—

LETTER 363. TO MR. MURRAY.
"Ravenna, March 23. 1820.

"I have received your letter of the 7th. Besides the four packets you have already received, I have sent the Pulci a few days after, and since (a few days ago) the four first Cantos of Dante's Prophecy, (the best thing I ever wrote, if it be not unintelligible,) and by last post a literal translation, word for word (versed like the original), of the episode of Francesca of Rimini. I want to hear what you think of the new Juans, and the translations, and the Vision. They are all things that are, or ought to be, very different from one another.

"If you choose to make a print from the Venetian, you may; but she don't correspond at all to the character you mean her to represent. On the contrary, the Contessa G. does (except that she is fair), and is much prettier than the Fornarina; but I have no picture of her except a miniature, which is very ill done; and, besides, it would not be proper, on any account whatever, to make such a use of it, even if you had a copy.

"Recollect that the two new Cantos only count with us for one. You may put the Pulci and Dante together: perhaps that were best. So you have put your name to Juan, after all your panic. You are a rare fellow. I must now put myself in a passion to continue my prose. Yours," &c.

"I have caused write to Thorwaldsen. Pray be careful in sending my daughter's picture—I mean, that it be not hurt in the carriage, for it is a journey rather long and jolting."

LETTER 364. TO MR. MURRAY.
"Ravenna, March 28. 1820.

"Enclosed is a 'Screed of Doctrine' for you, of which I will trouble you to acknowledge the receipt by next post. Mr. Hobhouse must have the correction of it for the press. You may show it first to whom you please.

"I wish to know what became of my two Epistles from St. Paul (translated from the Armenian three years ago and more), and of the letter to R——ts of last autumn, which you never have attended to? There are two packets with this.

"P.S. I have some thoughts of publishing the 'Hints from Horace,' written ten years ago,—if

Hobhouse can rummage them out of my papers left at his father's,—with some omissions and alterations previously to be made when I see the proofs."

LETTER 365. TO MR. MURRAY.

"Ravenna, March 29. 1820.

"Herewith you will receive a note (enclosed) on Pope, which you will find tally with a part of the text of last post. I have at last lost all patience with the atrocious cant and nonsense about Pope, with which our present * *s are overflowing, and am determined to make such head against it as an individual can, by prose or verse; and I will at least do it with good will. There is no bearing it any longer; and if it goes on, it will destroy what little good writing or taste remains amongst us. I hope there are still a few men of taste to second me; but if not, I'll battle it alone, convinced that it is in the best cause of English literature.

"I have sent you so many packets, verse and prose, lately, that you will be tired of the postage, if not of the perusal. I want to answer some parts of your last letter, but I have not time, for I must 'boot and saddle,' as my Captain Craigengelt (an officer of the old Napoleon Italian army) is in waiting, and my groom and cattle to boot.

"You have given me a screed of metaphor and what not about Pulci, and manners, and 'going without clothes, like our Saxon ancestors.' Now, the Saxons did not go without clothes; and, in the next place, they are not my ancestors, nor yours either; for mine were Norman, and yours, I take it by your name, were Gael. And, in the next, I differ from you about the 'refinement' which has banished the comedies of Congreve. Are not the comedies of Sheridan? acted to the thinnest houses? I know (as ex-committed) that 'The School for Scandal' was the worst stock piece upon record. I also know that Congreve gave up writing because Mrs. Centlivre's balderdash drove his comedies off. So it is not decency, but stupidity, that does all this; for Sheridan is as decent a writer as need be, and Congreve no worse than Mrs. Centlivre, of whom Wilks (the actor) said, 'not only her play would be damned, but she too.' He alluded to 'A Bold Stroke for a Wife.' But last, and most to the purpose, Pulci is not an indecent writer—at least in his first Canto, as you will have perceived by this time.

"You talk of refinement:—are you all more moral? are you so moral? No such thing. I know what the world is in England, by my own proper experience of the best of it—at least of the loftiest; and I have described it every where as it is to be found in all places.

"But to return. I should like to see the proofs of mine answer, because there will be something to omit or to alter. But pray let it be carefully printed. When convenient let me have an answer.

"Yours."

LETTER 366. TO MR. HOPPNER.

"Ravenna, March 31. 1820.

"Ravenna continues much the same as I described it. Conversazioni all Lent, and much better ones than any at Venice. There are small games at hazard, that is, faro, where nobody can point more than a shilling or two;—other card-tables, and as much talk and coffee as you please. Every body does and says what they please; and I do not recollect any disagreeable events, except being three times falsely accused of flirtation, and once being robbed of six sixpences by a nobleman of the city, a Count * * *. I did not suspect the illustrious delinquent; but the Countess V * * * and the Marquis L * * * told me of it directly, and also that it was a way he had, of filching money when he saw it before him; but I did not ax him for the cash, but contented myself with telling him that if he did it again, I should anticipate the law.

"There is to be a theatre in April, and a fair, and an opera, and another opera in June, besides the fine weather of nature's giving, and the rides in the Forest of Pine. With my best respects to Mrs. Hoppner, believe me ever, &c. BYRON.

"P.S. Could you give me an item of what books remain at Venice? I don't want them, but want to know whether the few that are not here are there, and were not lost by the way. I hope and trust you have got all your wine safe, and that it is drinkable. Allegra is prettier, I think, but as obstinate as a mule, and as ravenous as a vulture: health good, to judge of the complexion—temper tolerable, but for vanity and pertinacity. She thinks herself handsome, and will do as she pleases."

LETTER 367. TO MR. MURRAY.

"Ravenna, April 9. 1820.

"In the name of all the devils in the printing-office, why don't you write to acknowledge the receipt of the second, third, and fourth packets, viz. the Pulci translation and original, the Danticles, the Observations on, &c.? You forget that you keep me in hot water till I know whether they are arrived, or if I must have the bore of re-copying.

"Have you gotten the cream of translations, Francesca of Rimini, from the Inferno? Why, I have sent you a warehouse of trash within the last month, and you have no sort of feeling about you: a pastry-cook would have had twice the gratitude, and thanked me at least for the quantity.

"To make the letter heavier, I enclose you the Cardinal Legate's (our Campeius) circular for his conversazione this evening. It is the anniversary of the Pope's tiara-tion, and all polite Christians, even of the Lutheran creed, must go and be civil. And there will be a circle, and a faro-table, (for shillings, that is, they don't allow high play,) and all the beauty, nobility, and sanctity of Ravenna present. The Cardinal himself is a very good-natured little fellow, bishop of Muda, and legate here,—a decent believer in all the doctrines of the church. He has kept his housekeeper these forty years * * * *; but is reckoned a pious man, and a moral liver.

"I am not quite sure that I won't be among you this autumn, for I find that business don't go on—what with trustees and lawyers—as it should do, 'with all deliberate speed.' They differ about investments in Ireland.

> "Between the devil and deep sea,
> Between the lawyer and trustee,

I am puzzled; and so much time is lost by my not being upon the spot, what with answers, demurs, rejoinders, that it may be I must come and look to it; for one says do, and t'other don't, so that I know not which way to turn: but perhaps they can manage without me.

"Yours, &c.

"P.S. I have begun a tragedy on the subject of Marino Faliero, the Doge of Venice; but you sha'n't see it these six years, if you don't acknowledge my packets with more quickness and precision. Always write, if but a line, by return of post, when any thing arrives, which is not a mere letter.

"Address direct to Ravenna; it saves a week's time, and much postage."

LETTER 368. TO MR. MURRAY.

"Ravenna, April 16. 1820.

"Post after post arrives without bringing any acknowledgment from you of the different packets (excepting the first) which I sent within the last two months, all of which ought to be arrived long ere now; and as they were announced in other letters, you ought at least to say whether they are come or not. You are not expected to write frequent, or long letters, as your time is much occupied; but when parcels that have cost some pains in the composition, and great trouble in the copying, are sent to you, I should at least be put out of suspense, by the immediate acknowledgment, per return of post, addressed directly to Ravenna. I am naturally—knowing what continental posts are—anxious to hear that they are arrived; especially as I loathe the task of copying so much, that if there was a human being that could copy my blotted MSS. he should have all they can ever bring for his trouble. All I desire is two lines, to say, such a day I received such a packet. There are at least six unacknowledged. This is neither kind nor courteous.

"I have, besides, another reason for desiring you to be speedy, which is, that there is THAT brewing in Italy which will speedily cut off all security of communication, and set all your Anglo-travellers flying in every direction, with their usual fortitude in foreign tumults. The Spanish and French affairs have set the Italians in a ferment; and no wonder: they have been too long trampled on. This will make a sad scene for your exquisite traveller, but not for the resident, who naturally wishes a people to redress itself. I shall, if permitted by the natives, remain to see what will come of it, and perhaps to take a turn with them, like Dugald Dalgetty and his horse, in case of business; for I shall think it by far the most interesting spectacle and moment in existence, to see the Italians send the barbarians of all nations back to their own dens. I have lived long enough among them to feel more for them as a nation than for any other people in existence. But they want union, and they want principle; and I doubt their success. However, they will try, probably, and if they do, it will be a good cause. No Italian can hate an Austrian more than I do: unless it be the English, the Austrians seem to me the most obnoxious race under the sky.

"But I doubt, if any thing be done, it won't be so quietly as in Spain. To be sure, revolutions are not to be made with rose-water, where there are foreigners as masters.

"Write while you can; for it is but the toss up of a paul that there will not be a row that will somewhat retard the mail by and by.

"Yours," &c.

LETTER 369. TO MR. HOPPNER.

"Ravenna, April 18. 1820.

"I have caused write to Siri and Willhalm to send with Vincenza, in a boat, the camp-beds and swords left in their care when I quitted Venice. There are also several pounds of Mantons best powder in a Japan case; but unless I felt sure of getting it away from V. without seizure, I won't have it ventured. I can get it in here, by means of an acquaintance in the customs, who has offered to get it ashore for me; but should like to be certiorated of its safety in leaving Venice. I would not lose it for its weight in gold—there is none such in Italy, as I take it to be.

"I wrote to you a week or so ago, and hope you are in good plight and spirits. Sir Humphry Davy is here, and was last night at the Cardinal's. As I had been there last Sunday, and yesterday was warm, I did not go, which I should have done, if I had thought of meeting the man of chemistry. He called this morning, and I shall go in search of him at Corso time. I believe to-day, being Monday, there is no great conversazione, and only the family one at the Marchese Cavalli's, where I go as a relation sometimes, so that, unless he stays a day or two, we should hardly meet in public.

"The theatre is to open in May for the fair, if there is not a row in all Italy by that time,—the Spanish business has set them all a constitutioning, and what will be the end, no one knows—it is also necessary thereunto to have a beginning.

"Yours, &c.

"P.S. My benediction to Mrs. Hoppner. How is your little boy? Allegra is growing, and has increased in good looks and obstinacy."

LETTER 370. TO MR. MURRAY.

"Ravenna, April 23. 1820.

"The proofs don't contain the last stanzas of Canto second, but end abruptly with the 105th stanza.

"I told you long ago that the new Cantos were not good, and I also told you a reason. Recollect, I do not oblige you to publish them; you may suppress them, if you like, but I can alter nothing. I have erased the six stanzas about those two impostors * * * * (which I suppose will give you great pleasure), but I can do no more. I can neither recast, nor replace; but I give you leave to put it all into the fire, if you like, or not to publish, and I think that's sufficient.

"I told you that I wrote on with no good will—that I had been, not frightened, but hurt by the outcry, and, besides, that when I wrote last November, I was ill in body, and in very great distress of mind about some private things of my own; but you would have it: so I sent it to you, and to make it lighter, cut it in two—but I can't piece it together again. I can't cobble: I must 'either make a spoon or spoil a horn,'—and there's an end; for there's no remeid: but I leave you free will to suppress the whole, if you like it.

"About the Morgante Maggiore, I won't have a line omitted. It may circulate, or it may not; but all the criticism on earth sha'n't touch a line, unless it be because it is badly translated. Now you say, and I say, and others say, that the translation is a good one; and so it shall go to press as it is. Pulci must answer for his own irreligion: I answer for the translation only.

"Pray let Mr. Hobhouse look to the Italian next time in the proofs: this time, while I am scribbling to you, they are corrected by one who passes for the prettiest woman in Romagna, and even the Marches, as far as Ancona, be the other who she may.

"I am glad you like my answer to your enquiries about Italian society. It is fit you should like something, and be d——d to you.

"My love to Scott. I shall think higher of knighthood ever after for his being dubbed. By the way, he is the first poet titled for his talent in Britain: it has happened abroad before now; but on the Continent titles are universal and worthless. Why don't you send me Ivanhoe and the Monastery? I have never written to Sir Walter, for I know he has a thousand things, and I a thousand nothings, to do; but I hope to see him at Abbotsford before very long, and I will sweat his claret for him, though Italian abstemiousness has made my brain but a shilpit concern for a Scotch sitting 'inter pocula.' I love Scott, and Moore, and all the better brethren; but I hate and abhor that puddle of water-worms whom you have taken into your troop.

"Yours, &c.

"P.S. You say that one half is very good: you are wrong; for, if it were, it would be the finest poem in existence. Where is the poetry of which one half is good? is it the Æneid? is it Milton's? is it Dryden's? is it any one's except Pope's and Goldsmith's, of which all is good? and yet these two last are the poets your pond poets would explode. But if one half of the two new Cantos be good in your opinion, what the devil would you have more? No—no; no poetry is generally good—only by fits and starts—and you are lucky to get a sparkle here and there. You might as well want a midnight all stars as rhyme all perfect.

"We are on the verge of a row here. Last night they have overwritten all the city walls with 'Up with the republic!' and 'Death to the Pope!' &c. &c. This would be nothing in London, where the walls are privileged. But here it is a different thing: they are not used to such fierce political inscriptions, and the police is all on the alert, and the Cardinal glares pale through all his purple.

"April 24. 1820. 8 o'clock, P.M.

"The police have been, all noon and after, searching for the inscribers, but have caught none as yet. They must have been all night about it, for the 'Live republics—Death to Popes and Priests,' are innumerable, and plastered over all the palaces: ours has plenty. There is 'Down with the Nobility,' too; they are down enough already, for that matter. A very heavy rain and wind having come on, I did not go out and 'skirr the country;' but I shall mount to-morrow, and take a canter among the peasantry, who are a savage, resolute race, always riding with guns in their hands. I wonder they don't suspect the serenaders, for they play on the guitar here all night, as in Spain, to their mistresses.

"Talking of politics, as Caleb Quotem says, pray look at the conclusion of my Ode on Waterloo, written in the year 1815, and, comparing it with the Duke de Berri's catastrophe in 1820, tell me if I have not as good a right to the character of 'Vates' in both senses of the word, as Fitzgerald and Coleridge?

"'Crimson tears will follow yet—'

and have not they?

"I can't pretend to foresee what will happen among you Englishers at this distance, but I vaticinate a row in Italy; in whilk case, I don't know that I won't have a finger in it. I dislike the Austrians, and think the Italians infamously oppressed; and if they begin, why, I will recommend 'the erection of a sconce upon Drumsnab,' like Dugald Dalgetty."

LETTER 371. TO MR. MURRAY.
"Ravenna, May 8. 1820.

"From your not having written again, an intention which your letter of the 7th ultimo indicated, I have to presume that the 'Prophecy of Dante' has not been found more worthy than its predecessors in the eyes of your illustrious synod. In that case, you will be in some perplexity; to end which, I repeat to you, that you are not to consider yourself as bound or pledged to publish any thing because it is mine, but always to act according to your own views, or opinions, or those of your friends; and to be sure that you will in no degree offend me by 'declining the article,' to use a technical phrase. The prose observations on John Wilson's attack, I do not intend for publication at this time; and I send a copy of verses to Mr. Kinnaird (they were written last year on crossing the Po) which must not be published either. I mention this, because it is probable he may give you a copy. Pray recollect this, as they are mere verses of society, and written upon private feelings and passions. And, moreover, I can't consent to any mutilations or omissions of Pulci: the original has been ever free from such in Italy, the capital of Christianity, and the translation may be so in England; though you will think it strange that they should have allowed such freedom for many centuries to the Morgante, while the other day they confiscated the whole translation of the fourth Canto of Childe Harold, and have persecuted Leoni, the translator—so he writes me, and so I could have told him, had he consulted me before his publication. This shows how much more politics interest men in these parts than religion. Half a dozen invectives against tyranny confiscate Childe Harold in a month; and eight and twenty cantos of quizzing monks and knights, and church government, are let loose for centuries. I copy Leoni's account.

"'Non ignorerà forse che la mia versione del 4° Canto del Childe Harold fu confiscata in ogni parte: ed io stesso ho dovuto soffrir vessazioni altrettanto ridicole quanto illiberaii, ad arte che alcuni versi fossero esclusi dalla censura. Ma siccome il divieto non fa d'ordinario che accrescere la curiosita cosí quel carme sull' Italia è ricercato più che mai, e penso di farlo ristampare in Inghil-terra senza nulla escludere. Sciagurata condizione di questa mia patria! se patria si può chiamare una terra così avvilita dalla fortuna, dagli uomini, da se medesima.'

"Rose will translate this to you. Has he had his letter? I enclosed it to you months ago.

"This intended piece of publication I shall dissuade him from, or he may chance to see the inside of St. Angelo's. The last sentence of his letter is the common and pathetic sentiment of all his countrymen.

"Sir Humphry Davy was here last fortnight, and I was in his company in the house of a very pretty Italian lady of rank, who, by way of displaying her learning in presence of the great chemist, then describing his fourteenth ascension to Mount Vesuvius, asked 'if there was not a similar volcano in Ireland?' My only notion of an Irish volcano consisted of the lake of Killarney, which I naturally conceived her to mean; but, on second thoughts, I divined that she alluded to Iceland and to Hecla—and so it proved, though she sustained her volcanic topography for some time with all the amiable pertinacity of 'the feminie.' She soon after turned to me and asked me various questions about Sir Humphry's philosophy, and I explained as well as an oracle his skill in gasen safety lamps, and ungluing the Pompeian MSS. 'But what do you call him?' said she. 'A great chemist,' quoth I. 'What can he do?' repeated the lady. 'Almost any thing,' said I. 'Oh, then, mio caro, do pray beg him to give me something to dye my eyebrows black. I have tried a thousand things, and the colours all come off; and besides, they don't grow; can't he invent something to make them grow?' All this with the greatest earnestness; and what you will be surprised at, she is neither ignorant nor a fool, but really well educated and clever. But they speak like children, when first out of their convents; and, after all, this is better than an English blue-stocking.

"I did not tell Sir Humphry of this last piece of philosophy, not knowing how he might take it. Davy was much taken with Ravenna, and the PRIMITIVE Italianism of the people, who are unused to foreigners: but he only stayed a day.

"Send me Scott's novels and some news.

"P.S. I have begun and advanced into the second act of a tragedy on the subject of the Doge's conspiracy (i.e. the story of Marino Faliero); but my present feeling is so little encouraging on such matters, that I begin to think I have mined my talent out, and proceed in no great phantasy of finding a new vein.

"P.S. I sometimes think (if the Italians don't rise) of coming over to England in the autumn after the coronation, (at which I would not appear, on account of my family schism,) but as yet I can decide nothing. The place must be a great deal changed since I left it, now more than four years ago."

LETTER 372. TO MR. MURRAY.

"Ravenna, May 20. 1820.

"Murray, my dear, make my respects to Thomas Campbell, and tell him from me, with faith and friendship, three things that he must right in his poets: Firstly, he says Anstey's Bath Guide characters are taken from Smollett. 'Tis impossible:—the Guide was published in 1766, and Humphrey Clinker in 1771—dunque, 'tis Smollett who has taken from Anstey. Secondly, he does not know to whom Cowper alludes, when he says that there was one who 'built a church to God, and then blasphemed his name:' it was 'Deo erexit Voltaire' to whom that maniacal Calvinist and coddled poet alludes. Thirdly, he misquotes and spoils a passage from Shakspeare, 'to gild refined gold, to paint the lily,' &c.; for lily he puts rose, and bedevils in more words than one the whole quotation.

"Now, Tom is a fine fellow; but he should be correct; for the first is an injustice (to Anstey), the second an ignorance, and the third a blunder. Tell him all this, and let him take it in good part; for I might have rammed it into a review and rowed him—instead of which, I act like a Christian.

"Yours," &c.

LETTER 373. TO MR. MURRAY.

"Ravenna, May 20. 1820.

"First and foremost, you must forward my letter to Moore dated 2d January, which I said you might open, but desired you to forward. Now, you should really not forget these little things, because they do mischief among friends. You are an excellent man, a great man, and live among great men, but do pray recollect your absent friends and authors.

"In the first place, your packets; then a letter from Kinnaird, on the most urgent business; another from Moore, about a communication to Lady Byron of importance; a fourth from the mother of Allegra; and, fifthly, at Ravenna, the Countess G. is on the eve of being separated. But the Italian public are on her side, particularly the women,—and the men also, because they say that he had no business to take the business up now after a year of toleration. All her relations (who are numerous, high in rank, and powerful) are furious against him for his conduct. I am warned to be on my guard, as he is very capable of employing sicarii—this is Latin as well as Italian, so you can understand it; but I have arms, and don't mind them, thinking that I could pepper his ragamuffins, if they don't come unawares, and that, if they do, one may as well end that way as another; and it would besides serve you as an advertisement:—

"Man may escape from rope or gun, &c.
But he who takes woman, woman, woman, &c.

"Yours.
"P.S. I have looked over the press, but heaven knows how. Think what I have on hand and the post going out to-morrow. Do you remember the epitaph on Voltaire?

"'Ci-git l'enfant gâté,' &c.

The original is in Grimm and Diderot, &c. &c. &c."
LETTER 374. TO MR. MOORE.
"Ravenna, May 24. 1820.

"I wrote to you a few days ago. There is also a letter of January last for you at Murray's, which will explain to you why I am here. Murray ought to have forwarded it long ago. I enclose you an epistle from a countrywoman of yours at Paris, which has moved my entrails. You will have the goodness, perhaps, to enquire into the truth of her story, and I will help her as far as I can,— though not in the useless way she proposes. Her letter is evidently unstudied, and so natural, that the orthography is also in a state of nature.

"Here is a poor creature, ill and solitary, who thinks, as a last resource, of translating you or me into French! Was there ever such a notion? It seems to me the consummation of despair. Pray enquire, and let me know, and, if you could draw a bill on me here for a few hundred francs, at your banker's, I will duly honour it,—that is, if she is not an impostor. If not, let me know, that I may get something remitted by my banker Longhi, of Bologna, for I have no correspondence myself, at Paris: but tell her she must not translate;—if she does, it will be the height of ingratitude.

"I had a letter (not of the same kind, but in French and flattery) from a Madame Sophie Gail, of Paris, whom I take to be the spouse of a Gallo-Greek of that name. Who is she? and what is she? and how came she to take an interest in my poeshie or its author? If you know her, tell her, with my compliments, that, as I only read French, I have not answered her letter; but would have done so in Italian, if I had not thought it would look like an affectation. I have just been scolding my monkey for tearing the seal of her letter, and spoiling a mock book, in which I put rose leaves. I had a civet-cat the other day, too; but it ran away, after scratching my monkey's cheek, and I am in search of it still. It was the fiercest beast I ever saw, and like * * in the face and manner.

"I have a world of things to say; but, as they are not come to a dénouement, I don't care to begin their history till it is wound up. After you went, I had a fever, but got well again without bark. Sir Humphry Davy was here the other day, and liked Ravenna very much. He will tell you any thing you may wish to know about the place and your humble servitor.

"Your apprehensions (arising from Scott's) were unfounded. There are no damages in this country, but there will probably be a separation between them, as her family, which is a principal one, by its connections, are very much against him, for the whole of his conduct;—and he is old and obstinate, and she is young and a woman, determined to sacrifice every thing to her affections. I have given her the best advice, viz. to stay with him,—pointing out the state of a separated woman, (for the priests won't let lovers live openly together, unless the husband sanctions it,) and making the most exquisite moral reflections,—but to no purpose. She says, 'I will stay with him, if he will let you remain with me. It is hard that I should be the only woman in Romagna who is not to have her Amico; but, if not, I will not live with him; and as for the consequences, love, &c. &c. &c.'—you know how females reason on such occasions.

"He says he has let it go on till he can do so no longer. But he wants her to stay, and dismiss me; for he doesn't like to pay back her dowry and to make an alimony. Her relations are rather for the separation, as they detest him,—indeed, so does every body. The populace and the women are, as usual, all for those who are in the wrong, viz. the lady and her lover. I should have retreated, but honour, and an erysipelas which has attacked her, prevent me,—to say nothing of love, for I love her most entirely, though not enough to persuade her to sacrifice every thing to a frenzy. 'I see how it will end; she will be the sixteenth Mrs. Shuffleton.'

"My paper is finished, and so must this letter.

"Yours ever, B.

"P.S. I regret that you have not completed the Italian Fudges. Pray, how come you to be still in Paris? Murray has four or five things of mine in hand—the new Don Juan, which his back-shop synod don't admire;—a translation of the first Canto of Pulci's Morgante Maggiore, excellent;—short ditto from Dante, not so much approved; the Prophecy of Dante, very grand and worthy, &c. &c. &c.;—a furious prose answer to Blackwood's Observations on Don Juan, with a savage Defence of Pope—likely to make a row. The opinions above I quote from Murray and his Utican senate;—you will form your own, when you see the things.

"You will have no great chance of seeing me, for I begin to think I must finish in Italy. But, if you come my way, you shall have a tureen of macaroni. Pray tell me about yourself, and your intents.

"My trustees are going to lend Earl Blessington sixty thousand pounds (at six per cent.) on a Dublin mortgage. Only think of my becoming an Irish absentee!"

LETTER 375. TO MR. HOPPNER.

"Ravenna, May 25. 1820.

"A German named Ruppsecht has sent me, heaven knows why, several Deutsche Gazettes, of all which I understand neither word nor letter. I have sent you the enclosed to beg you to translate to me some remarks, which appear to be Goethe's upon Manfred—and if I may judge by two notes of admiration (generally put after something ridiculous by us) and the word 'hypocondrisch,' are any thing but favourable. I shall regret this, for I should have been proud of Goethe's good word; but I sha'n't alter my opinion of him, even though he should be savage.

"Will you excuse this trouble, and do me this favour?—Never mind—soften nothing—I am literary proof—having had good and evil said in most modern languages.

"Believe me," &c.

LETTER 376. TO MR. MOORE.

"Ravenna, June 1. 1820,

"I have received a Parisian letter from W.W., which I prefer answering through you, if that worthy be still at Paris, and, as he says, an occasional visiter of yours. In November last he wrote to me a well-meaning letter, stating, for some reasons of his own, his belief that a re-union might be effected between Lady B. and myself. To this I answered as usual; and he sent me a second letter, repeating his notions, which letter I have never answered, having had a thousand other things to think of. He now writes as if he believed that he had offended me by touching on the topic; and I wish you to assure him that I am not at all so,—but, on the contrary, obliged by his good nature. At the same time acquaint him the thing is impossible. You know this, as well as I,—and there let it end.

"I believe that I showed you his epistle in autumn last. He asks me if I have heard of my 'laureat' at Paris,—somebody who has written 'a most sanguinary Epître' against me; but whether in French, or Dutch, or on what score, I know not, and he don't say,—except that (for my satisfaction) he says it is the best thing in the fellow's volume. If there is any thing of the kind that I ought to know, you will doubtless tell me. I suppose it to be something of the usual sort;—he says, he don't remember the author's name.

"I wrote to you some ten days ago, and expect an answer at your leisure.

"The separation business still continues, and all the world are implicated, including priests and cardinals. The public opinion is furious against him, because he ought to have cut the matter short at first, and not waited twelve months to begin. He has been trying at evidence, but can get none sufficient; for what would make fifty divorces in England won't do here—there must be the most decided proofs.

"It is the first cause of the kind attempted in Ravenna for these two hundred years; for, though they often separate, they assign a different motive. You know that the continental incontinent are more delicate than the English, and don't like proclaiming their coronation in a court, even when nobody doubts it.

"All her relations are furious against him. The father has challenged him—a superfluous valour, for he don't fight, though suspected of two assassinations—one of the famous Monzoni of Forli. Warning was given me not to take such long rides in the Pine Forest without being on my guard; so I take my stiletto and a pair of pistols in my pocket during my daily rides.

"I won't stir from this place till the matter is settled one way or the other. She is as femininely firm as possible; and the opinion is so much against him, that the advocates decline to undertake his cause, because they say that he is either a fool or a rogue—fool, if he did not discover the liaison till now; and rogue, if he did know it, and waited, for some bad end, to divulge it. In short, there has been nothing like it since the days of Guido di Polenta's family, in these parts.

"If the man has me taken off, like Polonius 'say, he made a good end,'—for a melodrama. The principal security is, that he has not the courage to spend twenty scudi—the average price of a clean-handed bravo—otherwise there is no want of opportunity, for I ride about the woods every evening, with one servant, and sometimes an acquaintance, who latterly looks a little queer in solitary bits of bushes.

"Good bye.—Write to yours ever," &c.
LETTER 377. TO MR. MURRAY.
"Ravenna, June 7. 1820.
"Enclosed is something which will interest you, to wit, the opinion of the greatest man of Germany—perhaps of Europe—upon one of the great men of your advertisements, (all 'famous hands,' as Jacob Tonson used to say of his ragamuffins,)—in short, a critique of Goethe's upon Manfred. There is the original, an English translation, and an Italian one; keep them all in your archives,—for the opinions of such a man as Goethe, whether favourable or not, are always interesting—and this is more so, as favourable. His Faust I never read, for I don't know German; but Matthew Monk Lewis, in 1816, at Coligny, translated most of it to me vivâ voce, and I was naturally much struck with it; but it was the Steinbach and the Jungfrau, and something else, much more than Faustus, that made me write Manfred. The first scene, however, and that of Faustus are very similar. Acknowledge this letter.

"Yours ever.

"P.S. I have received Ivanhoe;—good. Pray send me some tooth-powder and tincture of myrrh, by Waite, &c. Ricciardetto should have been translated literally, or not at all. As to puffing Whistlecraft, it won't do. I'll tell you why some day or other. Cornwall's a poet, but spoilt by the detestable schools of the day. Mrs. Hemans is a poet also, but too stiltified and apostrophic,—and quite wrong. Men died calmly before the Christian era, and since, without Christianity: witness the Romans, and, lately, Thistlewood, Sandt, and Lovel—men who ought to have been weighed down with their crimes, even had they believed. A deathbed is a matter of nerves and constitution, and not of religion. Voltaire was frightened, Frederick of Prussia not: Christians the same, according to their strength rather than their creed. What does H * * H * * mean by his stanza? which is octave got drunk or gone mad. He ought to have his ears boxed with Thor's hammer for rhyming so fantastically."

The following is the article from Goethe's "Kunst und Alterthum," enclosed in this letter. The grave confidence with which the venerable critic traces the fancies of his brother poet to real persons and events, making no difficulty even of a double murder at Florence to furnish grounds for his theory, affords an amusing instance of the disposition so prevalent throughout Europe, to picture Byron as a man of marvels and mysteries, as well in his life as his poetry. To these exaggerated, or wholly false notions of him, the numerous fictions palmed upon the world of his romantic tours and wonderful adventures in places he never saw, and with persons that never existed, have, no doubt, considerably contributed; and the consequence is, so utterly out of truth and nature are the representations of his life and character long current upon the Continent, that it may be questioned whether the real "flesh and blood" hero of these pages,—the social, practical-minded, and, with all his faults and eccentricities, English Lord Byron,—may not, to the over-exalted imaginations of most of his foreign admirers, appear but an ordinary, unromantic, and prosaic personage.

"GOETHE ON MANFRED.

[1820.]

"Byron's tragedy, Manfred, was to me a wonderful phenomenon, and one that closely touched me. This singular intellectual poet has taken my Faustus to himself, and extracted from it the strongest nourishment for his hypochondriac humour. He has made use of the impelling principles in his own way, for his own purposes, so that no one of them remains the same; and it is particularly on this account that I cannot enough admire his genius. The whole is in this way so completely formed anew, that it would be an interesting task for the critic to point out not only the alterations he has made, but their degree of resemblance with, or dissimilarity to, the original: in the course of which I cannot deny that the gloomy heat of an unbounded and exuberant despair becomes at last oppressive to us. Yet is the dissatisfaction we feel always connected with esteem and admiration.

"We find thus in this tragedy the quintessence of the most astonishing talent born to be its own tormentor. The character of Lord Byron's life and poetry hardly permits a just and equitable appreciation. He has often enough confessed what it is that torments him. He has repeatedly pourtrayed it; and scarcely any one feels compassion for this intolerable suffering, over which he is ever laboriously ruminating. There are, properly speaking, two females whose phantoms for ever haunt him, and which, in this piece also, perform principal parts—one under the name of Astarte, the other without form or actual presence, and merely a voice. Of the horrid occurrence which took place with the former, the following is related:—When a bold and enterprising young man, he won the affections of a Florentine lady. Her husband discovered the amour, and murdered his wife; but the murderer was the same night found dead in the street, and there was no one on whom any suspicion could be attached. Lord Byron removed from Florence, and these spirits haunted him all his life after.

"This romantic incident is rendered highly probable by innumerable allusions to it in his poems. As, for instance, when turning his sad contemplations inwards, he applies to himself the fatal history of the king of Sparta. It is as follows:—Pausanias, a Lacedemonian general, acquires glory by the important victory at Platæa, but afterwards forfeits the confidence of his countrymen through his arrogance, obstinacy, and secret intrigues with the enemies of his country. This man draws upon himself the heavy guilt of innocent blood, which attends him to his end; for, while commanding the fleet of the allied Greeks, in the Black Sea, he is inflamed with a violent passion for a Byzantine maiden. After long resistance, he at length obtains her from her parents, and she is to be delivered up to him at night. She modestly desires the servant to put out the lamp, and, while groping her way in the dark, she overturns it. Pausanias is awakened from his sleep—apprehensive of an attack from murderers, he seizes his sword, and destroys his mistress. The horrid sight never leaves him. Her shade pursues him unceasingly, and he implores for aid in vain from the gods and the exorcising priests.

"That poet must have a lacerated heart who selects such a scene from antiquity, appropriates it to himself, and burdens his tragic image with it. The following soliloquy, which is overladen with gloom and a weariness of life, is, by this remark, rendered intelligible. We recommend it as an exercise to all friends of declamation. Hamlet's soliloquy appears improved upon here."

LETTER 378. TO MR. MOORE.

"Ravenna, June 9. 1820.

"Galignani has just sent me the Paris edition of your works (which I wrote to order), and I am glad to see my old friends with a French face. I have been skimming and dipping, in and over them, like a swallow, and as pleased as one. It is the first time that I had seen the Melodies without music; and, I don't know how, but I can't read in a music-book—the crotchets confound the words in my head, though I recollect them perfectly when sung. Music assists my memory through the ear, not through the eye; I mean, that her quavers perplex me upon paper, but they are a help when heard. And thus I was glad to see the words without their borrowed robes;—to my mind they look none the worse for their nudity.

"The biographer has made a botch of your life—calling your father 'a venerable old gentleman,' and prattling of 'Addison,' and 'dowager countesses.' If that damned fellow was to write my life, I would certainly take his. And then, at the Dublin dinner, you have 'made a speech' (do you recollect, at Douglas K.'s, 'Sir, he made me a speech?') too complimentary to the 'living poets,' and somewhat redolent of universal praise. I am but too well off in it, but * * *.

"You have not sent me any poetical or personal news of yourself. Why don't you complete an Italian Tour of the Fudges? I have just been turning over Little, which I knew by heart in 1803, being then in my fifteenth summer. Heigho! I believe all the mischief I have ever done, or sung, has been owing to that confounded book of yours.

"In my last I told you of a cargo of 'Poeshie,' which I had sent to M. at his own impatient desire;—and, now he has got it, he don't like it, and demurs. Perhaps he is right. I have no great opinion of any of my last shipment, except a translation from Pulci, which is word for word, and verse for verse.

"I am in the third Act of a Tragedy; but whether it will be finished or not, I know not: I have, at this present, too many passions of my own on hand to do justice to those of the dead. Besides the vexations mentioned in my last, I have incurred a quarrel with the Pope's carabiniers, or gens d'armerie, who have petitioned the Cardinal against my liveries, as resembling too nearly their own lousy uniform. They particularly object to the epaulettes, which all the world with us have on upon gala days. My liveries are of the colours conforming to my arms, and have been the family hue since the year 1066.

"I have sent a tranchant reply, as you may suppose; and have given to understand that, if any soldados of that respectable corps insult my servants, I will do likewise by their gallant commanders; and I have directed my ragamuffins, six in number, who are tolerably savage, to defend themselves, in case of aggression; and, on holidays and gaudy days, I shall arm the whole set, including myself, in case of accidents or treachery. I used to play pretty well at the broad-sword, once upon a time, at Angelo's; but I should like the pistol, our national buccaneer weapon, better, though I am out of practice at present. However, I can 'wink and hold out mine iron.' It makes me think (the whole thing does) of Romeo and Juliet—'now, Gregory, remember thy swashing blow.'

"All these feuds, however, with the Cavalier for his wife, and the troopers for my liveries, are very tiresome to a quiet man, who does his best to please all the world, and longs for fellowship and good will. Pray write. I am yours," &c.

LETTER 379. TO MR. MOORE.

"Ravenna, July 13. 1820.

"To remove or increase your Irish anxiety about my being 'in a wisp,' I answer your letter forth-with; premising that, as I am a 'Will of the wisp,' I may chance to flit out of it. But, first, a word on the Memoir;—I have no objection, nay, I would rather that one correct copy was taken and deposited in honourable hands, in case of accidents happening to the original; for you know that I have none, and have never even re-read, nor, indeed, read at all what is there written; I only know that I wrote it with the fullest intention to be 'faithful and true' in my narrative, but not impartial—no, by the Lord! I can't pretend to be that, while I feel. But I wish to give every body concerned the opportunity to contradict or correct me.

"I have no objection to any proper person seeing what is there written,—seeing it was written, like every thing else, for the purpose of being read, however much many writings may fail in arriving at that object.

"With regard to 'the wisp,' the Pope has pronounced their separation. The decree came yesterday from Babylon,—it was she and her friends who demanded it, on the grounds of her husband's (the noble Count Cavalier's) extraordinary usage. He opposed it with all his might because of the alimony, which has been assigned, with all her goods, chattels, carriage, &c. to be restored by him. In Italy they can't divorce. He insisted on her giving me up, and he would forgive every thing,— * *

"The friends and relatives, who are numerous and powerful, reply to him—'You, yourself, are either fool or knave,—fool, if you did not see the consequences of the approximation of these two young persons,—knave, if you connive at it. Take your choice,—but don't break out (after twelve months of the closest intimacy, under your own eyes and positive sanction) with a scandal, which can only make you ridiculous and her unhappy.'

"He swore that he thought our intercourse was purely amicable, and that I was more partial to him than to her, till melancholy testimony proved the contrary. To this they answer, that 'Will of this wisp' was not an unknown person, and that 'clamosa Fama' had not proclaimed the purity of my morals;—that her brother, a year ago, wrote from Rome to warn him that his wife would infallibly be led astray by this ignis fatuus, unless he took proper measures, all of which he neglected to take, &c. &c.

"Now he says that he encouraged my return to Ravenna, to see 'in quanti piedi di acqua siamo,' and he has found enough to drown him in. In short,

>"'Ce ne fut pas le tout; sa femme se plaignit—
>Procès—La parenté se joint en excuse et dit
>Que du Docteur venoit tout le mauvais ménage;
>Que cet homme étoit fou, que sa femme étoit sage.
>On fit casser le mariage.'

It is but to let the women alone, in the way of conflict, for they are sure to win against the field. She returns to her father's house, and I can only see her under great restrictions—such is the custom of the country. The relations behave very well:—I offered any settlement, but they refused to accept it, and swear she shan't live with G. (as he has tried to prove her faithless), but that he shall maintain her; and, in fact, a judgment to this effect came yesterday. I am, of course, in an awkward situation enough.

"I have heard no more of the carabiniers who protested against my liveries. They are not popular, those same soldiers, and, in a small row, the other night, one was slain, another wounded, and divers put to flight, by some of the Romagnuole youth, who are dexterous, and somewhat liberal of the knife. The perpetrators are not discovered, but I hope and believe that none of my ragamuffins were in it, though they are somewhat savage, and secretly armed, like most of the inhabitants. It is their way, and saves sometimes a good deal of litigation.

"There is a revolution at Naples. If so, it will probably leave a card at Ravenna in its way to Lombardy.

"Your publishers seem to have used you like mine. M. has shuffled, and almost insinuated that my last productions are dull. Dull, sir!—damme, dull! I believe he is right. He begs for the completion of my tragedy on Marino Faliero, none of which is yet gone to England. The fifth act is nearly completed, but it is dreadfully long—40 sheets of long paper of 4 pages each—about 150 when printed; but 'so full of pastime and prodigality' that I think it will do.

"Pray send and publish your Pome upon me; and don't be afraid of praising me too highly. I shall pocket my blushes.

"'Not actionable!'—Chantre d'enfer!—by * * that's 'a speech,' and I won't put up with it. A pretty title to give a man for doubting if there be any such place!

"So my Gail is gone—and Miss Mahony won't take Money. I am very glad of it—I like to be generous free of expense. But beg her not to translate me.

"Oh, pray tell Galignani that I shall send him a screed of doctrine if he don't be more punctual. Somebody regularly detains two, and sometimes four, of his Messengers by the way. Do, pray, entreat him to be more precise. News are worth money in this remote kingdom of the Ostrogoths.

"Pray, reply. I should like much to share some of your Champagne and La Fitte, but I am too Italian for Paris in general. Make Murray send my letter to you—it is full of epigrams.

"Yours," &c.

In the separation that had now taken place between Count Guiccioli and his wife, it was one of the conditions that the lady should, in future, reside under the paternal roof:—in consequence of which, Madame Guiccioli, on the 16th of July, left Ravenna and retired to a villa belonging to Count Gamba, about fifteen miles distant from that city. Here Lord Byron occasionally visited her—about once or twice, perhaps, in a month—passing the rest of his time in perfect solitude. To a mind like his, whose world was within itself, such a mode of life could have been neither new nor unwelcome; but to the woman, young and admired, whose acquaintance with the world and its pleasures had but just begun, this change was, it must be confessed, most sudden and trying. Count Guiccioli was rich, and, as a young wife, she had gained absolute power over him. She was proud, and her station placed her among the highest in Ravenna. They had talked of travelling to Naples, Florence, Paris,—and every luxury, in short, that wealth could command was at her disposal.

All this she now voluntarily and determinedly sacrificed for Byron. Her splendid home abandoned—her relations all openly at war with her—her kind father but tolerating, from fondness, what he could not approve—she was now, upon a pittance of 200l. a year, living apart from the world, her sole occupation the task of educating herself for her illustrious friend, and her sole reward the few brief glimpses of him which their now restricted intercourse allowed. Of the man who could inspire and keep alive so devoted a feeling, it may be pronounced with confidence that he could not have been such as, in the freaks of his own wayward humour, he represented himself; while, on the lady's side, the whole history of her attachment goes to prove how completely an Italian woman, whether by nature or from her social position, is led to invert the usual course of such frailties among ourselves, and, weak in resisting the first impulses of passion, to reserve the whole strength of her character for a display of constancy and devotedness afterwards.

LETTER 380. TO MR. MURRAY.

"Ravenna, July 17. 1820.

"I have received some books, and Quarterlies, and Edinburghs, for all which I am grateful: they contain all I know of England, except by Galignani's newspaper.

"The tragedy is completed, but now comes the task of copy and correction. It is very long, (42 sheets of long paper, of four pages each,) and I believe must make more than 140 or 150 pages, besides many historical extracts as notes, which I mean to append. History is closely followed. Dr. Moore's account is in some respects false, and in all foolish and flippant. None of the chronicles (and I have consulted Sanuto, Sandi, Navagero, and an anonymous Siege of Zara, besides the histories of Laugier, Daru, Sismondi, &c.) state, or even hint, that he begged his life; they merely say that he did not deny the conspiracy. He was one of their great men,— commanded at the siege of Zara,—beat 80,000 Hungarians, killing 8000, and at the same time kept the town he was besieging in order,—took Capo d'Istria,—was ambassador at Genoa, Rome, and finally Doge, where he fell for treason, in attempting to alter the government, by what Sanuto calls a judgment on him for, many years before (when Podesta and Captain of Treviso), having knocked down a bishop, who was sluggish in carrying the host at a procession. He 'saddles him,' as Thwackum did Square, 'with a judgment;' but he does not mention whether he had been punished at the time for what would appear very strange, even now, and must have been still more so in an age of papal power and glory. Sanuto says, that Heaven took away his senses for this buffet, and induced him to conspire. 'Però fù permesso che il Faliero perdette l'intelletto,' &c.

"I do not know what your parlour-boarders will think of the Drama I have founded upon this extraordinary event. The only similar one in history is the story of Agis, King of Sparta, a prince with the commons against the aristocracy, and losing his life therefor. But it shall be sent when copied.

"I should be glad to know why your Quartering Reviewers, at the close of 'The Fall of Jerusalem,' accuse me of Manicheism? a compliment to which the sweetener of 'one of the mightiest spirits' by no means reconciles me. The poem they review is very noble; but could they not do justice to the writer without converting him into my religious antidote? I am not a Manichean, nor an Any-chean. I should like to know what harm my 'poeshies' have done? I can't tell what people mean by making me a hobgoblin."

LETTER 381. TO MR. MURRAY.

"Ravenna, August 31. 1820.

"I have 'put my soul' into the tragedy (as you if it); but you know that there are d——d souls as well as tragedies. Recollect that it is not a political play, though it may look like it: it is strictly historical. Read the history and judge.

"Ada's picture is her mother's. I am glad of it—the mother made a good daughter. Send me Gifford's opinion, and never mind the Archbishop. I can neither send you away, nor give you a hundred pistoles, nor a better taste: I send you a tragedy, and you ask for 'facetious epistles;' a little like your predecessor, who advised Dr. Prideaux to 'put some more humour into his Life of Mahomet.'

"Bankes is a wonderful fellow. There is hardly one of my school or college contemporaries that has not turned out more or less celebrated. Peel, Palmerstone, Bankes, Hobhouse, Tavistock, Bob Mills, Douglas Kinnaird, &c. &c. have all talked and been talked about.

"We are here going to fight a little next month, if the Huns don't cross the Po, and probably if they do. I can't say more now. If any thing happens, you have matter for a posthumous work, in MS.; so pray be civil. Depend upon it, there will be savage work, if once they begin here. The French courage proceeds from vanity, the German from phlegm, the Turkish from fanaticism and opium, the Spanish from pride, the English from coolness, the Dutch from obstinacy, the Russian from insensibility, but the Italian from anger; so you'll see that they will spare nothing."

LETTER 382. TO MR. MOORE.

"Ravenna, August 31, 1820.

"D——n your 'mezzo cammin'—you should say 'the prime of life,' a much more consolatory phrase. Besides, it is not correct. I was born in 1788, and consequently am but thirty-two. You are mistaken on another point. The 'Sequin Box' never came into requisition, nor is it likely to do so. It were better that it had, for then a man is not bound, you know. As to reform, I did reform—what would you have? 'Rebellion lay in his way, and he found it.' I verily believe that nor you, nor any man of poetical temperament, can avoid a strong passion of some kind. It is the poetry of life. What should I have known or written, had I been a quiet, mercantile politician, or a lord in waiting? A man must travel, and turmoil, or there is no existence. Besides, I only meant to be a Cavalier Servente, and had no idea it would turn out a romance, in the Anglo fashion.

"However, I suspect I know a thing or two of Italy—more than Lady Morgan has picked up in her posting. What do Englishmen know of Italians beyond their museums and saloons—and some hack * *, en passant? Now, I have lived in the heart of their houses, in parts of Italy freshest and least influenced by strangers,—have seen and become (pars magna fui) a portion of their hopes, and fears, and passions, and am almost inoculated into a family. This is to see men and things as they are.

"You say that I called you 'quiet'—I don't recollect any thing of the sort. On the contrary, you are always in scrapes.

"What think you of the Queen? I hear Mr. Hoby says, 'that it makes him weep to see her, she reminds him so much of Jane Shore.'

> "Mr. Hoby the bootmaker's heart is quite sore,
> For seeing the Queen makes him think of Jane Shore;
> And, in fact, * *

Pray excuse this ribaldry. What is your poem about? Write and tell me all about it and you.
"Yours, &c.

"P.S. Did you write the lively quiz on Peter Bell? It has wit enough to be yours, and almost too much to be any body else's now going. It was in Galignani the other day or week."

LETTER 383. TO MR. MURRAY.

"Ravenna, September 7. 1820.

"In correcting the proofs you must refer to the manuscript, because there are in it various readings. Pray attend to this, and choose what Gifford thinks best, Let me hear what he thinks of the whole.

"You speak of Lady * *'s illness; she is not of those who die:—the amiable only do; and those whose death would do good live. Whenever she is pleased to return, it may be presumed she will take her 'divining rod' along with her: it may be of use to her at home, as well as to the 'rich man' of the Evangelists.

"Pray do not let the papers paragraph me back to England. They may say what they please, any loathsome abuse but that. Contradict it.

"My last letters will have taught you to expect an explosion here: it was primed and loaded, but they hesitated to fire the train. One of the cities shirked from the league. I cannot write more at large for a thousand reasons. Our 'puir hill folk' offered to strike, and raise the first banner, but Bologna paused; and now 'tis autumn, and the season half over. 'O Jerusalem! Jerusalem!' The Huns are on the Po; but if once they pass it on their way to Naples, all Italy will be behind them. The dogs—the wolves—may they perish like the host of Sennacherib! If you want to publish the Prophecy of Dante, you never will have a better time."

LETTER 384. TO MR. MURRAY.

"Ravenna, Sept. 11. 1820.

"Here is another historical note for you. I want to be as near truth as the drama can be.

"Last post I sent you a note fierce as Faliero himself, in answer to a trashy tourist, who pretends that he could have been introduced to me. Let me have a proof of it, that I may cut its lava into some shape.

"What Gifford says is very consolatory (of the first act). English, sterling genuine English, is a desideratum amongst you, and I am glad that I have got so much left; though Heaven knows how I retain it: I hear none but from my valet, and his is Nottinghamshire: and I see none but in your new publications, and theirs is no language at all, but jargon. Even your * * * * is terribly stilted and affected, with 'very, very' so soft and pamby.

"Oh! if ever I do come amongst you again, I will give you such a 'Baviad and Mæviad!' not as good as the old, but even better merited. There never was such a set as your ragamuffins (I mean not yours only, but every body's). What with the Cockneys, and the Lakers, and the followers of Scott, and Moore, and Byron, you are in the very uttermost decline and degradation of literature. I can't think of it without all the remorse of a murderer. I wish that Johnson were alive again to crush them!"

LETTER 385. TO MR. MURRAY.

"Ravenna, Sept. 14. 1820.

"What! not a line? Well, have it your own way.

"I wish you would inform Perry, that his stupid paragraph is the cause of all my newspapers being stopped in Paris. The fools believe me in your infernal country, and have not sent on their gazettes, so that I know nothing of your beastly trial of the Queen.

"I cannot avail myself of Mr. Gifford's remarks, because I have received none, except on the first act. Yours, &c.

"P.S. Do, pray, beg the editors of papers to say any thing blackguard they please; but not to put me amongst their arrivals. They do me more mischief by such nonsense than all their abuse can do."

LETTER 386. TO MR. MURRAY.

"Ravenna, Sept. 21. 1820.

"So you are at your old tricks again. This is the second packet I have received unaccompanied by a single line of good, bad, or indifferent. It is strange that you have never forwarded any further observations of Gifford's. How am I to alter or amend, if I hear no further? or does this silence mean that it is well enough as it is, or too bad to be repaired? If the last, why do you not say so at once, instead of playing pretty, while you know that soon or late you must out with the truth.

"Yours, &c.

"P.S. My sister tells me that you sent to her to enquire where I was, believing in my arrival, driving a curricle, &c. &c. into Palace-yard. Do you think me a coxcomb or a madman, to be capable of such an exhibition? My sister knew me better, and told you, that could not be me. You might as well have thought me entering on 'a pale horse,' like Death in the Revelations."

LETTER 387. TO MR. MURRAY.

"Ravenna, Sept. '23. 1820.

"Get from Mr. Hobhouse, and send me a proof (with the Latin) of my Hints from Horace; it has now the nonum prematur in annum complete for its production, being written at Athens in 1811. I have a notion that, with some omissions of names and passages, it will do; and I could put my late observations for Pope amongst the notes, with the date of 1820, and so on. As far as versification goes, it is good; and, on looking back to what I wrote about that period, I am astonished to see how little I have trained on. I wrote better then than now; but that comes of my having fallen into the atrocious bad taste of the times. If I can trim it for present publication, what with the other things you have of mine, you will have a volume or two of variety at least, for there will be all measures, styles, and topics, whether good or no. I am anxious to hear what Gifford thinks of the tragedy: pray let me know. I really do not know what to think myself.

"If the Germans pass the Po, they will be treated to a mass out of the Cardinal de Retz's Breviary. * *'s a fool, and could not understand this: Frere will. It is as pretty a conceit as you would wish to see on a summer's day.

"Nobody here believes a word of the evidence against the Queen. The very mob cry shame against their countrymen, and say, that for half the money spent upon the trial, any testimony whatever may be brought out of Italy. This you may rely upon as fact. I told you as much before. As to what travellers report, what are travellers? Now I have lived among the Italians—not Florenced, and Romed, and galleried, and conversationed it for a few months, and then home again; but been of their families, and friendships, and feuds, and loves, and councils, and correspondence, in a part of Italy least known to foreigners,—and have been amongst them of all classes, from the Conte to the Contadine; and you may be sure of what I say to you.

"Yours," &c.

LETTER 388. TO MR. MURRAY.

"Ravenna, Sept. 28. 1820.

"I thought that I had told you long ago, that it never was intended nor written with any view to the stage. I have said so in the preface too. It is too long and too regular for your stage, the persons too few, and the unity too much observed. It is more like a play of Alfieri's than of your stage (I say this humbly in speaking of that great man); but there is poetry, and it is equal to Manfred, though I know not what esteem is held of Manfred.

"I have now been nearly as long out of England as I was there during the time I saw you frequently. I came home July 14th, 1811, and left again April 25th, 1816: so that Sept. 28th, 1820, brings me within a very few months of the same duration of time of my stay and my absence. In course, I can know nothing of the public taste and feelings, but from what I glean from letters, &c. Both seem to be as bad as possible.

"I thought Anastasius excellent: did I not say so? Matthews's Diary most excellent; it, and Forsyth, and parts of Hobhouse, are all we have of truth or sense upon Italy. The Letter to Julia very good indeed, I do not despise * * * * * *; but if she knit blue stockings instead of wearing them, it would be better. You are taken in by that false stilted trashy style, which is a mixture of all the styles of the day, which are all bombastic (I don't except my own—no one has done more through negligence to corrupt the language); but it is neither English nor poetry. Time will show.

"I am sorry Gifford has made no further remarks beyond the first Act: does he think all the English equally sterling as he thought the first? You did right to send the proofs: I was a fool; but I do really detest the sight of proofs: it is an absurdity; but comes from laziness.

"You can steal the two Juans into the world quietly, tagged to the others. The play as you will—the Dante too; but the Pulci I am proud of: it is superb; you have no such translation. It is the best thing I ever did in my life. I wrote the play from beginning to end, and not a single scene without interruption, and being obliged to break off in the middle; for I had my hands full, and my head, too, just then; so it can be no great shakes—I mean the play; and the head too, if you like.

"P.S. Politics here still savage and uncertain. However, we are all in our 'bandaliers,' to join the 'Highlanders if they cross the Forth,' i.e. to crush the Austrians if they cross the Po. The rascals!—and that dog Liverpool, to say their subjects are happy! If ever I come back, I'll work some of these ministers.

"Sept. 29.

"I opened my letter to say, that on reading more of the four volumes on Italy, where the author says 'declined an introduction,' I perceive (horresco referens) it is written by a WOMAN!!! In that case you must suppress my note and answer, and all I have said about the book and the writer. I never dreamed of it until now, in my extreme wrath at that precious note. I can only say that I am sorry that a lady should say any thing of the kind. What I would have said to one of the other sex you know already. Her book too (as a she book) is not a bad one; but she evidently don't know the Italians, or rather don't like them, and forgets the causes of their misery and profligacy (Matthews and Forsyth are your men for truth and tact), and has gone over Italy in company—always a bad plan: you must be alone with people to know them well. Ask her, who was the 'descendant of Lady M.W. Montague,' and by whom? by Algarotti?

"I suspect that, in Marino Faliero, you and yours won't like the politics, which are perilous to you in these times; but recollect that it is not a political play, and that I was obliged to put into the mouths of the characters the sentiments upon which they acted. I hate all things written like Pizarro, to represent France, England, and so forth. All I have done is meant to be purely Venetian, even to the very prophecy of its present state.

"Your Angles in general know little of the Italians, who detest them for their numbers and their GENOA treachery. Besides, the English travellers have not been composed of the best company. How could they?—out of 100,000, how many gentlemen were there, or honest men?

"Mitchell's Aristophanes is excellent. Send me the rest of it.

"These fools will force me to write a book about Italy myself, to give them 'the loud lie.' They prate about assassination; what is it but the origin of duelling—and 'a wild justice,' as Lord Bacon calls it? It is the fount of the modern point of honour in what the laws can't or won't reach. Every man is liable to it more or less, according to circumstances or place. For instance, I am living here exposed to it daily, for I have happened to make a powerful and unprincipled man my enemy;—and I never sleep the worse for it, or ride in less solitary places, because precaution is useless, and one thinks of it as of a disease which may or may not strike. It is true that there are those here, who, if he did, would 'live to think on't;' but that would not awake my bones: I should be sorry if it would, were they once at rest."

LETTER 389. TO MR. MURRAY.

"Ravenna, 8bre 6°, 1820.

"You will have now received all the Acts, corrected, of the Marino Faliero. What you say of the 'bet of 100 guineas' made by some one who says that he saw me last week, reminds me of what happened in 1810: you can easily ascertain the fact, and it is an odd one.

"In the latter end of 1811, I met one evening at the Alfred my old school and form fellow (for we were within two of each other, he the higher, though both very near the top of our remove,) Peel, the Irish secretary. He told me that, in 1810, he met me, as he thought, in St. James's Street, but we passed without speaking. He mentioned this, and it was denied as impossible, I being then in Turkey. A day or two afterward, he pointed out to his brother a person on the opposite side of the way:—'There,' said he, 'is the man whom I took for Byron.' His brother instantly answered, 'Why, it is Byron, and no one else.' But this is not all:—I was seen by somebody to write down my name amongst the enquirers after the King's health, then attacked by insanity. Now, at this very period, as nearly as I could make out, I was ill of a strong fever at Patras, caught in the marshes near Olympia, from the malaria. If I had died there, this would have been a new ghost story for you. You can easily make out the accuracy of this from Peel himself, who told it in detail. I suppose you will be of the opinion of Lucretius, who (denies the immortality of the soul, but) asserts that from the 'flying off of the surfaces of bodies, these surfaces or cases, like the coats of an onion, are sometimes seen entire when they are separated from it, so that the shapes and shadows of both the dead and living are frequently beheld.'

"But if they are, are their coats and waistcoats also seen? I do not disbelieve that we may be two by some unconscious process, to a certain sign, but which of these two I happen at present to be, I leave you to decide. I only hope that t'other me behaves like a gemman.

"I wish you would get Peel asked how far I am accurate in my recollection of what he told me; for I don't like to say such things without authority.

"I am not sure that I was not spoken with; but this also you can ascertain. I have written to you such letters that I stop.

"Yours, &c.

"P.S. Last year (in June, 1819), I met at Count Mosti's, at Ferrara, an Italian who asked me 'if I knew Lord Byron?' I told him no (no one knows himself, you know). 'Then,' says he, 'I do; I met him at Naples the other day.' I pulled out my card and asked him if that was the way he spelt his name: he answered, yes. I suspect that it was a blackguard navy surgeon, who attended a young travelling madam about, and passed himself for a lord at the post-houses. He was a vulgar dog— quite of the cock-pit order—and a precious representative I must have had of him, if it was even so; but I don't know. He passed himself off as a gentleman, and squired about a Countess * * (of this place), then at Venice, an ugly battered woman, of bad morals even for Italy."

LETTER 390. TO MR. MURRAY.

"Ravenna, 8bre 8°, 1820.

"Foscolo's letter is exactly the thing wanted; firstly, because he is a man of genius; and, next, because he is an Italian, and therefore the best judge of Italics. Besides,

"He's more an antique Roman than a Dane;

that is, he is more of the ancient Greek than of the modern Italian. Though 'somewhat,' as Dugald Dalgetty says, 'too wild and salvage' (like 'Ronald of the Mist'), 'tis a wonderful man, and my friends Hobhouse and Rose both swear by him; and they are good judges of men and of Italian humanity.

"Here are in all two worthy voices gain'd:

Gifford says it is good 'sterling genuine English,' and Foscolo says that the characters are right Venetian. Shakspeare and Otway had a million of advantages over me, besides the incalculable one of being dead from one to two centuries, and having been both born blackguards (which ARE such attractions to the gentle living reader); let me then preserve the only one which I could possibly have—that of having been at Venice, and entered more into the local spirit of it. I claim no more.

"I know what Foscolo means about Calendaro's spitting at Bertram; that's national—the objection, I mean. The Italians and French, with those 'flags of abomination,' their pocket handkerchiefs, spit there, and here, and every where else—in your face almost, and therefore object to it on the stage as too familiar. But we who spit nowhere—but in a man's face when we grow savage—are not likely to feel this. Remember Massinger, and Kean's Sir Giles Overreach—

"Lord! thus I spit at thee and at thy counsel!

Besides, Calendaro does not spit in Bertram's face; he spits at him, as I have seen the Mussulmans do upon the ground when they are in a rage. Again, he does not in fact despise Bertram, though he affects it—as we all do, when angry with one we think our inferior. He is angry at not being allowed to die in his own way (although not afraid of death); and recollect that he suspected and hated Bertram from the first. Israel Bertuccio, on the other hand, is a cooler and more concentrated fellow: he acts upon principle and impulse; Calendaro upon impulse and example.

"So there's argument for you.

"The Doge repeats;—true, but it is from engrossing passion, and because he sees different persons, and is always obliged to recur to the cause uppermost in his mind. His speeches are long:—true, but I wrote for the closet, and on the French and Italian model rather than yours, which I think not very highly of, for all your old dramatists, who are long enough too, God knows:—look into any of them.

"I return you Foscolo's letter, because it alludes also to his private affairs. I am sorry to see such a man in straits, because I know what they are, or what they were. I never met but three men who would have held out a finger to me: one was yourself, the other William Bankes, and the other a nobleman long ago dead: but of these the first was the only one who offered it while I really wanted it; the second from good will—but I was not in need of Bankes's aid, and would not have accepted it if I had (though I love and esteem him); and the third —— ——.

"So you see that I have seen some strange things in my time. As for your own offer, it was in 1815, when I was in actual uncertainty of five pounds. I rejected it; but I have not forgotten it, although you probably have.

"P.S. Foscolo's Ricciardo was lent, with the leaves uncut, to some Italians, now in villeggiatura, so that I have had no opportunity of hearing their decision, or of reading it. They seized on it as Foscolo's, and on account of the beauty of the paper and printing, directly. If I find it takes, I will reprint it here. The Italians think as highly of Foscolo as they can of any man, divided and miserable as they are, and with neither leisure at present to read, nor head nor heart to judge of any thing but extracts from French newspapers and the Lugano Gazette.

"We are all looking at one another, like wolves on their prey in pursuit, only waiting for the first falling on to do unutterable things. They are a great world in chaos, or angels in hell, which you please; but out of chaos came Paradise, and out of hell—I don't know what; but the devil went in there, and he was a fine fellow once, you know.

"You need never favour me with any periodical publication, except the Edinburgh Quarterly, and an occasional Blackwood; or now and then a Monthly Review; for the rest I do not feel curiosity enough to look beyond their covers.

"To be sure I took in the British finely. He fell precisely into the glaring trap laid for him. It was inconceivable how he could be so absurd as to imagine us serious with him.

"Recollect, that if you put my name to 'Don Juan' in these canting days, any lawyer might oppose my guardian right of my daughter in Chancery, on the plea of its containing the parody;—such are the perils of a foolish jest. I was not aware of this at the time, but you will find it correct, I believe; and you may be sure that the Noels would not let it slip. Now I prefer my child to a poem at any time, and so should you, as having half a dozen.

"Let me know your notions.

"If you turn over the earlier pages of the Huntingdon peerage story, you will see how common a name Ada was in the early Plantagenet days. I found it in my own pedigree in the reign of John and Henry, and gave it to my daughter. It was also the name of Charlemagne's sister. It is in an early chapter of Genesis, as the name of the wife of Lamech; and I suppose Ada is the feminine of Adam. It is short, ancient, vocalic, and had been in my family; for which reason I gave it to my daughter."

LETTER 391. TO MR. MURRAY.

"Ravenna, 8bre 12°, 1820.

"By land and sea carriage a considerable quantity of books have arrived; and I am obliged and grateful: but 'medio de fonte leporum, surgit amari aliquid,' &c. &c.; which, being interpreted, means,

> "I'm thankful for your books, dear Murray;
> But why not send Scott's Monastery?

the only book in four living volumes I would give a baioccolo to see—'bating the rest of the same author, and an occasional Edinburgh and Quarterly, as brief chroniclers of the times. Instead of this, here are Johnny Keats's * * poetry, and three novels by God knows whom, except that there is Peg * * *'s name to one of them—a spinster whom I thought we had sent back to her spinning. Crayon is very good; Hogg's Tales rough, but RACY, and welcome.

"Books of travels are expensive, and I don't want them, having travelled already; besides, they lie. Thank the author of 'The Profligate' for his (or her) present. Pray send me no more poetry but what is rare and decidedly good. There is such a trash of Keats and the like upon my tables that I am ashamed to look at them. I say nothing against your parsons, your S * *s and your C * *s—it is all very fine—but pray dispense me from the pleasure. Instead of poetry, if you will favour me with a few soda-powders, I shall be delighted: but all prose ('bating travels and novels NOT by Scott) is welcome, especially Scott's Tales of my Landlord, and so on.

"In the notes to Marino Faliero, it may be as well to say that 'Benintende' was not really of the Ten, but merely Grand Chancellor, a separate office (although important): it was an arbitrary alteration of mine. The Doges too were all buried in St. Mark's before Faliero. It is singular that when his predecessor, Andrea Dandolo, died, the Ten made a law that all the future Doges should be buried with their families, in their own churches,—one would think by a kind of presentiment. So that all that is said of his ancestral Doges, as buried at St. John's and Paul's, is altered from the fact, they being in St. Mark's. Make a note of this, and put Editor as the subscription to it.

"As I make such pretensions to accuracy, I should not like to be twitted even with such trifles on that score. Of the play they may say what they please, but not so of my costume and dram. pers. they having been real existences.

"I omitted Foscolo in my list of living Venetian worthies, in the notes, considering him as an Italian in general, and not a mere provincial like the rest; and as an Italian I have spoken of him in the preface to Canto 4th of Childe Harold.

"The French translation of us!!! oimè! oimè!—the German; but I don't understand the latter and his long dissertation at the end about the Fausts. Excuse haste. Of politics it is not safe to speak, but nothing is decided as yet.

"I am in a very fierce humour at not having Scott's Monastery. You are too liberal in quantity, and somewhat careless of the quality, of your missives. All the Quarterlies (four in number) I had had before from you, and two of the Edinburgh; but no matter; we shall have new ones by and by. No more Keats, I entreat:—flay him alive; if some of you don't, I must skin him myself. There is no bearing the drivelling idiotism of the manikin.

"I don't feel inclined to care further about 'Don Juan.' What do you think a very pretty Italian lady said to me the other day? She had read it in the French, and paid me some compliments, with due DRAWBACKS, upon it. I answered that what she said was true, but that I suspected it would live longer than Childe Harold. 'Ah but' (said she). 'I would rather have the fame of Childe Harold for three years than an IMMORTALITY of Don Juan!' The truth is that it is TOO TRUE, and the women hate many things which strip off the tinsel of sentiment; and they are right, as it would rob them of their weapons. I never knew a woman who did not hate De Grammont's Memoirs for the same reason: even Lady * * used to abuse them.

"Rose's work I never received. It was seized at Venice. Such is the liberality of the Huns, with their two hundred thousand men, that they dare not let such a volume as his circulate."

LETTER 392. TO MR. MURRAY.

"Ravenna, 8bre 16°, 1820.

"The Abbot has just arrived; many thanks; as also for the Monastery—when you send it!!!

"The Abbot will have a more than ordinary interest for me, for an ancestor of mine by the mother's side, Sir J. Gordon of Gight, the handsomest of his day, died on a scaffold at Aberdeen for his loyalty to Mary, of whom he was an imputed paramour as well as her relation. His fate was much commented on in the Chronicles of the times. If I mistake not, he had something to do with her escape from Loch Leven, or with her captivity there. But this you will know better than I.

"I recollect Loch Leven as it were but yesterday. I saw it in my way to England in 1798, being then ten years of age. My mother, who was as haughty as Lucifer with her descent from the Stuarts, and her right line from the old Gordons, not the Seyton Gordons, as she disdainfully termed the ducal branch, told me the story, always reminding me how superior her Gordons were to the southern Byrons, notwithstanding our Norman, and always masculine descent, which has never lapsed into a female, as my mother's Gordons had done in her own person.

"I have written to you so often lately, that the brevity of this will be welcome. Yours," &c.

LETTER 393. TO MR. MURRAY.

"Ravenna, 8bre 17°, 1820.

"Enclosed is the Dedication of Marino Faliero to Goethe. Query,—is his title Baron or not? I think yes. Let me know your opinion, and so forth.

"P.S. Let me know what Mr. Hobhouse and you have decided about the two prose letters and their publication.

"I enclose you an Italian abstract of the German translator of Manfred's Appendix, in which you will perceive quoted what Goethe says of the whole body of English poetry (and not of me in particular). On this the Dedication is founded, as you will perceive, though I had thought of it before, for I look upon him as a great man."

The very singular Dedication transmitted with this letter has never before been published, nor, as far as I can learn, ever reached the hands of the illustrious German. It is written in the poet's most whimsical and mocking mood; and the unmeasured severity poured out in it upon the two favourite objects of his wrath and ridicule compels me to deprive the reader of some of its most amusing passages.

DEDICATION TO BARON GOETHE, &c. &c. &c.

"Sir,—In the Appendix to an English work lately translated into German and published at Leipsic, a judgment of yours upon English poetry is quoted as follows: 'That in English poetry, great genius, universal power, a feeling of profundity, with sufficient tenderness and force, are to be found; but that altogether these do not constitute poets,' &c. &c.

"I regret to see a great man falling into a great mistake. This opinion of yours only proves that the 'Dictionary of ten thousand living English Authors' has not been translated into German. You will have read, in your friend Schlegel's version, the dialogue in Macbeth—

"'There are ten thousand!
Macbeth. Geese, villain?
Answer. Authors, sir.'

Now, of these 'ten thousand authors,' there are actually nineteen hundred and eighty-seven poets, all alive at this moment, whatever their works may be, as their booksellers well know; and amongst these there are several who possess a far greater reputation than mine, although considerably less than yours. It is owing to this neglect on the part of your German translators that you are not aware of the works of * * *.

"There is also another, named * * * *

"I mention these poets by way of sample to enlighten you. They form but two bricks of our Babel, (WINDSOR bricks, by the way,) but may serve for a specimen of the building.

"It is, moreover, asserted that 'the predominant character of the whole body of the present English poetry is a disgust and contempt for life.' But I rather suspect that, by one single work of prose, you yourself have excited a greater contempt for life than all the English volumes of poesy that ever were written. Madame de Staël says, that 'Werther has occasioned more suicides than the most beautiful woman;' and I really believe that he has put more individuals out of this world than Napoleon himself, except in the way of his profession. Perhaps, Illustrious Sir, the acrimonious judgment passed by a celebrated northern journal upon you in particular, and the Germans in general, has rather indisposed you towards English poetry as well as criticism. But you must not regard our critics, who are at bottom good-natured fellows, considering their two professions,—taking up the law in court, and laying it down out of it. No one can more lament their hasty and unfair judgment, in your particular, than I do; and I so expressed myself to your friend Schlegel, in 1816, at Coppet.

"In behalf of my 'ten thousand' living brethren, and of myself, I have thus far taken notice of an opinion expressed with regard to 'English poetry' in general, and which merited notice, because it was YOURS.

"My principal object in addressing you was to testify my sincere respect and admiration of a man, who, for half a century, has led the literature of a great nation, and will go down to posterity as the first literary character of his age.

"You have been fortunate, Sir, not only in the writings which have illustrated your name, but in the name itself, as being sufficiently musical for the articulation of posterity. In this you have the advantage of some of your countrymen, whose names would perhaps be immortal also—if any body could pronounce them.

"It may, perhaps, be supposed, by this apparent tone of levity, that I am wanting in intentional respect towards you; but this will be a mistake: I am always flippant in prose. Considering you, as I really and warmly do, in common with all your own, and with most other nations, to be by far the first literary character which has existed in Europe since the death of Voltaire, I felt, and feel, desirous to inscribe to you the following work,—not as being either a tragedy or a poem, (for I cannot pronounce upon its pretensions to be either one or the other, or both, or neither,) but as a mark of esteem and admiration from a foreigner to the man who has been hailed in Germany 'THE GREAT GOETHE.'

"I have the honour to be,
"With the truest respect,
"Your most obedient and
"Very humble servant,
"BYRON.
"Ravenna, 8bre 14°, 1820.
"P.S. I perceive that in Germany, as well as in Italy, there is a great struggle about what they call 'Classical' and 'Romantic,'—terms which were not subjects of classification in England, at least when I left it four or five years ago. Some of the English scribblers, it is true, abused Pope and Swift, but the reason was that they themselves did not know how to write either prose or verse; but nobody thought them worth making a sect of. Perhaps there may be something of the kind sprung up lately, but I have not heard much about it, and it would be such bad taste that I shall be very sorry to believe it."

FOOTNOTES:

It will be perceived that, as far as this, the original matter of the third Act has been retained.

"Raven-stone (Rabenstein), a translation of the German word for the gibbet, which in Germany and Switzerland is permanent, and made of stone."

This fine soliloquy, and a great part of the subsequent scene, have, it is hardly necessary to remark been retained in the present form of the Drama.

Altered in the present form, to "some strange things in them, Herman."

An allusion (such as often occurs in these letters) to an anecdote with which he had been amused.

A tragedy, by the Rev. Mr. Maturin.

A country-house on the Euganean hills, near Este, which Mr. Hoppner, who was then the English Consul-General at Venice, had for some time occupied, and which Lord Byron afterwards rented of him, but never resided in it.

So great was the demand for horses, on the line of march of the Austrians, that all those belonging to private individuals were put in requisition for their use, and Lord Byron himself received an order to send his for the same purpose. This, however, he positively refused to do, adding, that if an attempt were made to take them by force, he would shoot them through the head in the middle of the road, rather than submit to such an act of tyranny upon a foreigner who was merely a temporary resident in the country. Whether his answer was ever reported to the higher authorities I know not; but his horses were suffered to remain unmolested in his stables.

On this paragraph, in the MS. copy of the above letter, I find the following note, in the handwriting of Mr. Gifford:— "There is more good sense, and feeling, and judgment in this passage, than in any other I ever read, or Lord Byron wrote."

A paper in the Edinburgh Magazine, in which it was suggested that the general conception of Manfred, and much of what is excellent in the manner of its execution, had been borrowed from "The Tragical History of Dr. Faustus," of Marlow.

"Vide your letter."

Beppo.

This possibly may have been the subject of the Poem given in p. 152. of the first volume.

Having seen by accident the passage in one of his letters to Mr. Murray, in which he denounces, as false and worthless, the poetical system on which the greater number of his contemporaries, as well as himself, founded their reputation, I took an opportunity, in the next letter I wrote to him, of jesting a little on this opinion, and his motives for it. It was, no doubt (I ventured to say), excellent policy in him, who had made sure of his own immortality in this style of writing, thus to throw overboard all us poor devils, who were embarked with him. He was, in fact, I added, behaving towards us much in the manner of the methodist preacher who said to his congregation—"You may think, at the Last Day, to get to heaven by laying hold on my skirts; but I'll cheat you all, for I'll wear a spencer, I'll wear a spencer!"

"His father's sense, his mother's grace

In him, I hope, will always fit so;
With (still to keep him in good case)
The health and appetite of Rizzo."

Having ascertained that the utmost this translator could expect to make by his manuscript was two hundred francs, Lord Byron offered him that sum, if he would desist from publishing. The Italian, however, held out for more; nor could he be brought to terms, till it was intimated to him pretty plainly from Lord Byron that, should the publication be persisted in, he would horsewhip him the very first time they met. Being but little inclined to suffer martyrdom in the cause, the translator accepted the two hundred francs, and delivered up his manuscript, entering at the same time into a written engagement never to translate any other of the noble poet's works. Of the qualifications of this person as a translator of English poetry, some idea may be formed from the difficulty he found himself under respecting the meaning of a line in the Incantation in Manfred,—"And the wisp on the morass,"—which he requested of Mr. Hoppner to expound to him, not having been able to find in the dictionaries to which he had access any other signification of the word "wisp" than "a bundle of straw."

A continuation of Vathek, by the author of that very striking and powerful production. The "Tales" of which this unpublished sequel consists are, I understand, those supposed to have been related by the Princes in the Hall of Eblis.

There follows, in this place, among other matter, a long string of verses, in various metres, to the amount of about sixty lines, so full of light gaiety and humour, that it is with some reluctance I suppress them. They might, however, have the effect of giving pain in quarters where even the author himself would not have deliberately inflicted it;—from a pen like his, touches may be wounds, and without being actually intended as such.

"Byron, while you make gay what circle fits ye,
Bandy Venetian slang with the Benzòn,
Or play at company with the Albrizzi,
The self-pleased pedant, and patrician crone,
Grimanis, Mocenigos, Balbis, Rizzi,
Compassionate our cruel case,—alone,
Our pleasure an academy of frogs,
Who nightly serenade us from the bogs," &c. &c.

"I have hunted out a precedent for this unceremonious address."
I had said, I think, in my letter to him, that this practice of carrying one stanza into another was "something like taking on horses another stage without baiting."
I had, in first transcribing the above letter for the press, omitted the whole of this caustic, and, perhaps, over-severe character of Mr. Hunt; but the tone of that gentleman's book having, as far as himself is concerned, released me from all those scruples which prompted the suppression, I have considered myself at liberty to restore the passage.

"Venice, August, 1818. "We came from Padua hither in a gondola; and the gondolier, among other things, without any hint on our part, began talking of Lord Byron. He said he was a 'Giovanotto Inglese,' with a 'nome stravagante,' who lived very luxuriously, and spent great sums of money. "At three o'clock I called on Lord Byron. He was delighted to see me, and our first conversation of course consisted in the object of our visit. He took me in his gondola, across the Laguna, to a long, strandy sand, which defends Venice from the Adriatic. When we disembarked, we found his horses waiting for us, and we rode along the sands, talking. Our conversation consisted in histories of his own wounded feelings, and questions as to my affairs, with great professions of friendship and regard for me. He said that if he had been in England, at the time of the Chancery affair, he would have moved heaven and earth to have prevented such a decision. He talked of literary matters,—his fourth Canto, which he says is very good, and indeed repeated some stanzas, of great energy, to me. When we returned to his palace, which is one if the most magnificent in Venice," &c. &c.

In the preface also to this poem, under the fictitious name of Count Maddalo, the following just and striking portrait of Lord Byron is drawn:— "He is a person of the most consummate genius, and capable, if he would direct his energies to such an end, of becoming the redeemer of his degraded country. But it is his weakness to be proud: he derives, from a comparison of his own extraordinary mind with the dwarfish intellects that surround him, an intense apprehension of the nothingness of human life. His passions and his powers are incomparably greater than those of other men, and instead of the latter having been employed in curbing the former, they have mutually lent each other strength. His ambition preys upon itself for want of objects which it can consider worthy of exertion. I say that Maddalo is proud, because I can find no other word to express the concentred and impatient feelings which consume him; but it is on his own hopes and affections only that he seems to trample, for in social life no human being can be more gentle, patient, and unassuming than Maddalo. He is cheerful, frank, and witty. His more serious conversation is a sort of intoxication. He has travelled much; and there is an inexpressible charm in his relation of his adventures in different countries."

Deeply is it, for many reasons, to be regretted that this friendly purpose did not succeed. This little child had been sent to him by its mother about four or five months before, under the care of a Swiss nurse, a young girl not above nineteen or twenty years of age, and in every respect unfit to have the charge of such an infant, without the superintendence of some more experienced person. "The child, accordingly," says my informant, "was but ill taken care of;—not that any blame could attach to Lord Byron, for he always expressed himself most anxious for her welfare, but because the nurse wanted the necessary experience. The poor girl was equally to be pitied; for, as Lord Byron's household consisted of English and Italian men servants, with whom she could hold no converse, and as there was no other female to consult with and assist her in her charge, nothing could be more forlorn than her situation proved to be." Soon after the date of the above letter, Mrs. Hoppner, the lady of the Consul General, who had, from the first, in compassion both to father and child, invited the little Allegra occasionally to her house, very kindly proposed to Lord Byron to take charge of her altogether, and an arrangement was

accordingly concluded upon for that purpose.
"I had one only fount of quiet left,
And that they poison'd! My pure household gods
Were shivered on my hearth." MARINO FALIERO.

"Lost the unbalanced scale."

This passage also remains uncorrected.
"Nell' Aprile del 1819, io feci la conoscenza di Lord Byron; e mi fu presentato a Venezia dalla Contessa Benzoni nella di lei società. Questa presentazione che ebbe tante consequenze per tutti e due fu fatta contro la volontà d'entrambi, e solo per condiscendenza l'abbiamo permessa. Io stanca più che mai quella sera par le ore tarde che si costuma fare in Venezia andai con molta ripugnanza e solo per ubbidire al Conte Guiccioli in quella società. Lord Byron che scansava di fare nuove conoscenze, dicendo sempre che aveva interamente rinunciato alle passioni e che non voleva esporsi più alle loro consequenze, quando la Contessa Benzoni la pregò di volersi far presentare a me eglì recusò, e solo per la compiàcenza glielo permise. La nobile e bellissima sua fisonomia, il suono della sua voce, le sue maniere, i mille incanti che lo circondavano lo rendevano un essere così differente, così superiore a tutti quelli che io aveva sino allora veduti che non potei a meno di non provarne la più profonda impressione. Da quella sera in poi in tutti i giorni che mi fermai in Venezia ei siamo seinpre veduti."—MS.

This story, as given in the Preface to the "Vampire," is as follows:— "It appears that one evening Lord B., Mr. P.B. Shelley, two ladies, and the gentleman before alluded to, after having perused a German work called Phantasmagoria, began relating ghost stories, when his Lordship having recited the beginning of Christabel, then unpublished, the whole took so strong a hold of Mr. Shelley's mind, that he suddenly started up, and ran out of the room. The physician and Lord Byron followed, and discovered him leaning against a mantel-piece, with cold drops of perspiration trickling down his face. After having given him something to refresh him, upon enquiring into the cause of his alarm, they found that his wild imagination having pictured to him the bosom of one of the ladies with eyes (which was reported of a lady in the neighbourhood where he lived), he was obliged to leave the room in order to destroy the impression."

A clerk of the English Consulate, whom he at this time employed to control his accounts.

The Po.

Though Lord Byron, like most other persons, in writing to different friends, was sometimes led to repeat the same circumstances and thoughts, there is, from the ever ready fertility of his mind, much less of such repetition in his correspondence than in that, perhaps, of any other multifarious letter-writer; and, in the instance before us, where the same facts and reflections are, for the second time, introduced, it is with such new touches, both of thought and expression, as render them, even a second time, interesting;—what is wanting in the novelty of the matter being made up by the new aspect given to it.

There were, in the former edition, both here and in a subsequent letter, some passages reflecting upon the late Sir Samuel Romilly, which, in my anxiety to lay open the workings of Lord Byron's mind upon a subject in which so much of his happiness and character were involved, I had been induced to retain, though aware of the erroneous impression under which they were written;—the evident morbidness of the feeling that dictated the attack, and the high, stainless reputation of the person assailed, being sufficient, I thought, to neutralise any ill effects such reflections might otherwise have produced. As I find it, however, to be the opinion of all those whose opinions I most respect, that, even with these antidotes, such an attack upon such a man ought not to be left on record, I willingly expunge all trace of it from these pages.

"Tal qual di ramo in ramo si raccoglie
Per la pineta in sul lito di Chiassi,
Quando Eolo Scirocco fuor discioglie."
DANTE, PURG. Canto xxviii.

"Partendo io da Venezia egli promise di venir a vedermi a Ravenna. La Tomba di Dante, il classico bosco di pini, gli avvanzi di antichità che a Ravenna si trovano davano a me ragioni plausibili per invitarlo a venire, ed a lui per accettare l'invito. Egli venne difatti nel mese Guigno, e giunse a Ravenna nel giorno della Solennità del Corpus Domini, mentre io attaccata da una malattia de consunzione ch' ebbe principio dalla mia partenza da Venezia ero vicina a morire.

L'arrivo in Ravenna d'un forestiero distinto, in un paese così lontano dalle strade che ordinariamente tengono i viaggiatori era un avvenimento del quale molto si parlava, indagandosene i motivi, che involontariamente poi egli feci conoscere. Perchè avendo egli domandato di me per venire a vedermi ed essendogli risposto 'che non potrebbe vedermi più perchè ero vicina a morire'—egli rispose che in quel caso voleva morire egli pure; la qual cosa essendosi poi ripetata si conobbe cosi l'oggetto del suo viaggio. "Il Conte Guiccioli visitò Lord Byron, essendolo conosciuto in Venezia, e nella speranza che la di lui compagnia potesse distrarmi ed essermi di qualche giovamento nello stato in cui mi trovavo egli lo invitò di venire a visitarmi. Il giorno appresso egli venne. Non si potrebbero descrivere le cure, i pensieri delicati, quanto egli fece per me. Per molto tempo egli non ebbe per le mani che dei Libri di Medicina; e poco confidandosi nel miei medici ottenne dal Conte Guiccioli il permesso di far venire un valente medico di lui amico nel quale egli aveva molta confidanza. Le cure del Professore Aglietti (cosi si chiama questo distinto Italiano) la tranquillità, anzi la felicità inesprimibile che mi cagionava la presenza di Lord Byron migliorarono così rapidamente la mia salute che entro lo spazio di due mesi potei seguire mio marito in un giro che egli doveva fare per le sue terre."—
MS.

That this task of "governing" him was one of more ease than, from the ordinary view of his character, might be concluded, I have more than once, in these pages, expressed my opinion, and shall here quote, in corroboration of it, the remark of his own servant (founded on an observation of more than twenty years), in speaking of his master's matrimonial fate:— "It is very odd, but I never yet knew a lady that could not manage my Lord, except my Lady." "More knowledge," says Johnson, "may be gained of a man's real character by a short conversation with one of his servants than from the most formal and studied narrative."

The Vice-Consul of Mr. Hoppner.

An English widow lady, of considerable property in the north of England, who, having seen the little Allegra at Mr. Hoppner's, took an interest in the poor child's fate, and having no family of her own, offered to adopt and provide for this little girl, if Lord Byron would consent to renounce all claim to her. At first he seemed not disinclined to enter into her views—so far, at least, as giving permission that she should take the child with her to England and educate it; but the entire surrender of his paternal authority he would by no means consent to. The proposed arrangement accordingly was never carried into effect.

"During my illness," says Madame Guiccioli, in her recollections of this period, "he was for ever near me, paying me the most amiable attentions, and when I became convalescent he was constantly at my side. In society, at the theatre, riding, walking, he never was absent from me. Being deprived at that time of his books, his horses, and all that occupied him at Venice, I begged him to gratify me by writing something on the subject of Dante, and, with his usual facility and rapidity, he composed his 'Prophecy.'"—"Durante la mia malattia L.B. era sempre presso di me, prestandomi le più sensibili cure, e quando passai allo stato di convalescenza egli era sempre al mio fianco;—e in società, e al teatro, e cavalcando, e passeggiando egli non si allontanava mai da me. In quel' epoca essendo egli privo de' suoi libri, e de' suoi cavalli, e di tuttociò che lo occupava in Venezia io lo pregai di volersi occupare per me scrivendo qualche cosa sul Dante; ed egli colla usata sua facilita e rapidita scrisse la sua Profezia."

The "Dama," in whose company he witnessed this representation, thus describes its effect upon him:—"The play was that of Mirra; the actors, and particularly the actress who performed the part of Mirra, seconded with much success the intentions of our great dramatist. Lord Byron took a strong interest in the representation, and it was evident that he was deeply affected. At length there came a point of the performance at which he could no longer restrain his emotions;—he burst into a flood of tears, and, his sobs preventing him from remaining any longer in the box, he rose and left the theatre.—I saw him similarly affected another time during a representation of Alfieri's 'Philip,' at Ravenna."—"Gli attori, e specialmente l' attrice che rappresentava Mirra secondava assai bene la mente del nostro grande tragico. L.B. prece molto interesse alla rappresentazione, e si conosceva che era molto commosso. Venne un punto poi della tragedia in cui non potè più frenare la sua emozione,—diede in un diretto pianto e i singhiozzi gl' impedirono di più restare nel palco; onde si levò, e parti dal teatro. In uno stato simile lo viddi un altra volta a Ravenna ad una rappresentazione del Filippo d'Alfieri."

It appeared afterwards in the Liberal.

"I knew Madame de Staël well,—better than she knew Italy,—but I little thought that, one day, I should think with her thoughts, in the country where she has laid the scene of her most attractive productions. She is sometimes right, and often wrong, about Italy and England; but almost always true in delineating the heart, which is of but one nation, and of no country,—or, rather, of all. "BYRON. "Bologna, August 23. 1819."

"Oh Love! what is it, in this world of ours,

> Which makes it fatal to be loved? ah! why
> With cypress branches hast thou wreath'd thy bowers,
> And made thy best interpreter a sigh?
> As those who dote on odours pluck the flowers,
> And place them on their breasts—but place to die.—
> Thus the frail beings we would fondly cherish
> Are laid within our bosoms but to perish."

"Am I now reposing on a bed of flowers?"

"Il Conte Guiccioli doveva per affari ritornare a Ravenna; lo stato della mia salute esiggeva che io ritornassi in vece a Venezia. Egli acconsentì dunque che Lord Byron, mi fosse compagno di viaggio. Partimmo da Bologna alli 15 di Sre.—visitammo insieme i Colli Euganei ed Arquà; scrivemmo i nostri nomi nel libro che si presenta a quelli che fanno quel pellegrinaggio. Ma sopra tali rimembranze di felicità non posso fermarmi, caro Signr. Moore; l'opposizione col presente é troppo forte, e se un anima benedetta nel pieno godimento di tutte le felicità celesti fosse mandata quaggiù e condannata a sopportare tutte le miserie della nostra terra non potrebbe sentire più terribile contrasto frà il passato ed il presente di quello che io sento dacchè quella terribile parola è giunta alle mie orecchie, dacchè ho perduto la speranza di più vedere quello di cui uno sguardo valeva per me più di tutte le felicità della terra. Giunti a Venezia i medici mi ordinarono di respirare l'aria della campagna. Egli aveva una villa alla Mira,—la cedesse a me, e venne meco. Là passammo l'autunno, e là ebbi il bene di fare la vostra conoscenza."—MS.

The title of Segretario is sometimes given, as in this case, to a head-servant or house-steward. That this was the case with Milton is acknowledged by Richardson, who admired both Milton and the Arts too warmly to make such an admission upon any but valid grounds. "He does not appear," says this writer, "to have much regarded what was done with the pencil; no, not even when in Italy, in Rome, in the Vatican. Neither does it seem Sculpture was much esteemed by him." After an authority like this, the theories of Hayley and others, with respect to the impressions left upon Milton's mind by the works of art he had seen in Italy, are hardly worth a thought. Though it may be conceded that Dante was an admirer of the Arts, his recommendation of the Apocalypse to Giotto, as a source of subjects for the pencil, shows, at least, what indifferent judges poets are, in general, of the sort of fancies fittest to be embodied by the painter.

The writer here, no doubt, alludes to such questionable liberalities as those exercised towards the husbands of his two favourites, Madame S * * and the Fornarina.

The circumstance here alluded to may be most clearly, perhaps, communicated to my readers through the medium of the following extract from a letter which Mr. Barry (the friend and banker of Lord Byron) did me the favour of addressing to me, soon after his Lordship's death:—
"When Lord Byron went to Greece, he gave me orders to advance money to Madame G * *; but that lady would never consent to receive any. His Lordship had also told me that he meant to

leave his will in my hands, and that there would be a bequest in it of 10,000l. to Madame G * *. He mentioned this circumstance also to Lord Blessington. When the melancholy news of his death reached me, I took for granted that this will would be found among the sealed papers he had left with me; but there was no such instrument. I immediately then wrote to Madame G * *, enquiring if she knew any thing concerning it, and mentioning, at the same time, what his Lordship had said is to the legacy. To this the lady replied, that he had frequently spoken to her on the same subject, but that she had always cut the conversation short, as it was a topic she by no means liked to hear him speak upon. In addition, she expressed a wish that no such will as I had mentioned would be found; as her circumstances were already sufficiently independent, and the world might put a wrong construction on her attachment, should it appear that her fortunes were, in any degree, bettered by it."

This will remind the reader of Molière's avowal in speaking of wit:—"C'est mon bien, et je le prends partout où je le trouve."

The History of Agathon, by Wieland.

Between Wieland, the author of this Romance, and Lord Byron, may be observed some of those generic points of resemblance which it is so interesting to trace in the characters of men of genius. The German poet, it is said, never perused any work that made a strong impression upon him, without being stimulated to commence one, himself, on the same topic and plan; and in Lord Byron the imitative principle was almost equally active,—there being few of his poems that might not, in the same manner, be traced to the strong impulse given to his imagination by the perusal of some work that had just before interested him. In the history, too, of their lives and feelings, there was a strange and painful coincidence,—the revolution that took place in all Wieland's opinions, from the Platonism and romance of his youthful days, to the material and Epicurean doctrines that pervaded all his maturer works, being chiefly, it is supposed, brought about by the shock his heart had received from a disappointment of its affections in early life. Speaking of the illusion of this first passion, in one of his letters, he says,—"It is one for which no joys, no honours, no gifts of fortune, not even wisdom itself can afford an equivalent, and which, when it has once vanished, returns no more."

"'Tis but a portrait of his son and wife,
And self; but such a woman! love in life!"
BEPPO, Stanza xii.

"Egli viene per vedere le meraviglie di questa Città, e sono certa che nessuno meglio di lui saprebbe gustarle. Mi sarà grato che vi facciate sua guida come potrete, e voi poi me ne avrete obbligo. Egli è amico de Lord Byron—sà la sua storia assai più precisamente di quelli che a voi la raccontarono. Egli dunque vi racconterà se lo interrogherete la forma, le dimensioni, e tuttociò che vi piacerà del Castello ove tiene imprigionata una giovane innocente sposa, &c. &c. Mio caro Pietro, quando ti sei bene sfogato a ridere, allora rispondi due righe alla tua sorella, che t' ama e t' amerà sempre colla maggiore tenerezza."

Mr. Hoppner, before his departure from Venice for Switzerland, had, with all the zeal of a true friend, written a letter to Lord Byron, entreating him "to leave Ravenna while yet he had a whole skin, and urging him not to risk the safety of a person he appeared so sincerely attached to—as well as his own—for the gratification of a momentary passion, which could only be a source of regret to both parties." In the same letter Mr. Hoppner informed him of some reports he had heard lately at Venice, which, though possibly, he said, unfounded, had much increased his anxiety respecting the consequences of the connection formed by him.

"This language" (says Mr. Hoppner, in some remarks upon the above letter) "is strong, but it was the language of prejudice; and he was rather apt thus to express the feelings of the moment, without troubling himself to consider how soon he might be induced to change them. He was at this time so sensitive on the subject of Madame * *, that, merely because some persons had disapproved of her conduct, he declaimed in the above manner against the whole nation. I never" (continues Mr. Hoppner) "was partial to Venice; but disliked it almost from the first month of my residence there. Yet I experienced more kindness in that place than I ever met with in any country, and witnessed acts of generosity and disinterestedness such as rarely are met with elsewhere."

I beg to say that this report of my opinion of Venice is coloured somewhat too deeply by the feelings of the reporter.

The following curious particulars of his delirium are given by Madame Guiccioli:—"At the beginning of winter Count Guiccioli came from Ravenna to fetch me. When he arrived, Lord Byron was ill of a fever, occasioned by his having got wet through;—a violent storm having surprised him while taking his usual exercise on horseback. He had been delirious the whole night, and I had watched continually by his bedside. During his delirium he composed a good many verses, and ordered his servant to write them down from his dictation. The rhythm of these verses was quite correct, and the poetry itself had no appearance of being the work of a delirious mind. He preserved them for some time after he got well, and then burned them."—"Sul cominciare dell' inverno il Conte Guiccioli venne a prendermi per ricondurmi a Ravenna. Quando egli giunse Ld. Byron era ammalato di febbri prese per essersi bagnato avendolo sorpreso un forte temporale mentre faceva l' usato suo esercizio a cavallo. Egli aveva delirato tutta la notte, ed io aveva sempre vegliato presso al suo letto. Nel suo delirio egli compose molti versi che ordinò al suo domestico di scrivere sotto la sua dittatura. La misura dei versi era esatissima, e la poesia pure non pareva opera di una mente in delirio. Egli la conservò lungo tempo dopo restabilito—poi l' abbrucciò." I have been informed, too, that, during his ravings at this time, he was constantly haunted by the idea of his mother-in-law,—taking every one that came near him for her, and reproaching those about him for letting her enter his room.

"Tu sei, e sarai sempre mio primo pensier. Ma in questo momento sono in un' stato orribile non sapendo cosa decidere;—temendo, da una parte, comprometterti in eterno col mio ritorno a Ravenna, e colle sue consequenze; e, dal' altra perderti, e me stesso, e tutto quel che ho conosciuto o gustato di felicità, nel non vederti più. Ti prego, ti supplico calmarti, e credere che non posso cessare ad amarti che colla vita."

"Io parto, per salvarti, e lascio un paese divenuto insopportabile senza di te. Le tue lettere alla F

* *, ed anche a me stesso fanno torto ai miei motivi; ma col tempo vedrai la tua ingiustizia. Tu parli del dolor—io lo sento, ma mi mancano le parole. Non basta lasciarti per dei motivi dei quali tu eri persuasa (non molto tempo fa)—non basta partire dall' Italia col cuore lacerato, dopo aver passato tutti i giorni dopo la tua partenza nella solitudine, ammalato di corpo e di anima—ma ho anche a sopportare i tuoi rimproveri, senza replicarti, e senza meritarli. Addio—in quella parola è compresa la morte di mia felicità." The close of this last sentence exhibits one of the very few instances of incorrectness that Lord Byron falls into in these letters;—the proper construction being "della mia felicità."

"Egli era tutto vestito di viaggio coi guanti fra le mani, col suo bonnet, e persino colla piccola sua canna; non altro aspettavasi che egli scendesse le scale, tutti i bauli erano in barca. Milord fa la pretesta che se suona un ora dopo il mezzodi e che non sia ogni cosa all' ordine (poichè le armi sole non erano in pronto) egli non partirebbe più per quel giorno. L'ora suona ed egli resta."

"La F * * ti avra detta, colla sua solita sublimità, che l'Amor ha vinto. Io non ho potuto trovare forza di anima per lasciare il paese dove tu sei, senza vederti almeno un' altra volta:—forse dipenderà da te se mai ti lascio più. Per il resto parleremo. Tu dovresti adesso sapere cosa sarà più convenevole al tuo ben essere la mia presenza o la mia lontananza. Io sono cittadino del mondo—tutti i paesi sono eguali per me. Tu sei stata sempre (dopo che ci siamo conosciuti) l'unico oggetto di miei pensieri. Credeva che il miglior partito per la pace tua e la pace di tua famiglia fosse il mio partire, e andare ben lontano; poichè stare vicino e non avvicinarti sarebbe per me impossibile. Ma tu hai deciso che io debbo ritornare a Ravenna—tornaro—e farò—e sarò ciò die tu vuoi. Non posso dirti di più."

This is one of the many mistakes into which his distance from the scene of literary operations led him. The gentleman, to whom the hostile article in the Magazine is here attributed, has never, either then or since, written upon the subject of the noble poet's character or genius, without giving vent to a feeling of admiration as enthusiastic as it is always eloquently and powerfully expressed.

"Gehenna of the waters! thou Sea-Sodom!"
MARINO FALIERO.

The word here, being under the seal, is illegible.
It has been suggested to me that usbergo is obviously the same as hauberk, habergeon, &c. all from the German halsberg, or covering of the neck.
"The prostitution of his Muse and wife,
Both beautiful, and both by him debased,
Shall salt his bread and give him means of life."

"In some of the editions, it is, 'diro,' in others 'faro;'—an essential difference between 'saying' and 'doing,' which I know not how to decide. Ask Foscolo. The d——d editions drive me mad."

When making the observations which occur in the early part of this work, on the singular preference given by the noble author to the "Hints from Horace," I was not aware of the revival of this strange predilection, which (as it appears from the above letter, and, still more strongly, from some that follow) took place so many years after, in the full maturity of his powers and taste. Such a delusion is hardly conceivable, and can only, perhaps, be accounted for by that tenaciousness of early opinions and impressions by which his mind, in other respects so versatile, was characterised.

Of Don Juan.

According to his desire, I waited upon this young lady, having provided myself with a rouleau of fifteen or twenty Napoleons to present to her from his Lordship; but, with a very creditable spirit, my young countrywoman declined the gift, saying that Lord Byron had mistaken the object of her application to him, which was to request that, by allowing her to have the sheets of some of his works before publication, he would enable her to prepare early translations for the French booksellers, and thus afford her the means of acquiring something towards a livelihood.

M. Lamartine.

Of this kind are the accounts, filled with all sorts of circumstantial wonders, of his residence in the island of Mytilene;—his voyages to Sicily,—to Ithaca, with the Countess Guiccioli, &c. &c. But the most absurd, perhaps, of all these fabrications, are the stories told by Pouqueville, of the poet's religious conferences in the cell of Father Paul, at Athens; and the still more unconscionable fiction in which Rizo has indulged, in giving the details of a pretended theatrical scene, got up (according to this poetical historian) between Lord Byron and the Archbishop of Arta, at the tomb of Botzaris, in Missolonghi.

The critic here subjoins the soliloquy from Manfred, beginning "We are the fools of time and terror," in which the allusion to Pausanias occurs.

An Irish phrase for being in a scrape.

The title given him by M. Lamartine, in one of his Poems.

I had congratulated him upon arriving at what Dante calls the "mezzo cammin" of life, the age of thirty-three.

I had mistaken the concluding words of his letter of the 9th of June.

The angry note against English travellers appended to this tragedy, in consequence of an assertion made by some recent tourist, that he (or as it afterwards turned out, she) "had repeatedly declined an introduction to Lord Byron while in Italy."

The paragraph is left thus imperfect in the original.

Printed in Poland
by Amazon Fulfillment
Poland Sp. z o.o., Wrocław